ReFocus: The Films of William Friedkin

ReFocus: The American Directors Series

Series Editors: Robert Singer, Frances Smith, and Gary D. Rhodes

Editorial Board: Kelly Basilio, Donna Campbell, Claire Perkins, Christopher Sharrett, and Yannis Tzioumakis

ReFocus is a series of contemporary methodological and theoretical approaches to the interdisciplinary analyses and interpretations of neglected American directors, from the once-famous to the ignored, in direct relationship to American culture—its myths, values, and historical precepts.

Titles in the series include:

ReFocus: The Films of Preston Sturges
Edited by Jeff Jaeckle and Sarah Kozloff

ReFocus: The Films of Delmer Daves
Edited by Matthew Carter and Andrew Nelson

ReFocus: The Films of Amy Heckerling
Edited by Frances Smith and Timothy Shary

ReFocus: The Films of Budd Boetticher
Edited by Gary D. Rhodes and Robert Singer

ReFocus: The Films of Kelly Reichardt
E. Dawn Hall

ReFocus: The Films of William Castle
Edited by Murray Leeder

ReFocus: The Films of Barbara Kopple
Edited by Jeff Jaeckle and Susan Ryan

ReFocus: The Films of Elaine May
Edited by Alexandra Heller-Nicholas and Dean Brandum

ReFocus: The Films of Spike Jonze
Edited by Kim Wilkins and
Wyatt Moss-Wellington

ReFocus: The Films of Paul Schrader
Edited by Michelle E. Moore and
Brian Brems

ReFocus: The Films of John Hughes
Edited by Timothy Shary and
Frances Smith

ReFocus: The Films of Doris Wishman
Edited by Alicia Kozma and
Finley Freibert

ReFocus: The Films of Albert Brooks
Edited by Christian B. Long

ReFocus: The Films of William Friedkin
Steve Choe

edinburghuniversitypress.com/series/refoc

ReFocus:
The Films of William Friedkin

Steve Choe

Edinburgh University Press is one of the leading university presses in the UK. We publish academic books and journals in our selected subject areas across the humanities and social sciences, combining cutting-edge scholarship with high editorial and production values to produce academic works of lasting importance. For more information visit our website: edinburghuniversitypress.com

© Steve Choe, 2021, 2023

Edinburgh University Press Ltd
The Tun—Holyrood Road
12 (2f) Jackson's Entry
Edinburgh EH8 8PJ

First published in hardback by Edinburgh University Press 2021

Typeset in 11/13 Ehrhardt MT by
IDSUK (DataConnection) Ltd, and

A CIP record for this book is available from the British Library

ISBN 978 1 4744 3137 8 (hardback)
ISBN 978 1 4744 3138 5 (paperback)
ISBN 978 1 4744 3139 2 (webready PDF)
ISBN 978 1 4744 3140 8 (epub)

The right of Steve Choe to be identified as author of this work has been asserted in accordance with the Copyright, Designs and Patents Act 1988 and the Copyright and Related Rights Regulations 2003 (SI No. 2498).

Contents

List of Figures — vi
Acknowledgments — vii

Introduction — 1

1 Spaces of Melodrama
 The Night They Raided Minsky's, *The Birthday Party*,
 The Boys in the Band, and *The French Connection* — 14

2 Policing the Police
 To Live and Die in L.A., *Rules of Engagement*, and
 The Hunted — 52

3 Criminal Desires
 Cruising, *Jade*, and *Killer Joe* — 86

4 Justice at the Limits of Popular Cinema
 The People v. Paul Crump, *Rampage*, *12 Angry Men*, and *Bug* — 124

5 "The Power of Cinema Compels You"
 The Exorcist and *Sorcerer* — 164

Bibliography — 202
Index — 208

Figures

1.1	"Madame Fifi" incites the audience	18
1.2	Stanley is trapped	25
1.3	The face, skin, and soul	35
1.4	Men of vice meeting in front of the Capitol Building	42
2.1	Accusing the accusers	53
2.2	An exchange of counterfeit currency	64
2.3	Sentimental fidelity justifies the flouting of the law	74
2.4	Rembrandt's *Sacrifice of Isaac* (1635)	81
3.1	Male bodies fill the frame	91
3.2	"Who's here? I'm here. You're here."	99
3.3	Matt reveals his knowledge of Trina's exploits	111
3.4	Smith family dinner	118
4.1	Interview with Paul Crump	129
4.2	PET scan of insanity	141
4.3	Remembering past films	149
4.4	Peter threatens his consultant Dr. Sweet	159
5.1	Scanning for Regan's malady	171
5.2	Innocence and defilement	180
5.3	Male collaboration	189
5.4	An alien landscape	194

Acknowledgments

I am grateful to the editors of the ReFocus series for providing me with the opportunity to research and write this book. This project came at a fortuitous time in the course of my thinking about the moving image, after my book on contemporary Korean cinema was published in 2016, which allowed me to continue to think about the issues around politics, emotions, and ethics I raised there. I knew *The Exorcist* since I was a teenager and saw *The French Connection* while in college but I became engrossed with *Sorcerer* a bit later. The audacious aims of the film and its hallucinatory ending were particularly striking for me. Before I knew much about the rest of Friedkin's oeuvre, I was fascinated that these films, each different from the other in genre and scope, were made one after another and by the same director. *Sorcerer* has typically been understood as exemplary of the outsized pretensions of New Hollywood filmmaking in the late '70s, along with Michael Cimino's *Heaven's Gate*, Martin Scorsese's *New York, New York*, and Francis Ford Coppola's *One From the Heart*. I don't dispute this historicization, as it helps periodize this era of Hollywood filmmaking, but the more I learned about Friedkin, the more I realized that *Sorcerer* was also about a series of ideas that span much of his work, despite their variety and diverse range. I began to think about *Sorcerer* as a film about the lived experience of time, allegorized through the timespan of the cinema. The project has allowed me to pursue deeper research into other films by this auteur, many of which were forgotten or received negatively by critics at the time, and to consider ideas that critics, scholars, and Friedkin himself may have missed. Coincidentally, some of these problems were those I had been analyzing in my previous work and so I was thrilled to develop them further within a new historical context.

I am especially grateful to colleagues, friends, and students who have entertained dialogue with me about Friedkin and his cinema. These individuals include Jinsoo An, Keung Yoon "Becky" Bae, Michelle Cho, Pablo Lorenzo Riquelme Cuartero, Theresa Geller, Steffen Handke, Mayumo Inoue Jordon Jacobson, Kyu Hyun Kim, Jordan Klein, Rachel Park, Celine Parreñas Shimizu, Amy Rust, Britta Holly Sjogren, Damon Young, and Chang-Min Yu. I am grateful to the librarians at the Margaret Herrick Library, who provided me with assistance with the William Friedkin Papers, as well as to the students in my New Hollywood Cinema classes at San Francisco State University. Their support and enthusiasm have energized me to sustain work on this book. Many thanks to Ryan Semans for his excellent transcription work. I am thankful to Fiona Screen for her sustained attention to the style and language of the entire manuscript. Finally, I am grateful to Mr. Friedkin himself, who allowed an interview on October 27, 2017 of over three hours at his home. It was one of the most thrilling afternoons in my professional career, not only because of the occasion, but also because it was moving to hear a Hollywood director speak so profoundly about his own life and work.

Finally, I would like to acknowledge Jeffrey Winter. My hope is that the final results of this project have realized some of its initial aspirations.

December 2020

Introduction

On February 25, 2016, William Friedkin, the Hollywood director of *The French Connection* in 1971 and *The Exorcist* in 1973, was interviewed by Marc Maron on his podcast, *WTF with Marc Maron*. In his two-hour conversation with the comedian, the 81-year-old filmmaker speaks about the films, music, and art that inspired him and the television programs, operas, and films he directed. Friedkin has an excellent capacity for recall, particularly for names and dates, and is an engrossing storyteller. On the podcast he eloquently recounts stories about meetings for lunch with Billy Wilder and dinner parties at the house of Francis Ford Coppola (with the food prepared by George Lucas), and reveals thoughtful insights about working with Gene Hackman, Tommy Lee Jones, and others on his most well-known as well as his lesser-known productions. Although Friedkin was bar mitzvahed, the director, perhaps inexplicably, tells Maron of his long admiration for the "teachings of Jesus." In fact, while he was in Turin to direct Verdi's *Aida* at the Teatro Regio, he was invited to see the Shroud of Turin by the last surviving relative of the Savoia kings, Serge of Yugoslavia. While he was aware of the issues surrounding the authenticity of the Shroud, it proved to be an especially dramatic experience:

> Serge arranged this private showing for eight people to which Sherry and I were invited. After the noon mass had completely let out, a big black limousine came around the corner with the Bishop of Piedmonte and two or three priests accompanying him. And Serge said to us, "You will have to kiss his ring." We kissed the ring, both of us. Then we went inside to the empty basilica. As you walk toward the rather ornate altar, on the left-hand side is a long room, covered from outside with leaded glass and from inside with velvet drapes that remained shut for a hundred years.

> Serge handed the keys to this room to the bishop who opened the doors. They rolled back the drapes and now we are in a room that was probably twice as big as this room, fifteen by ten, probably thirty by twenty. And the only thing you see in the room is just to the left of the altar. The only thing you see in the room is a painting of Jesus, and I don't know who it was by, it does not seem to be a well-known or famous portrait, and you see a rug. The priests—there were eight of us—and the priests rolled back the rug, and there's a foot pedal. The bishop placed his foot on the pedal, at Serge's invitation, and up from the floor rises this table that's about fifteen feet long. After the rug is rolled back, it's covered by a red velvet cloth with an embroidered gold crucifix. They roll that back, and beneath leaded glass on the table is the outline of a crucified man in blood. The most current DNA has shown, and they're pretty good with the DNA now, that that image of the crucified man is not paint, certainly not photography, because its existence has been known since the third century, photography goes back to the nineteenth century. It is in fact type AB blood. It's the outline of a crucified man including the outline of a crown of thorns and there's an outline of blood in the chest where the Centurian Spear was supposed to have gone. You're looking at the image of a crucified man whose palms are crossed but they have been nailed through. His ankles are crossed with one nail through both ankles. You see the outlines in blood of this image. And my wife and I and everyone else in the room burst into tears. As I think of it now my eyes tear up. And we see what is the image of a crucified man. In other words, we see, before us, man's inhumanity to man. Bang. I don't know if it's Jesus . . . My wife and I, who are both Jewish, burst into uncontrollable tears because of the power of this image.

The drama of "man's inhumanity to man" compelled Friedkin and his partner, Sherry Lansing, who was CEO of Paramount from 1992 to 2004, to break down and weep before the sight of the Shroud. The traces of blood indicate that the man wrapped in it was subjected to violence and suffered in pain. Friedkin's reaction, as he recalls it, was induced by the "power of this image," even as its authenticity remains in question. Nevertheless it was an image that solicited a dramatic, emotional, bodily response. One is reminded here of André Bazin's essay on photography and a footnote making the connection between the Shroud and visual media explicit: "Let us merely note in passing that the Holy Shroud of Turin combines the features alike of relic and photograph."[1] The Shroud has inscribed on it traces of the past, allowing the viewer to take in the image of a man who once lived and is no longer, while functioning as an *aide-mémoire* for the story of how he died. This story is not only significant within the theological context—Friedkin performed a great deal of research on Jesus and his historical milieu—but in the context of universal, secular humanity as well. It attests to the capacity for humans to sympathize with the suffering of others and, perhaps, the melodramatic character of this image of suffering.

In an interview that I conducted with the director in 2017, I brought up this experience he related to Maron and asked about his relationship to Christianity and with Catholicism more specifically. To be sure, Friedkin recognizes that his interest in Catholic faith is as an outsider, of someone who was not raised within this tradition. He nevertheless believes in its wisdom and, as it turns out, some of its basic tenets will find their way into his films as well.

> All I can tell you in answer to that is I strongly believe inherently in the teachings of Jesus Christ. But I'm not a Catholic, I'm not a Christian. I was raised in the Jewish faith. I never felt particularly close to it because I never understood the language. The religion that interests me the most is Catholicism, but not the practice of it . . . So the value of religion: people need something to hold onto that's greater than themselves. I do. To the extent that you rely on that, that's an individual thing, but it's the mystery of faith.

The "mystery of faith" will be a key phrase for interpreting a number of Friedkin's films. For this mystery is relevant not only for understanding the role Catholicism plays in the filmmaker's life but also for how it raises questions around belief in the image, cinematic and otherwise. The filmmaker's experience of the Shroud is exemplary, then, for the power of the image, even when it may be suspected of being inauthentic or fake, can still move viewers to tears. It can raise problems around violence, around its ethics and justification, the relationship between morality and law, the spectacle of suffering and its solicitation of sympathy, and around the possibility of redemption. These are issues that for Friedkin have become like obsessions and are articulated within the mode of popular cinema.

* * *

This book is an attempt to refocus our understanding of the films of William Friedkin, particularly those that have not been celebrated or recognized, and to try to bring the issues that concern them as a whole into greater relief. *The Exorcist* and the Academy Award-winning *The French Connection*, two paramount films of the New Hollywood generation of filmmaking, are his most successful and well-known works. These films set new standards for the scope of the genres in which they are typically categorized and now occupy a kind of mythic status in our culture. They are the ones that have received the lion's share of attention by scholars and critics, and Friedkin himself discusses *The Exorcist* and *The French Connection* most often in public. On the other hand, many filmgoers will have at least heard of or be familiar with *To Live and Die in L.A.* from 1985. Others will perhaps know that in 1970 Friedkin made a film adaptation of Mart Crowley's off-Broadway play, *The Boys in the Band*, that he directed the ambitious *Sorcerer*, which was met with crushing failure at the box office, and perhaps be aware that he made the highly controversial *Cruising* in 1980, which incited protests during its filming and release. Most will likely not know that he adapted Harold Pinter's play, *The Birthday Party*, that he filmed an interview with the octogenarian German director Fritz Lang in 1975, that he remade *12 Angry Men* as a television movie in 1997, or that he took on smaller film projects, working on a scale more typical of independent filmmaking, in more recent adaptations of two intense plays by Tracy Letts. The director of a horror film that is often called the scariest movie of all time made almost twenty feature films and over a dozen fictional and documentary productions for television. And while only a few of these could be counted as belonging to the horror genre, which is typically how *The Exorcist* is categorized, his oeuvre encompasses a wide range of popular genres, from crime thrillers and dramas to action and adventure films, including even a couple of comedies. The director is aware that *The Exorcist* is often understood by critics and historians as a pivotal text in horror film history but he will typically reiterate that he became interested in William Peter Blatty's *The Exorcist* after he first read it in 1971 because he understood it as a story about the "mystery of faith."[2] His filmic adaptation was intended not only to be horrifying but also "transcendent, as Blatty has intended."[3] Indeed, it is this experience of transcendence, realized by a largely secular individual who has a particular admiration for the discourse of the Catholic church, that can be linked to his response to the Shroud. Reconsidering and rethinking most of his feature-length productions, this book will attempt to renew our estimation of them, and in doing so, allow us to consider his well-regarded films in conjunction with those that are less known and even disliked.

The failure of Friedkin's *Sorcerer* in 1977 is typically understood, by critics and the filmmaker himself, as being a watershed moment in his career. As he was filming and editing it, he thought that this remake of Henri-Georges Clouzot's *The Wages of Fear* would constitute his magnum opus, the work that would sum up his ideas surrounding the relationship between human agency and fate. "Here was a film," he remarked in 1990, "that I set out to do, that was more than I realized at the time expressing my own cynicism, my own dark side, and I felt that it was pretty good."[4] Friedkin also believed, with some hubris, that it would be as successful as *The Exorcist* at the box office and predicted that it would gross at least $90 million, about the same amount the 1973 film garnered at the time *Sorcerer* was in production in 1976. "Was this bluster and bravado?

Hardly. I believed it," the director recalls.[5] It opened to terrible reviews and also had the unfortunate fate of being released one month after *Star Wars*. George Lucas's film opened to a limited number of cinemas but it quickly became a runaway blockbuster hit as well as originating a franchise that has since attained mythic pop culture status. Friedkin's film played for only a week at the Chinese Theater in Los Angeles before it was overtaken by *Star Wars*. Critics at the time wondered why anyone would want to remake Clouzot's masterpiece and charged the director for "sinfully" creating an inferior copy of the original.[6] Following a complicated production process that involved two major studios, Paramount and Universal, and a final cost that went way over budget, Friedkin was devastated when the film earned less than one-tenth of what he expected. Indeed, other New Hollywood directors such as Martin Scorsese, Peter Bogdanovich, and Michael Cimino experienced failure by the end of the 1970s, due at least to the changing conditions of production, distribution, and exhibition in Hollywood. As David A. Cook writes, many well-known auteurs of the 1970s "experienced a reversal of fortune from the beginning to the end of the decade because so much changed so rapidly. Friedkin's was simply more dramatic than most, because he had been briefly at the pinnacle of the blockbuster pyramid in the process of its formation."[7]

Sorcerer was followed by a string of films that received either lukewarm or intensely adverse responses from critics and audiences. *The Brink's Job*, *Cruising*, *Deal of the Century*, *Rampage*, *The Guardian*, *Jade*: with one underperforming release after another, the 1980s and much of the 90s were particularly unkind to the director. In a *Sight and Sound* article called "Whatever Happened to William Friedkin?," the author explains that the filmmaker, "as a 'man of the 70s', went on making genre films with an uncompromisingly dark view of man and society, at a time when that darkness grew increasingly unfashionable, first with audiences, and then with the (always craven) critics."[8] In his personal life, Friedkin suffered a heart attack in 1981 while driving on the freeway. He fortunately recovered but had to undergo physical therapy for months in order to relearn how to walk. When the director returned to full health, he vowed to learn from his past mistakes and produce better films. But his new releases would invariably be compared to *The Exorcist* and *The French Connection*, and critics typically echoed uninformed or even unfair comparisons to these unique works. In 2012, a reviewer recounts a list of "nonsense" that has "riddled" Friedkin's résumé since 1973 and then writes that the director's newest production at the time, *Killer Joe*, "continues that downward trend, and with any luck it will be the last we hear of William Friedkin."[9] Despite the craven wishes of critics that he somehow go away, and though his films never enjoyed the incredible success of his earlier ones, the man of the '70s continued to produce and never compromised on his thematic preoccupations. Each film is driven by a set of questions that enable us to think of all the films of Friedkin as a body of work.

Meanwhile, *The Boys in the Band* was remade in 2020, directed by Joe Mantello and distributed on Netflix, and a feature-length film of *The Exorcist* is reportedly in the works for theatrical release in 2021. This time around, film critics seem to be more forgiving of the ostensible sin of remaking original films of the past. A documentary directed by Francesco Zippel called *Friedkin Uncut* was shown at festivals and cinemas in 2019, featuring interviews with collaborators and actors with whom he worked. In 2020, another documentary, called *Leap of Faith: William Friedkin on The Exorcist*, was released, this one directed by Alexandre O. Philippe and which delves into the ideas that informed Friedkin during the production of his 1973 blockbuster. In an ironic turn of fate, a number of the director's works, including *Sorcerer* and *Cruising*, have more recently enjoyed a reassessment within the popular and scholarly discourse. The writer Stephen King, in an article for the BFI, remarks that, "My favourite film of all time—this may surprise you—is *Sorcerer*, William Friedkin's remake of the great Henri-Georges Clouzot's *The Wages of Fear*. Some may argue that the Clouzot film is better; I beg to disagree."[10] When the Blu-ray disc of *Cruising* was released in 2019, critics did not denounce it as a homophobic screed that linked homosexuality with violence, as they did when the film was first released in theaters. One contemporary reviewer has called it a "gloriously messy BDSM thriller" while others acknowledge its daring and unabashed portrayal of gay desire, before the AIDS crisis would make such depictions increasingly rare in Hollywood. Film scholars have devoted essays, book chapters, and even an entire monograph to *Cruising*.[11] Meanwhile, an excellent anthology of essays devoted to *The Boys in the Band* was published in 2016. And more recently, a selection of interviews featuring the director was published in the "Conversations with Filmmakers Series" through the University of Mississippi Press.[12]

These studies are preceded by Friedkin's own memoirs, *The Friedkin Connection*, which is the arguably the most significant of the more recent books that have been written about the director. Published in 2013 when he was seventy-eight years old, it is striking for its honesty and general lack of sentimentality about his failures. *The Friedkin Connection* recounts the director's upbringing in the North Side neighborhood of Chicago, the beginnings of his cinema career, his experience of phenomenal success in the early 1970s, struggles with producers, censors, and actors, his professional disappointments, the gradual diversification of his creative activity in film, television, and opera, and then a kind of resigned acceptance of his career trajectory. And while one would be well-advised to maintain some degree of hesitation about the anecdotes reported in it, and to remember that they are to be taken as an article of faith, fascinating flashes of humility and self-reflection repeatedly appear about his own life and career. These flashes of insight were apparently inspired by Elia Kazan's 1988 autobiography. "It's the greatest book about film ever written," Friedkin remarked to me, "[a]bout a life in film, and the book is called *A Life*. It was a tremendous influence on my autobiography. Especially the candor with which he described everything equally that he did, good and bad. And he doesn't boast or brag, he's self-critical, and completely honest about all of his shortcomings." The reception of Friedkin's films, both good and bad, has had a great deal to do with what he calls the "mystery of fate," a mystery that may be related to the mystery of faith, and which he invokes to explain unforeseen events and surprising developments in his life. The director repeatedly claims ignorance about how his films would be received by critics and audiences and throughout *The Friedkin Connection* his tendency is to chalk up unanticipated setbacks to the hand of fate. It is in this way that he is able to bring the narrative of his life and career together, to reconsider his work retrospectively, and refocus the thematic and aesthetic obsessions that reappear in most of his films.

It is in the spirit of these more recent writings on the films of William Friedkin—by critics, scholars, and the director himself—that this book proceeds and continues the critical reassessment of this American auteur. I argue that his work raises the nature of moral character in the cinema and the problem of faith in the modern era in order to seek more capacious, humane ways of relating to others. In provocative narrative moments and explosive scenes that violate how spectators typically think and feel in the cinema, Friedkin lays bare the logic of extra-judicial violence by critically interrogating the nature of moral judgment and its relationship to legal justice. Not only in *The Exorcist* and *The French Connection* but also in *Sorcerer*, *Cruising*, *To Live and Die in L.A.*, *Rules of Engagement*, *Killer Joe* and other films, key characters knowingly transgress moral norms; yet in doing so, the images of these characters provide viewers with the opportunity to critically think the logic of violence that underpins their actions. Indeed, it is precisely the depiction of transgression that defines much of Friedkin's work. In their pursuit of transgressive experience, which takes root in the everyday yet strives to overcome it, his films test the limits of what it means to be a moral human being in postwar American life. Policemen who brutalize civilians with impunity, soldiers who lash out in anger, lawmen who become vigilantes and take the law into their own hands, but also murderers who are put to death: these characters and situations from Friedkin's films raise the question of justice and interrogate the moral lines that separate victims from victimizers. We shall see that his work habitually gravitates toward the delineation of moral contradictions and ethical ambiguities. In doing so, Friedkin asks difficult questions around who is worthy of sympathy and grief, who must be held accountable for wrongdoing, and in what measure.

Narration will be a key area of analysis throughout this book, and we will look closely at its aesthetic form and solicitation of viewer sympathy within popular cinema. But these are areas of critical analysis that will be opened up in order to bring them into crisis. In Friedkin's cinema, denouements are deliberately obscured and plots are knowingly fractured, as if to defy classic Hollywood narration. In tension with the dramatic spectacle that so moved the director when he and his wife encountered the Shroud of Turin, his films have generally eschewed attempts to evoke powerful sentiment. Friedkin explicitly described his own work as "unsentimental" in my interview with him. But it is precisely within this tension between moral sentiment and the lack of it that the mystery of faith in secular life can be brought into relief. To be moved by the image of suffering, an image that attests to universal humanity, even when the authenticity of the image remains in doubt, equates to a kind of belief in the cinema for Friedkin, in what the cinema can do and the discursive effects that it can mobilize in the world. And to maintain a critical stance toward this sentimentality is to pose the problem not only of whether what viewers see and hear in the cinema counts as true but also of whether it can still provide us with the experience of redemption.

Friedkin's career came of age in the wake of the counterculture of the late 1960s, when public sentiment had already turned decisively against the Vietnam War, and confidence in public institutions had soured in the midst of the Watergate scandal and in the subsequent handling of the legacy of Richard Nixon's presidency. Films like *The French Connection* (1971), Francis Ford Coppola's *The Godfather* (1972), Robert Altman's *The Long Goodbye* (1973), Sidney Lumet's *Serpico* (1973), Alan Pakula's *The Parallax View* (1974), Sydney Pollack's *Three Days of the Condor* (1975), and Martin Scorsese's *Taxi Driver* (1976) spoke to younger, radicalized audiences who sought out films that reflected the social and political turmoil that raged outside the theater. The generation of directors that comprised the New Hollywood of the late 1960s to the early 1980s produced work after the collapse of the studios and the Production Code, while contending with the challenges of television and broad changes in the American economy after the dismantling of the Bretton Woods agreement in 1971. Friedkin's films challenge viewers to think critically about the melodrama that is seemingly inextricably linked with politics in America. Compromised individuals in his cinema are asked to render justice in a fair and impartial manner, but this responsibility is repeatedly disrupted and subverted in his films, often by figures of law enforcement. While the American populace was losing faith in the legitimacy of its institutions, Friedkin's work considered the extent to which these institutions were already compromised and impoverished, motivated by moralizing gestures and performative politics. His cynical films show how moral righteousness, fueled by fear and rage, often serves as justification to commit amoral and illegal acts. They resonate with politics in the 1970s in this regard and particularly with the public discourse throughout this decade surrounding the Watergate scandal. In 1973, Nixon famously declared that "I am not a crook." Beleaguered and hounded by the press, he quickly lost legitimacy as commander-in-chief in the eyes of the public.

These are questions that would continue to be addressed in Friedkin's work into the 1980s and beyond, questions that critically reflect on what legitimates the exercise of moral judgment and how others may be deemed guilty or innocent. At a time when traditional morality and structures of authority were being questioned, a number of films inspired viewers to overcome the values of the previous generation through an appeal to a kind of critical pointlessness or to what Todd Berliner, in his book on American film in the 1970s, calls "narrative incoherence."[13] The late Thomas Elsaesser has noted that the heroes in New Hollywood demonstrate a sense of

> inconsequential action, of pointlessness and uselessness: stances which are not only interpretable psychologically, but speak of a radical scepticism about American virtues of ambition, vision, drive; themselves the unacknowledged, because firmly underpinning, architecture of the classical Hollywood action genres.[14]

As Friedkin's career continued into the 1980s and after, some key themes would continue to reappear, despite the changing conditions of production for his films and the changing historical circumstances. We will see how his cinema critiques the ethical thinking of popular narration while striving to discover and delineate one of its own.

This book is organized into five chapters, each introducing concepts and lines of ethical thinking that are key to understanding Friedkin's oeuvre as a whole. Each chapter places two, three, or four films within historical and theoretical contexts. This work is meant to be read straight through, ideally in conjunction with screenings of the work under discussion, as one chapter builds upon ideas developed in the previous ones. Within each chapter, the films are analyzed in chronological order. The reader may notice that I have chosen only sixteen of Friedkin's films to analyze in detail. Although I make at least passing reference to almost all of the director's films and television productions, the works I have chosen for this study I believe are the most effective at articulating thematic obsessions that are distinctive to the director's sensibility and style.

Chapter One, "Spaces of Melodrama," introduces a small cluster of concepts that will be key to understanding the approach I will be taking throughout this book. It begins by focusing on *The Night They Raided Minsky's*, *The Birthday Party*, and *The Boys in the Band*, three of Friedkin's earliest films. On the one hand, I will discuss the analytical virtues of thinking New Hollywood cinema against the backdrop of what Linda Williams calls the "melodramatic mode."[15]

Following the dismantling of the Production Code and the industry's shift toward younger audiences, movies in the late 1960s became more explicit and risqué, transgressing the moral boundaries that would have run counter to the Code's aim of "moral uplift." On the other hand, Friedkin's early films take place in enclosed interior spaces, implicitly delineating inside from outside, and bring us quickly into the experience of these spaces as claustrophobic. Claustrophobic spaces affect characters by both heightening the sense of desperation for the individuals within the diegesis and by inducing anxiety for the spectator sitting in the enclosed space of the cinema theater. *The French Connection*, as we know, is set in outdoor locations in Marseille and New York. Here, for the first time in Friedkin's films, we see the character of the policeman who crosses the thin blue line to pursue criminals by having recourse to morally and legally questionable methods. Those who enforce the law become violators of the law, emboldened by their own outrage at the transgressions of others and their growing frustration at the inability to capture the French drug traffickers.

Chapter Two, "Policing the Police," further considers this crossing from policeman to criminal. In *To Live and Die in L.A.*, law and lawlessness are made exchangeable with each other, like real and counterfeit money, or cops who impersonate crooks. Friedkin boasts that the fake currency used in the film was successfully exchanged by a crew member's son for candy at a supermarket, allowing us to ponder the difference between truth and fiction in the cinema. Moreover, *To Live and Die in L.A.*, with its "dirty" cops and car chase set piece, is read here as a reiteration of themes and problems taken over from *The French Connection*. The later film seems to "impersonate" the earlier. Where the heroin in the earlier film was real, the money in the later one is fake, bought by real money procured from the federal government. At stake in these exchanges is the question of legitimacy—of what legitimizes paper as legal tender—but also of identities based on gender, sexuality, and criminality. These issues are also raised in *Rules of Engagement* and *The Hunted*, both films that feature military soldiers who act out with impunity under conditions of emergency. Male camaraderie and loyalty are invoked in them to justify the transgression of law. Procedure and protocol in fact merely stand in the way of their moral righteousness, and are seen to be frustrating impediments toward the heroic recognition of virtue, however perverse, within the melodramatic mode. *The Hunted* is explicitly structured as a chase film and it is precisely the chase that sanctions the chaos it typically produces as well as the suspension of legal and moral norms.

The next chapter, "Criminal Desires," looks at *Cruising*, *Jade*, and *Killer Joe*, three films that have raised controversy for their explicit representations of and linkage between violence and sexuality. While the characters in these films exhibit signs of criminal desire that are sexual in nature, I am less interested in performing psychoanalytic analyses that will reveal their interiority. Rather, we shall see that for Friedkin, working with the formulation attributed to T. S. Eliot that states that "action is character," characterization is a consequence of legible actions and not the other way around.[16] Sexuality and criminality are manifest through legible performatives and not simply the expressions of a psychic condition. In this way, dissimulation and impersonation become key themes in *Cruising* and *Jade*, as identity is constituted in both films through the display of surfaces that are available for scrutiny within the melodramatic mode. *Killer Joe*, adapted from the play by Tracy Letts, also works with the thin line between policeman and criminal, taking the justification of violence that Friedkin has interrogated in previous films to its limits. We shall see that the transactional relations that comprise the ethics of the characters in this claustrophobic community of poor individuals, who have been trapped in desperate situations, seem to implode from within, culminating with the film's explosive conclusion.

Chapter Four, "Justice at the Limits of Popular Cinema," takes a look at four films in order to consider the impulse toward transgression within the context of melodrama. Taken together, they span almost the entirety of Friedkin's filmmaking career: *The People v. Paul Crump*, *Rampage*, *12 Angry Men*, and *Bug*. The first three films of the chapter raise the question of how justice may be realized through the form of popular narrative. *The People v. Paul Crump* and *Rampage* both deal with the morality of capital punishment but differ in their approach toward its ethics. While the earlier film offers a clear critique of the death penalty, by 1987 Friedkin seems to have shifted in his position and makes the case that state-sanctioned death for the victimizer can achieve some measure of justice for the victimized. The 1997 film *12 Angry Men* is a remake of the well-known 1957 Sidney Lumet film of the same name. In his remake Friedkin makes subtle changes to the script that places the film into dialogue with issues of race and justice that were raised during the O. J. Simpson trial, the so-called "Trial of the Century," that unfolded on American televisions in 1995. Finally, *Bug* is another adaptation of a play by Letts that takes the dichotomy between interiority and exteriority to its limits, showing what happens to the spaces of melodrama when they are plunged into crisis. The protagonists of the film become obsessed with bugs that are simultaneously inside and outside their bodies, inducing an experience of paranoia for the characters in the diegesis, but perhaps for spectators sitting inside the cinema theater as well.

The last chapter, "The Power of Cinema Compels You," culminates with Friedkin's most ambitious films, bringing the mysteries of faith and fate to the fore most explicitly. *The Exorcist* and *Sorcerer* were made relatively early in the director's career, one a major success with most critics and audiences and the other a failure with viewers at the time. But these films introduce broad themes to which his later ones will repeatedly return. They bring us back to questions that refer to the power of the cinema image. *The Exorcist* and *Sorcerer* ask viewers to have faith in what it reveals, on the one hand, and also lead us to reflect upon the unfolding of one's life through film's own temporal unfolding. When Friedkin speaks about fate, he is referring to the arrival of that which cannot be anticipated, yet an event that is nevertheless certain to occur. *The Exorcist* take the limits of what can be seen and heard in the cinema to its breaking point, raising the problem of faith in the cinema through the allegory of religious faith. *Sorcerer* plays out a narrative of human individuals who are placed in extreme conditions and, because they have nothing more to lose, risk their lives by choosing to pursue a goal in a state of constant precariousness. The four main protagonists deliver highly combustible explosives on rickety trucks through dilapidated roads, over hundreds of miles of treacherous terrain.

After the disappointment of this film's poor reception with audiences, Friedkin continued to direct, perhaps with a similar sense of precariousness that reminded him of his own status as a filmmaker in Hollywood. At the Cannes festival in 2016, Friedkin reflects upon this constant reminder that followed him throughout his long career, according to his interviewer:

> "Inside of every one of us who has ever created anything there is an almost constant record of failure," he told the festival audience. "That's what we think about. That's what involves our thought process. I know some of the most successful filmmakers and songwriters, and inside these giant talents is a little mouse."[17]

Refocusing our understanding of the films of Friedkin must be undertaken with an appreciation of the way in which this auteur has dealt with a long period of disappointment following an experience of stunning, but short-lived, success. The *Spectator* journalist who interviewed him reports that Friedkin arrived at the festival "basking in sort of adoration he hadn't known for half a lifetime."[18] When I spoke to the director at his Bel-Air home, he had just returned from one of the many retrospectives of his work that were taking place in New York, France, Italy, and other locations where international festivals celebrated his career. I asked him what he thought about the recent recognition of his work and he replied, with characteristic brute honesty, that he "doesn't give a damn." I laughed at this somewhat flippant response and then, with the same lack of sentimentality, we moved on to discuss his rich life and career.

NOTES

1. André Bazin, "The Ontology of the Photographic Image," in *What is Cinema? Vol. 1*, trans. Hugh Gray (Berkeley: University of California Press, 1984), 14.
2. William Friedkin, *The Friedkin Connection* (New York: Harper, 2013), 232.
3. Friedkin, *The Friedkin Connection*, 232.
4. Christopher Lane, ed., *William Friedkin: Interviews*, Conversations with Filmmakers Series (Jackson: University of Mississippi Press, 2020), 51.

5. Friedkin, *The Friedkin Connection*, 345.
6. Gary Arnold, "A Sinful Copy of 'The Wages of Fear,'" *The Washington Post*, June 27, 1977.
7. David A. Cook, *Lost Illusions: American Cinema in the Shadow of Watergate and Vietnam* (Berkeley: University of California Press, 2000), 106.
8. Larry Gross, "Whatever Happened to William Friedkin?," *Sight and Sound* 12 (December 1995), 15.
9. Josh Rosenblatt, "Friedkin Continues Career Dive," *The Texas Observer* 104, no. 8 (2012), 42.
10. Stephen King, "Stephen King's Favorite Films," *BFI*, December 8, 2017, accessed November 1, 2020, <https://www2.bfi.org.uk/news-opinion/news-bfi/features/stephen-king-favourite-films>
11. Chris Ludovici, "Williams Friedkin's '*Cruising*' Remains a Gloriously Messy BDSM Thriller," *The Spool*, September 25, 2019, accessed November 1, 2020, <https://thespool.net/reviews/movies/2019/09/william-friedkins-cruising-blu-ray-review>. See Eugenio Ercolani and Marcus Stiglegger, *Cruising* (Liverpool: Liverpool University Press, 2020).
12. See Matt Bell, ed., *The Boys in the Band: Flashpoints of Cinema, History, and Queer Politics* (Detroit: Wayne State University Press, 2016) and Lane, *William Friedkin: Interviews*.
13. See Todd Berliner, *Hollywood Incoherent: Narration in Seventies Cinema* (Austin: University of Texas Press, 2010).
14. Thomas Elsaesser, "The Pathos of Failure: American Films in the 1970s," in Thomas Elsaesser, Alexander Horwath, and Noel King, eds., *The Last Great American Picture Show* (Amsterdam: Amsterdam University Press, 2004), 282.
15. See Linda Williams, *Playing the Race Card: Melodramas of Black and White from Uncle Tom to O. J. Simpson* (Princeton: Princeton University Press, 2002).
16. Friedkin, *The Friedkin Connection*, 472.
17. Lane, *William Friedkin: Interviews*, 142.
18. Lane, *William Friedkin: Interviews*, 140.

CHAPTER 1

Spaces of Melodrama

THE NIGHT THEY RAIDED MINSKY'S (1968)

The premise of *The Night They Raided Minsky's* (hereafter *Minsky's*), Friedkin's second fictional feature, embodies a number of contradictions that will be reiterated throughout his work. The film begins with a series of intertitles written in the second person and read by a vaudeville announcer (spoken by Rudy Vallée). While the text states that the story is based on "really true incidents that actually happened," Vallée's hyperbolic and flamboyant voice indicates that the ensuing film will have a campy tone. The intertitles acknowledge its "real sophisticated audience," addressing them with a wink and smile. They then entice the viewer with the premise of the scandalous story that will follow: "In 1925 there was this real religious girl and by accident she invented the striptease. This real religious girl. In 1925." The repetition of the "real religious girl" and the year, 1925, seems intended to saucily emphasize the tension produced by the juxtaposition of the virtues of faith and the questionable scruples of striptease. Further tensions are also indicated in the text's reference to religious naivety and the excesses of the Roaring Twenties as well as to the perceived incongruity between the sexual mores of 1925 and those of 1968, the time of the viewer. The presence of the intertitles harks back to the silent period of film history and Vallée's radio voice to the youth culture of the 1930s.

The credit sequence further plays out these contradictions through montage. *Minsky's* cuts to black-and-white footage of smiling flappers dancing with their partners and robust men performing stunts in front of clapping audiences. This sequence then settles into depictions of New York's bustling Lower East Side, featuring working-class women shopping in its outdoor markets and men pushing heavy carts through its busy streets. In the midst of this bustle, shots of the same market, filmed contemporaneously in color to the era of the spectator, are intercut throughout the archival footage. With the location established, images of the elevated New York subway take us to a close-up shot of a young woman riding a subway car. She has red hair and wears a prayer kapp, a traditional Amish head covering. As the woman disembarks from the train and walks through the market, the viewer is shown color images of the settings taken from the 1960s, then in black-and-white from the 1920s, then back again, switching between footage that was recently filmed and that sourced from the archives. On the one hand, *Minsky's* opening montage sequence attempts to nostalgically transport the viewer's imagination to the time signified in the diegesis, while adding a sense of historical authenticity to Friedkin's images. On the other hand, this sequence acknowledges the historicity of the film medium itself, of a period pre-dating what the cinema was in 1968, signaled through cuts in this opening scene to documentary footage not taken by Friedkin. Switching back and forth between the diegesis of the film and archival material, *Minsky's* nostalgically recalls an earlier era of bawdy entertainment that has all but disappeared.

Minsky's editor, Ralph Rosenblum, recalls in his memoirs that he stumbled upon the idea to intercut between the old and new shots of the Lower East Side through experimentation. Looking for inspiration in archival footage of the Amish, Rosenblum made an unanticipated connection, as he writes:

> The head of *Minsky's* is the opening sequence of the Amish girl arriving in New York. I worked and reworked this scene, trying to incorporate some of the stock footage. The process is tedious, rarely offering much return on a day's labor, but it yielded my first inkling of how I might transform the film. As I intercut the scenes, I realized that the orthodox Amish farmers looked similar to some of the extras in the original shooting, men with beards and big hats who were supposed to be Orthodox Jews. It seemed a perfect binding element to bolster the important opening minutes. As Britt Ekland arrives in New York, the flash cuts of the Amish would highlight the emotional impact of her entering this alien but strangely similar world.[1]

The dynamic intercutting that constitutes the film's opening sequence was conceived as Rosenblum recognized a resemblance between the Pennsylvania Amish and Orthodox Jews in New York. Comparisons between two religious groups gave way, for him, to comparisons between the two historical moments of 1925 and 1968. Friedkin would take these juxtapositions further, however, in order to express a series of moral contradictions that underpin the film as a whole. As this book proceeds, such juxtapositions will repeatedly return as a series of problematics characterizing Friedkin's films throughout his career.

We soon find out that the name of the young Amish woman is Rachel Schpitendavel, played by the young Swedish actress Britt Ekland. She continues to wander through the market until she reaches the National Winter Garden Theater. Standing at its front doors is Professor Spats, played by the then seventy-two-year-old Bert Lahr who is perhaps best known for his role as the Cowardly Lion in *The Wizard of Oz*, another film that switches between color and black-and-white thematically. In his earlier life, Lahr enjoyed a long and successful career in the vaudeville theater circuit and his presence here underscores *Minsky's* homage to a past period of popular entertainment. A sign above the theater entrance reads, "The Poor Man's Follies," which implicitly compares the gaudy shows that take place inside with the much more elaborate *Ziegfeld Follies* on Broadway. Rachel asks Spats if she has arrived at the National Winter Garden and he answers in the affirmative. "Could I move inside," she implores in awkward English, perhaps meant to emphasize her naivety, "I'd feel safe forever." Spats winks and smiles. And with this, as if to whisk Rachel and the viewer to another world (perhaps somewhere "over the rainbow"), the film cuts to the raucous pit orchestra of the theater. Almost immediately, the film's soundtrack begins to play waltz-like and sentimental music while a montage of vaudeville stage acts follows. The audience sees joyous musical numbers, line dancers, and close-ups of costumed actors performing in comedy sketches. Over these shots the credits roll and the full title of the film, "The Night They Raided Minsky's," flashes on the screen. Despite the merriment, this opening montage seems also to evoke a sense of bittersweet nostalgia, setting a tone that juxtaposes merriment with wistfulness.

Minsky's quickly settles into its story. Rachel, the "real religious girl" indicated in the opening intertitles, has arrived in New York in defiance of her father. She wants to dance on the stage at the Winter Garden, but the young Amish woman only knows how to dance to stories from the Bible. She certainly does not have the experience to perform the garish bopping and swaying that typically takes place in the Lower East Side theater. As Rachel elaborates on her intentions and as the film unfolds, two vaudeville performers, Raymond (Jason Robards) and Chick (Norman Wisdom), compete for her attention. Both men enjoy ribbing on each other while making a game out of sleeping with attractive women. The older Raymond remarks that Chick has the "curse of the three Ds, you are decent, devoted, and dependable—good qualities in a dog, disastrous in a man." Conversely, Raymond calls himself a "BFC," a "Bastard First Class," and claims that "women like bastards." *Minsky's* is a comedic film, yet it also takes up the cruel premise set out in *Les Liaisons dangereuses*, an epistolary novel by Pierre Choderlos de Laclos that tells the story of two manipulative, competitive men who possess a particular talent for seduction.

Raymond and Chick devise a plan to exploit the naive young Rachel, not only to win her sexually, but also to humiliate the police, who have been hassling the theater to clean up their act and have sought to revoke Minsky's license. Together, Raymond and Chick conspire to put Rachel on stage and bill her as "Madame Fifi," the lascivious performer who "drove a million Frenchmen wild." The head of the New York vice squad, Vance Fowler (Denholm Elliott), hears of the licentious midnight show and threatens that, "if Mademoiselle Fifi puts one foot on stage tonight, we raid tonight!" The intent is to shame the police when they raid the theater, for they will only discover a "real religious girl" dancing chastely to Bible stories. Throughout all this, Rachel's desire remains only to break away from her traditional, virtuous past so that she may look forward to adopting her new life as a stage dancer.

While Raymond and Chick make plans to expose the self-righteousness and over-zealousness of the police, it is the naive Amish girl who is cruelly shamed in *Minsky's* final scene. Their plans are revealed to the entire cast and crew. "It was all a plan to trick Fowler," Billy Minsky (Elliot Gould) explains, "he thought he was going to raid the real Fifi, and we were gonna send this one out on stage. But she's a kid. She dances stories from the Bible." The camera moves to a close-up of Rachel's face and her eyes well up with tears. She is hearing about this scheme for the first time. "Like that, we were gonna embarrass Fowler," he continues, "and have him run out of town. I didn't want to send her out on stage. She can't dance. She's not talented. Raymond tricked her. He told her that if she came in here she'd be able to go out on stage. She's nothin'. It was all just a big joke." Realizing that Raymond and Chick planned to take advantage of her, Rachel becomes disillusioned and begins to feel sorry for herself.

As soon as he finishes explaining his plan, Rachel's stern Amish father (Harry Andrews) storms into the backstage area of the theater and approaches his daughter. Rachel is just about to go on. Referring to her as "Jezebel," her father tears off her coat to reveal the skimpy dancing outfit underneath, accuses her of sinful pride, and explicitly calls her a whore. With tears now running down her cheeks, Rachel defiantly announces, "You heard my father, I'm a whore," and marches out on stage to enthusiastic applause. Though apprehensive at first, she is encouraged by the orchestra drummer to twist and thrust her hips toward cheering men in various sections of the audience. Rachel's father becomes outraged and tries to grab and tear her away from the stage, only to rip a section of her dress and expose her bare leg. This incites the crowd to jeer and clap more loudly. As she becomes increasingly aware of the audience reaction at the spectacle of her state of undress, Rachel, who has now become Madame Fifi, removes her gloves, exposes her legs further by ripping her dress more, and throws off the green scarf that covers her top (Figure 1.1). She looks back at the group standing in the wings, including performers and the police,

Figure 1.1 "Madame Fifi" incites the audience

and sees Raymond's disapproving face. The experienced performer places his hat on his head, dons his coat and suitcase, and turns to leave. Rachel apparently wants to retain his affection and when she reaches out toward him, her dress falls to the floor. With her exposed breasts on view, the crowd applauds even more wildly and the police promptly scuttle in, shutting down Minsky's theater. As Rachel is escorted out of the theater by the police, both the men and the women in the audience clap and cheer. She even stops for a photo, posing and smiling, aware that she has already become a star. And with this, so the story goes, the modern striptease was born—from the grand, bawdy tradition of American vaudeville theater.

When *Minsky's* begins, we are introduced to an innocent Amish girl who wants to perform on stage and break away from her provincial upbringing. By the end of the film, she has definitively broken away from her father – and from Raymond and Chick as well. But in the end, it is the young Rachel who exploits Raymond for her own personal gain, and in doing so it is she, now all grown up, who defies all the men that have tried to control her throughout the film. She is crudely billed as "the hottest little cooch artist in the world" by the businessmen and male performers who plan to exploit her. And yet, despite her feelings of remorse for disappointing both Raymond and especially her father, she nevertheless feels that her potential as a performer must be realized. Contradicting her characterization as, according to Roger Ebert, "wide-eyed and innocent as anyone since the young Debbie Reynolds," it remains unclear whether Rachel has been taken or is taking advantage of these situations.[2] Nevertheless, by the end of the film she quickly defines her own sexuality, determines how it should be presented, and takes control of the contexts in which it is to be utilized. And so, by affirming her incendiary power to "drive a million men wild," Rachel flouts the patriarchal constraints on her gender and, ostensibly, takes control of her own destiny. Still, despite her sexual liberation, it remains uncertain whether viewers are supposed to sympathize with her character.

The character of Rachel is exploited by the film's narrative to tell the history of how the movies grew up and how audiences matured to accept more explicit, more provocative representations of sex and sexuality. She functions as the agent by which traditional tastes and moral standards were incited to change toward more modern visual pleasures, as if to manifest the progression from 1925 to 1968. *Minsky's* works with memories of a time before the fall of virtue, when audiences could appreciate the art of vaudeville and burlesque performance, before the obscene and the explicit infiltrated the stage and screen and brought into question the mission of "moral uplift" typically associated with reputable entertainment. By depicting a time that predates the year of its production by thirty-three years, Friedkin's film seems to nostalgically reflect, in an age when more provocative representations increasingly appeared on film screens and living room televisions, on the final moments of cinema's moral innocence. *Minsky's* also seems to look back on a time when cinema profits and audiences were more certain, from the vantage point of an emerging generation of New Hollywood directors who were interested in themes around disillusionment and alienation (Mike Nichols's *The Graduate* [1967]), more explicit scenes of violence and new anti-heroes (Sam Peckinpah's *The Wild Bunch* [1969] and Arthur Penn's *Bonnie and Clyde* [1967]), and the emerging counterculture (Dennis Hopper's *Easy Rider* [1969]). Hollywood at this transitional moment invited innovation in order to cultivate younger audiences. Meanwhile, long-lens and wide-angle lens shots provided filmmakers with new ways of distorting and shaping the image of reality through expansive establishing shots, intense close-ups, documentary authenticity and stylized flattening. Portable sound equipment lent this reality a greater immediacy as well. In *Minsky's*, released in late 1968, Friedkin was indulging the changing desires of these new audiences by self-reflexively flirting with transgressive desires that were largely denied during the era of the Production Code.

The year 1968 was a turning point in the ongoing war in Vietnam, particularly in the public perception of America's moral righteousness in the world after 1945. The Tet Offensive that began in the first few months of that year revealed the cost, in lives and money, of the continued involvement of the U.S. in imperial missions abroad. Shocking NBC footage of a South Vietnamese officer executing a Viet Cong officer, which was broadcast worldwide in February, galvanized the anti-war movement and further divided the American public. On April 4, Martin Luther King Jr. was assassinated, causing violence and race riots in many cities throughout the U.S. In June, Senator Robert F. Kennedy was killed while giving a speech in Los Angeles, by an assassin who disagreed with his support of Israel in the midst of the Arab-Israeli conflict. A couple of months later, the Democratic National Convention in Chicago brought student activist leaders and anti-war protestors into violent melee with armed police, conflicts that were filmed and widely publicized in the news media. *Chariots of the Gods* was written in 1968, a book that proposed that extraterrestrial aliens influenced human technology long ago, and it eventually became a *New York Times* bestseller. In November of that same year, *The White Album* by the Beatles was released, and it would come to serve as the grounding text for Charles Manson's fantasies about a coming race war and be cited to justify his murderous rampage in Los Angeles in 1969. And about a month before *Minsky's* premiered in theaters, Richard Nixon became the thirty-seventh president of the U.S., defeating Democratic incumbent Hubert Humphrey. His campaign promised the upkeep of law and order throughout the land, especially in the cities, and assured voters that he would end the Vietnam War. Nixon would remain in office throughout the production of Friedkin's most successful films, including *The French Connection* and *The Exorcist*.

The character of Rachel in *Minsky's* may be read to allegorize these transformations and the loss of innocence. She is both the subject of and subject to changes—aesthetic, moral, and technological—in how these transformations are represented, serving as the figure that both initiates and marks radical shifts from old to new. Renata Adler's review for the *New York Times*, commenting positively on the authenticity of the Lower East Side depicted in Friedkin's film, seems to express this nostalgia. "The nicest thing about the movie," Adler writes,

> which is a little broad in plot and long in spots, is its denseness and care in detail: The little ugly cough that comes from one room of a shoddy hotel; the thoughtfully worked out, poorly danced vaudeville routines; the beautifully timed, and genuinely funny, gags. "I hear the man say impossible," a man on the stage says when the man here hasn't said a word. And the vaudeville routines of innocence forever victimized, for the amusement of an audience of fall guys, works pretty much as it must have worked in its time.[3]

And yet, while *Minsky's* pays homage to a more innocent past, its ironic tone nevertheless seems to acknowledge that this past remains one that exists only in the imagination and that the recovery of this innocence will be impossible. While honoring an American art form that has lost its contemporary relevance, and through this inspiring a consciousness of history and historicity, Friedkin's film acknowledges that this form will not be resurrected. "The zeitgeist was changing," the director writes of this film, "and a nostalgic piece of fluff about a bygone era was out of step with the rise of independent cinema."[4]

It is thus significant that Friedkin's film appeared at a moment when the Production Code, instituted in 1924 by Will Hays, was being abandoned and replaced by Jack Valenti's ratings system. *Minsky's* flies in the face of many of the Code's guiding principles, not to mention its specific interdictions. Indeed, if the aim of the Code was to ensure that films would not lower the moral standards of American audiences and that the depiction of sex and violence be shown in a manner that would uphold "the correct standards of life," Friedkin's film seems, like Rachel's performance, defiant of such normative criteria.[5] As if to affirm this, near the beginning of the film Billy Minsky (Elliott Gould) explains to his father that his burlesque shows are "supposed to be frank, it makes fun of life, but dirty." Rachel's show pushes the limits of what sort of entertainment may be considered "clean" or "dirty," what may be considered morally acceptable with respect to the depiction of nudity, and, by co-extension, how relations between men and women may be depicted in the cinema. As one of the first films to be scrutinized by the new system, *Minsky's* would receive an "M" ("Mature") rating for its indiscretions. It would foreshadow the kinds of thematic contradictions that would appear in Friedkin's films, as we shall see: legal and sexual transgression; the challenge to established morality; and protagonists that seem to inspire the divided sympathies of the viewer. Allegorizing the brazen but— paradoxically—also tentative manner by which Hollywood changed after the fall of the Production Code, Rachel bares her breasts to an audience eager for new, more risqué forms of entertainment. (This moment seems to anticipate a well-known scene in which Cybill Shepherd removes her clothes at a skinny-dipping party in Peter Bogdanovich's *The Last Picture Show*). Friedkin's films will flourish because of these relaxed interdictions around the representation of sex, crime, violence, and immoral behavior in this period.

At the time of *Minsky's* production, however, Friedkin claims that he was uncertain of what he was doing. In 2013, he comments that while the film is "charming, innocent, and touching in many ways," the director was "in over my head" during the production process.[6] Friedkin did not know much about the burlesque tradition or about musical comedy and admits that "*Minsky's* was a disaster that set me back in every possible way."[7] When filming took place in the Fall of 1967, the crew were on the verge of mutiny, sensing the director's lack of experience. Production ended in December of that year, but the first cut was deemed unacceptable and sent back to the editing room. The film was not granted a theatrical release until December 23rd of 1968, a full year later. However, the young director had already left for London to begin work on his next film, leaving his editor alone in New York to redo the failing first cut. The difficulties around post-production delayed its release, as he and Rosenblum freely confess, until after his next project was released in theaters. While *Minsky's* displays some of the themes that Friedkin would pursue throughout his career, it admittedly lacks the vision and intensity that would come to characterize his later work. Nevertheless, it has allowed us to introduce a number of key themes and contexts, and in a moment we shall see how the film director will become entrenched in the aesthetic and dramatic possibilities offered by the theatrical stage.

THE BIRTHDAY PARTY (1968)

The scene of Stanley Webber's (Robert Shaw) birthday toast, which occurs at the midway point of *The Birthday Party*, is filled not with celebration but insolence, depravity, and foreboding. Friedkin's film is an adaptation of Harold Pinter's 1958 play of the same name and features scenes of intimidation that are antithetical to the typical birthday celebration. In the small, drab boarding house in which the entirety of the story takes place, Stanley, a concert pianist, looks miserable as a flashlight shines in his face. The lights have been switched off. He is surrounded by two menacing strangers, McCann (Patrick Magee) and Goldberg (Sydney Tafler), and the elderly landlady of the boarding house, Meg Bowles (Dandy Nichols). They are the "guests" at Stanley's birthday party. Meg offers some trite words of affection, remarking that the despondent pianist is a "good boy, though sometimes he's bad," and then breaks down in tears of appreciation. Her comments and treatment of him are infantilizing, as if she were speaking about an ineffectual son. While Meg celebrates her adult boarder, a young, buxom woman named Lulu (Helen Fraser), a visitor to the boarding house, comes in the door. The lights of the small room are switched on and she is offered a drink. Then, as Goldberg, the most eloquent of the four, raises a glass to begin his toast, he once more commands, firmly, that Stanley sit down. The disheveled piano player peers at the condescendingly smiling man and hesitates to do so. In the moments leading up to this scene, an intense and heated struggle revolving around sitting and around who is going to sit, had taken place, a struggle that infused the birthday party with violence and bullying terror.

Goldberg delivers a droll speech about "real, true warmth" between friends and the "quality" of affection he sees shared between Meg and Stanley. Indeed, their relationship seems to oscillate between maternal solicitude and erotic longing throughout the film. With the lights turned off once again and the flashlight shining on Stanley's irritated face, they all wish him a happy birthday. Lulu asks Goldberg where he learned to speak so marvelously. "Well, my first chance to stand up and give a lecture," he answers, "was at the Ethical Hall, Bayswater. A wonderful opportunity. I'll never forget it. They were all there that night. Charlotte Street was empty. Of course, that's a good while ago." We know little about the intimidating Goldberg, but the fact that he has been given opportunities to lecture reveals that he possesses some form of expertise. He tells us that the topic of his lecture, significant in light of the violence that preceded the birthday party scene, was the "Necessary and the Possible."

In fact, Goldberg had just briefly extemporized on this topic during his and McCann's verbal assault on Stanley. In the twenty-five or so minutes leading up to this seemingly festive scene, the small boarding house had served as the claustrophobic stage for a violent confrontation between the nervous, irritated pianist and the two strange men. Their first uneasy meeting on screen escalated—through the exchange of threats and sarcastic remarks—to their raising chairs to strike each other. The increasing tension between the three men was diffused only with the entrance of Meg Bowles. At one point, McCann and Goldberg assaulted Stanley with a series of impossible questions, in the end all pointless, rapidly delivered as if each were a shot from a machine gun:

GOLDBERG. Do you recognise an external force?
STANLEY. What?
GOLDBERG. Do you recognise an external force?
MCCANN. That's the question!
GOLDBERG. Do you recognise an external force, responsible for you, suffering for you?
STANLEY. It's late.
GOLDBERG. Late! Late enough! When did you last pray?
MCCANN. He's sweating!
GOLDBERG. When did you last pray?
MCCANN. He's sweating!
GOLDBERG. Is the number 846 possible or necessary?
STANLEY. Neither.
GOLDBERG. Wrong! Is the number 846 possible or necessary?
STANLEY. Both.
GOLDBERG. Wrong! It's necessary but not possible.
STANLEY. Both.
GOLDBERG. Wrong! Why do you think the number 846 is necessarily possible?
STANLEY. Must be.
GOLDBERG. Wrong! It's only necessarily necessary! We admit possibility only after we grant necessity. It is possible because necessary but by no means necessary through possibility. The possibility can only be assumed after the proof of necessity.[8]

The Birthday Party cuts between quick close-up shots of the grotesque faces of McCann and Goldberg as they leave Stanley flummoxed with their unrelenting questions. In his notes for this moment, Friedkin writes, "Necessary-possible: Run it all together – don't break it up –."[9] Evidently, he wanted the dialogue to unfold quickly and aggressively. The two men then go on to accuse the victimized pianist of lechery, heresy, and of being a traitor (to what is not made clear). Inquiring about whether Stanley believes in an "external force, responsible for you, suffering for you," when he last prayed, and the significance of the number 846, their line of questioning seems arbitrary at best. Yet McCann and Goldberg also propose arbitrary answers to their own impossible inquiries, leaving little doubt that their intentions are to barrage Stanley rather than to find definitive resolutions. In passages like these, language seems to lose its power to signify, creating not meaningful speech but signification that remains empty and futile, speech acts whose purpose seems only to assault. In a lecture delivered by Pinter in 1962, he calls this empty speech a kind of "silence" that is constituted through garrulous talk, a silence which at the same time prattles on and conceals "a language locked beneath it."[10] This language, obscured by unnecessary and impossible speech, is one that is close to the expressive body and demands that it burst forth through Pinter's dialogue.

Indeed, the problem of whether a particular number is "necessary or possible" seems to speak to a question that remains central to *The Birthday Party*. McCann and Goldberg, who together constitute a violent external force, have come to the boarding house to take Stanley away (Figure 1.2). They never reveal the reason why, never explain the reasons for his guilt, and do not reference any of his past actions that might justify and help viewers understand Stanley's seemingly inevitable incarceration. At one point, the audience overhears McCann and Goldberg speaking about someone named Monty, who apparently is the leader of "the organization," but these entities remain shrouded in mystery. What are their motives? Why is it "necessary" that they pursue Stanley, and in such a threatening manner? Did they arrive to "shoot the piano player"? Who is Monty and are they all members of a gang or of law enforcement? How did such treatment of Stanley become "possible"? Vincent Canby, in his review of the film, calls *The Birthday Party* "a horror story that has no reasonable antecedents," suggesting that it depicts a violent story that had already been unfolding, as if the reasons for Stanley's seizure were so evident that they need not be made explicit.[11]

Moreover, and confounding this Kafkaesque predicament further, certain moments in the film indicate that Stanley's presumption of innocence may not be so clear, as he himself becomes a force of intimidating violence, not unlike McCann and Goldberg. At the end of the second act, following the celebratory toasts, the party guests coerce Stanley into a game of blind man's bluff. His glasses forcibly removed, the hapless pianist blindly searches the room with his hands and stumbles about. He inadvertently steps into the toy drum that was his birthday present from Meg. McCann, holding Stanley's glasses, snaps

Figure 1.2 Stanley is trapped

them in half. Meanwhile Stanley continues dragging the drum with his foot and somehow finds Meg in the dark. He begins to strangle her. Goldberg and McCann throw him off the motherly landlord and suddenly the lights go out again. In the darkness, they search for the light. Lulu screams in terror. When McCann finds a flashlight and shines it on Stanley once more, the piano player is bent over Lulu and sexually assaulting her. Caught in the spotlight, he is wide-eyed, as if to betray guilt through his look. Stanley backs away toward the wall and lets out a high-pitched giggle, an excruciating sound that seems to express both perverse pleasure and pent-up anguish. This horrific scene reveals, ostensibly, the violent resentment that has remained latent in Stanley's character and which was allowed to momentarily manifest itself in the darkness. If he was capable of carrying out these acts of brutality and sadism, what did he do previously that necessitated the aggressive intrusion of Goldberg and McCann? The film suggests the possibility that Stanley is, in fact, not a just victim of violence but may have himself been a victimizer. These questions, which concern the virtue of the characters as well as the extent to which the audience is supposed to sympathize with them, are left unanswered in Pinter's story and in Friedkin's film.

These problematics concerning characterization and sympathy in *The Birthday Party* revolve around discursive presuppositions that underpin the melodramatic mode. Encompassing a scope that extends far beyond the typical understanding of melodrama in film and media studies as primarily a genre or an aesthetic of excess, "melodrama proper," according to Peter Brooks, should be understood as a dominant mode of popular entertainment whose lineage may be traced back to late eighteenth-century French theater.[12] The Revolution was a decisive moment in this regard, constituting the culmination of a process of secularization that began with the Renaissance and which emblemizes the retreat of sacred myth from the ethical life of individuals in modernity. Popular theater and melodrama restore a sense of coherence to the void left by this retreat through its presumption of an invisible "moral occult" that must be interpreted from empirical signs: costumes, *mise-en-scène*, lighting, music, mute gestures, physiognomy. In this, the increasing preponderance of melodrama since the onset of modernity gives further proof of the waning legitimacy of the sacred, particularly in its social and political representations. As Brooks writes:

> We might, finally, do well to recognize the melodramatic mode as a central fact of the modern sensibility (I take Romanticism to be the genesis of the modern, of the sensibility within which we are still living), in that modern art has typically felt itself to be constructed on, and over, the voice, postulating meanings and symbolic means which have no certain justification because they are backed by no theology and no universally accepted social code.[13]

This sensibility, "within which we are still living," spares us from directly confronting the horror of living in a world devoid of universal moral and ethical presuppositions. Within this regime, the human being presupposes the presence of an individual humanity through the recognition of signs while also assigning motives to these very signs. This humanity is delineated as separate from the authority of the church and the promises of religious faith, and because of this secularization, this process of individualization, the human is assumed to seek expression in the world. Melodrama teaches audiences how to become sensitive to this modern world and embarks them on a search for virtue and authenticity beyond appearances.

The aim of melodrama is, through narration, to externalize and make legible this moral occult and, in turn, to constitute what is typically called "character" or the "persona" of a signifying body on screen. The modern belief in the presence of an invisible moral occult compels the desire for it to be discovered, to determine whether a character possesses a "moral compass" through the reading of details. Audiences of popular theater and eventually of the cinema, thinking and feeling within the melodramatic mode, are compelled to seek evidence of personalities on stage or screen that embody a Manichean struggle between good and evil, that play out discursive imperatives that transcend the self, and are the site of societal contradictions and psychological drives. Melodrama successfully functions when this personality is realized and known, when a fictional character becomes a sympathetic, "fleshed-out" human being. It restores faith in the belief that the other can be recognized and, in securing this faith, that the other can be morally judged. If morality is a crucial axis (along with other discourses such as race, gender, and sexuality) in which we taxonomize and consolidate the individual in modernity, melodrama is the means by which this taxonomization is made possible at all.

Yet human characters are not the only entities in the sensible world that are available for scrutiny in melodrama; inanimate and non-organic objects are subject to this hermeneutic gaze as well. A dilapidated, seaside boarding house, a toy drum, a pair of glasses, or even the sound of newspaper ripping: each of these signifiers from Friedkin's film function to both conceal and betray a hidden moral, and contribute to the construction of a meaningful diegetic world through narration. Close-ups of objects and faces, made possible with the cinema camera, insist upon the melodramatization of the world in ways not possible in the theater. Writing of the gaze and the attention to detail performed by the narrators in Balzac's novels, Brooks notes that his "descriptions reiterate the mental operation upon landscape, the effort of optical vision to become moral vision and to create a state for moral figurations. Everything in the real—facades, furniture, clothing, posture, gesture—must become sign."[14] The world is constituted in melodrama as a series of surfaces that are to be read. Everything subject to the gaze, both living and non-living, becomes an object of moral judgment for the viewer steeped in the melodramatic mode and acquires significance within a universe circumscribed by secularized notions of good and evil. Such signs give evidence that meaningful events took place and demand, like ruins, to be interpreted as inextricably linked to an inaccessible past moment.

Linda Williams has gone furthest in helping us think about melodrama within the cinematic context. In a wide-ranging claim, she writes that melodrama "most often typifies American narrative in literature, stage, film, and television when it seeks to engage with moral questions."[15] Williams emphasizes Brooks's insight that in both the theater and cinema, gesture and pantomime constitute a form of mute speech, speech that may be felt as a moral good. Typically, the aim of this feeling is to make legible the true villain or innocent victim of the story and, in doing so, move the politics of the narrative forward through the identification of enemies and allies. Williams pays particular attention to the spectacle of pathos and its framing of the injured body as one that compels sympathetic judgment and is worthy of recognition. "The key function of victimization," she writes, "is to orchestrate the moral legibility crucial to the mode, for if virtue is not obvious, suffering—often depicted as the literal suffering of an agonized body—is."[16] Images of victimization and suffering, then, serve the aims of moral legibility, enticing audiences to think and feel with individuals in a narrative.[17] Suffering functions as a sign for virtue through a process that, at once, recognizes the signs of suffering and assigns the body that bears these signs with virtue. To read the sign of suffering and feel sympathy for the one who suffers, and to participate in this regime of moral sentiment, means also to experience a sense of moral righteousness and to enjoy a kind of Cartesian certainty that inheres in one's moralizing stance. In doing so, the audience is compelled to judge the signifying body on screen, to jump to conclusions about who they are morally. The enticement toward sympathy in melodrama typically leads to the demand for justice, for action, or even violent retaliation, that will recompense the grief and pain unfairly inflicted upon the virtuous. Melodrama thus functions to domesticate and channel affect along political lines.

The Birthday Party, of course, operates within this mode of moral articulation, inviting audiences to engage with its Manichean conflict between good and evil. Yet its explosive effect on the viewer may be attributed to its refusal to follow through on this invitation, to confound the experience of moral certainty that is at the core of melodrama's mission. From the moment Friedkin's film begins, with its non-descript shots of empty beach chairs, the viewer is provided with images that evoke a vague sense of isolation. The sound of paper ripping comes on the soundtrack as the viewer is taken on a drive through a largely vacant, English seaside town. Having an odd effect, it remains purely acousmatic, having no visual reference during the entire ride, and defies efforts by the listener to understand its meaning. From these establishing shots, the film settles into the world of Pinter's play, the shabby boarding house run by Meg and her weary husband. The violence toward Meg and Lulu that erupts at the end of the birthday party, which many critics of the play have aspired to understand, may be attributed to Stanley being "deprived of all but the social identity to which he will be carried by Goldberg and McCann."[18] This moment of dramatic intensity culminates "with the total dissolution of his personality and his reversion into primitivism."[19] The irritation evoked by the ripping paper at the opening of Friedkin's film not only anticipates a point-of-audition shot that will appear later but also seems to signal the irritation that will be evoked through its anti-melodramatic narrative.

Understanding *The Birthday Party* in terms of melodrama reveals the emotional conflicts that engender its volatility. Stanley suffers under the aggressions of Goldberg and McCann, who have come to taunt and terrorize, while eliciting audience sympathy and inspiring curiosity about what he did to deserve such treatment. *The Birthday Party* also provides us with an opportunity to rethink the discursive presuppositions that underpin analyses of Pinter's play that delve into the psyches of its characters. According to one account, Stanley could be read as acting out "the wish to interact sexually with the mother and the wish to punish her for her infidelity with the father" and in replaying out this Oedipal drama, his violence comes to be understood as symptomatic of his male psyche.[20]

This assessment, and others that attempt to delve into Stanley's interiority in Pinter's script as well Friedkin's film, nevertheless fall within the scope of melodrama and its humanizing mission of making legible a hidden moral occult. Analyses of Pinter's play typically interrogate Stanley's psychic, existential, or ontological interiority in order to explain the logic of his character. Indeed, the aim of psychoanalysis, particularly in its interpretation of somatic symptoms, coincides with that of melodrama and its attention to visible signs. Brooks notes that psychoanalysis as a hermeneutic "reformulates melodrama's concerns and realizes its possibilities," while "relaying" the melodramatic impulse.[21] However, instead of communicating the content of characters on screen, approaching moving image narrative through the melodramatic enables us to critically work through the ways in which popular narrative moves viewers transactionally, as an exchange of affect between audiences and the cinema. As we move forward in our analysis of Friedkin's films, we will see how they continue to challenge and overturn assumptions of the melodramatic mode while still operating within it. Through this, we can begin to think critically about how the representation of grievance and the retrieval of innocence affects viewers.

Beyond the emotional hang-ups exhibited by the protagonists of *The Birthday Party*, its destabilizing power arises from its refusal to secure the experience of moral certainty for the viewer. Pinter's script provides only scant backstory to the characters, unsettling the audience as to how the tensions between Stanley, Goldberg, and McCann are to be judged. And as disappointment, frustration, and dread culminate in the explosive scene at the end of the birthday party, Stanley becomes a sympathetic victim to the bullying of the story's strange intruders. However, when we see, even momentarily, that this seemingly mild-mannered man harbors the capacity to violently lash out and victimize others, determination of the piano player's virtue becomes confused and one wonders once again about who Stanley is and what he has done. This confusion is borne from the incapacity of this key narrative moment to satisfy expectations around the individual and his personality. Are Goldberg and McCann carrying out justice or meting out revenge? We may be reminded, once more, of the ways in which the characterization of a human being only becomes real when external signs are understood as somehow integral to a specific narrative trajectory. The melodramatic sign, in other words, connects the past to the future, from cause to effect, manifesting itself as the realization of a consequence to memory while anticipating what is to come. This linkage is foreclosed in *The Birthday Party*.

Instead, we are left posing questions about the necessary and possible once again. Of what does Stanley stand guilty? Why do Goldberg and McCann utilize scare tactics to capture Stanley? Why are they compelled to exercise a tactics of menace and do they allegorize the force of legal violence? As we pose these inquiries once more, however, such questions collapse in on themselves. What Stanley is fearful of, what he did to provoke "the organization," these key narrative details remain unclear. Without the necessary information, we are left with the possibility that Pinter's script is about the fear of fear itself, and perhaps about the ethics of justice. Thus, by taking melodrama to its discursive limits in this manner, *The Birthday Party* allows audiences to question its underlying ethics as its narrative trajectory repeatedly refuses to definitively separate virtue from vice.

As a filmed play, Friedkin's *The Birthday Party* works within the spatial limitations on *mise-en-scène* delineated by the theatrical stage. Almost the entirety of the film takes place in the small living room of Peg's dingy boarding house. Medium shots and close-ups facilitate the drama and Pinter's dialogue also adds to a sense of things being suffocatingly closed in. It is as if the confines of the house were not just delineated by its walls but also by the frame of the screen. Exterior shots bookend the film, featuring absent streets of an English seaside town and the sound of cawing seagulls. Both of these location shots depict a gray sky, as if to signify that no time has passed between the beginning and end of the film. The violence that took place in the boarding house seems inconsequential in this dreary world. Somehow alienated even from this seemingly remote, unnamed English town, the events of *The Birthday Party* take place in a space of exception separated from the drab, everyday reality of life outside. Friedkin's film conforms closely to what film critic Leo Braudy, writing in 1976, calls the "closed" film:

> In a closed film the world of the film is the only thing that exists; everything within it has its place in the plot of the film—every object, every character, every gesture, every action. In an open film the world of the film is a momentary frame around an ongoing reality.[22]

The closed film enframes its diegesis with the frame of the screen, where no sound is allowed from outside it, and thereby constitutes this closed space as self-sufficient, with everything represented in it placed within a schematic form. Significantly for the aims of revealing the moral occult within the melodramatic mode, the closed film "asserts that all details are the expression of an invisible order."[23] In contrast to the endlessness that extends beyond the frame of the open film, the closed film, typified for Braudy in the cinema of Lang and Hitchcock, emphasizes interiority and implicitly places the viewer in a position of an outsider looking in.

THE BOYS IN THE BAND (1970)

Friedkin's next film is also based on a theater script and unfolds in the relatively closed living quarters of one of its main protagonists. An adaptation of Mart Crowley's off-Broadway play written in 1968, *The Boys in the Band* takes place in an Upper East Side apartment in New York City. As in *The Birthday Party*, it begins with a montage of establishing shots, but here they establish not the place but the characters that will then be featured in the claustrophobic rooms in which the remainder of the film will unfold. Harpers Bizarre's 1967 cover of Cole Porter's "Anything Goes" plays on the soundtrack in its opening shots, while Michael (Kenneth Nelson), wearing a business suit, walks with purpose through the streets of New York. The film cuts to Donald (Frederick Combs) driving his Volkswagen convertible through a tunnel, passing a truck while crossing the double yellow lines. Emory (Cliff Gorman) picks up his white toy poodle and closes up his lavishly furnished and decorated office. Hank (Laurence Luckinbill) sweats while playing basketball in a gym. Larry (Keith Prentice) takes photographs of two fashion models. Alan (Peter White) disembarks a plane. This opening continues to depict these six characters engaged in various activities and tasks: walking through Manhattan, picking up a gift, buying crab legs, entering a Doubleday book store, and briefly cruising for men. Hank confronts Larry in a bar and from their facial expressions it is clear that they know each other well and seem to be engaged in some sort of quarrel. This prelude, which introduces the characters before the film's plot begins, is constructed through montage and is a stylistic feature that will be utilized to introduce characters in a number of Friedkin's films.

Alan is alone in a hotel room, pacing nervously. He reaches for the phone and places a call. The film then cuts to Michael just as he is returning to his apartment. The phone rings and he rushes to answer it, but misses the call. Cut to Donald. He makes a call from a parking garage as his red Volkswagen is being retrieved. Cutting back, Michael, this time, answers the phone. Donald tells him that his psychoanalyst has cancelled their appointment and asks Michael if he could come over. The telephone connects some of the characters from the film's introduction who were separated through the editing of the montage. Later, the telephone will become a central device that connects these men to individuals from their past. And as we shall see, it will function as the means by which the individuals trapped inside Michael's apartment may be connected with those outside it.

Donald and Michael continue talking in Michael's bedroom. We soon find out that they are preparing for a birthday party for their mutual acquaintance Harold. Seven guests have been invited over, who Michael describes as "six tired screaming fairy queens and one anxious queer." They converse about getting older, traveling, loneliness, disappointment, and their upbringings while making references to Bette Davis and Victor Mature. Words like "faggot" and "fairy" easily fall from their lips. Though they banter affectionately, their tone is sarcastic and self-deprecating, full of sexual innuendo and biting humor. Film historian Vito Russo, in his seminal history of gay cinema *The Celluloid Closet*, reminds us that the production of a film with the sensibilities of *The Boys in the Band* would have been difficult, if not impossible, during the era of the Production Code.[24] The rest of the dialogue will proceed in this edgy, caustic tone that is, in fact, central to its sensibility. The phone suddenly rings again and this time it is Alan. He is distraught and asks if he might come over later in the evening for a drink. Michael says that he is having a birthday party for a friend and tells Alan that he will not be able to invite him over. "Well, kiddo, it just wouldn't work out." After they hang up, Michael tells Donald that Alan, an old friend from college, is "straight, and square city!"

As in Friedkin's adaptation of Pinter's play, *The Boys in the Band* tells the story of a group of individuals gathered in an enclosed space to celebrate a birthday. Utilizing many close-up shots, both films focus on psychological interiority while careful blocking reveals the close quarters of Meg's boarding house and Michael's apartment, spaces that force faces and bodies to confront each other. In this, *The Birthday Party* and *The Boys in the Band* may be contrasted to their theatrical versions, for the film camera allows for close-ups of these faces and significant objects to be given melodramatic scrutiny. Both films feature intruders, characters who interrupt the domesticity of the party, as the primary sources of their narrative drama.

The planned birthday party will gather individuals to mark the advancement of age and to provide an opportunity for friends to reflect upon what was and could have been within the privacy of Michael's apartment. "It wouldn't work out" with Alan because his conventional sexuality would create tension and misunderstanding at this get-together of eight gay friends (seven plus a hustler named Cowboy Tex [Robert La Tourneaux] hired to help celebrate Harold's birthday). And this is precisely what happens after his arrival at Michael's apartment. Alan does have some rapport with Hank, a married schoolteacher who is currently living with Larry, but the clean-cut, straight businessman is clearly uncomfortable with the presence of the other participants. In an outburst of homophobic rage, Alan has a physical altercation with Emory, perhaps the most expressively flamboyant of the group, hitting him in the face and giving him a bleeding lip. At this moment of high tension, Harold finally rings the doorbell. Michael, flustered from the violent struggle, quickly gains his composure, opens the door, and tells the newcomer that he is late. Harold acerbically responds that he "is a thirty-two-year-old, ugly, pockmarked Jew fairy, and if it takes me a little while to pull myself together, and if I smoke a little grass before I get up the nerve to show my face to the world, it's nobody's god damned business but my own. And how are you this evening?" With this caustic and sarcastic entrance, the birthday boy has arrived.

Alan will stay for the remainder of the party, which continues on the apartment patio. They dance, eat lasagna, drink wine, and smoke a joint. Yet as time wears on, the banter between the participants, which had been teasing and occasionally goading but friendly, becomes increasingly self-loathing and aggressive. The presence of the outsider seems to have provoked the admission of unspoken thoughts as well as the release of long-held grievances. Rain starts to fall and the party quickly moves indoors. Meanwhile Michael continues drinking and becomes increasingly belligerent. With the sound of thunder rumbling outside, he announces that they will play a party game, one that will forcibly bring secret desires and harbored resentments to light. Each person is to call a person from their past, "the one person we truly believed we have loved." Making the call scores one point; if the intended person answers, the caller receives two points; if someone else answers, one point; if nobody answers, "you're screwed." If the person calling tells the intended recipient who he is, the caller receives two more points. Finally, if he confesses their long-held love for receiver, they receive five points. Listening quietly to these rules, Harold sardonically calls the game "hateful."

Michael serves as the scorekeeper. One by one the guests play this cruel game, calling and confessing their affection to childhood crushes, married men with children, and a dentist. Hank calls Larry (or rather Larry's voicemail) and tells him that he loves him. This confession perturbs Alan, who seems concerned above all with his status as being the only straight male at the party. Michael then cajoles him to call, insinuating that he is a "closet queen." "What about Justin Stewart," he accusingly asks, "you were in love with him, . . . and that's who you're gonna call!" Alan takes the phone and dials a number. He tells the person on the other end that "it's Alan," that he's in New York, and that, "I love you." Michael grabs the phone away from him and realizes that it is not Justin, but Alan's wife Fran. Alan will not receive the grand prize of five points as his attempt to out his college friend as a closeted homosexual is stymied. Michael quickly becomes disconcerted and agitated.

This phone game proceeds along lines that may be likened to the hermeneutics of the melodramatic mode. At stake in this sequence is the spectacle of unexpressed longings and, through this, the scrutinizing of expressive surfaces and performances to reveal the secret of one's sexuality. The characters out each other, exposing backstories and shared secrets, in order to make what can come to light into objects of scorn, praise, and moral judgment. Ramzi Fawaz helps us understand why this ordeal of bringing to light remains important for the exercise of critical judgment. Calling Crowley's play "one of the longest and most searing public 'bitch sessions' ever performed on the American stage," Fawaz writes that the insults the characters hurl at each other and at the heterosexual world outside Michael's apartment should not simply be understood as indignant cries of social injustice.[25] The invectives do express their grievance, but their exchange also induces a form of community building, of a kind of affective intimacy connected to issues of insecurity and unrequited desire, and which is consolidated through a shared sense of victimization. "If gay male judgmentalness," Fawaz remarks, "can produce alternative intimacies outside the gaze of societal and clinical homophobia, *critical judgment* serves as a tool for holding other gay men accountable for their speech and actions."[26] This exercise of critical judgment constitutes a kind of alternative public sphere, consolidated through the expression of what Lauren Berlant calls the "unfinished business of sentimentality."[27] At issue here is the question of who judges and to what end. For within the privacy of Michael's apartment, gay men judge each other, not to put down, but to keep friends and lovers in check, ironically by appropriating and critically reiterating the discourse of homophobic judgment of the straight world outside. This claustrophobic space of minoritization is constituted by the pressure of the outside coming in, allegorized explicitly by Alan's presence at the party and which delineates the discursive space where the melodramatic will take place. The performance of critical judgment may seem cruel and self-righteous throughout *The Boys in the Band*, but this is just a means of coping with the constant possibility of withering judgment that awaits them outside. In turn, as a means of connecting this outside with the intimacy delineated by the walls of Michael's apartment, the telephone functions as a way for these men to cautiously out themselves, to individuals from their past and by co-extension to the straight world, while confronting hitherto unexpressed disappointments and resentments. The telephone allows them to make these connections while remaining within the safe space of the apartment.

After the phone game has ended and most of the guests have left, Michael breaks down in tears, exhausted by the rising intensity of the party. He begs Donald not to leave and implores him to "learn not to hate ourselves quite so much." This emotional culmination makes itself available for melodramatic interpretation, one that is inextricably linked to the question of Michael's sexuality. One may deduce that gay men hate themselves because society hates them; that they have internalized the hate that society outside harbors toward them. Such deductions are realized by "reading into" the characters of the play and, in so doing, reasserting the fact of their melodramatic victimization. At the conclusion, we see an ostensible truth that has remained invisible, bubbling underneath the film's surfaces. Speaking to this in relation to the beauty of the young Cowboy, Harold remarks:

> How could this beauty ever compare with my soul? And although I've never seen my soul, I understand from my mother's Rabbi that it's a knockout. I, however, cannot seem to locate it for a gander. And if I could, I'd sell it in a flash, for some skin-deep, transitory, meaningless beauty.

Here the birthday boy critically responds to judgments that impute an essential "soul" as somehow related to the question of beauty. In contrast to the theater, cinematic close-ups provide the viewer intimate access not only to this skin-deep beauty but also to Harold's pock-marked face and the beads of sweat on Michael's forehead. Yet such judgments also reinscribe the definition of the moral human being as constituted through the dichotomy between exteriority and interiority, and reiterate the persistence of the truth of sexuality which is somehow related to the question of moral virtue. While Michael's pathos solicits the sympathy of the viewer as one victimized by straight society outside, we also remember that he imposed the phone game on the party by playing the victimizer.

In his review of the film for the *New York Times*, Vincent Canby follows this line of thinking even as he sets out to critique the original play's failures: "There is something basically unpleasant, however, about a play that seems to have been created in an inspiration of love-hate and that finally does nothing more than exploit its (I assume) sincerely conceived stereotypes."[28] Harold would likely have none of it. Indeed, this representation of gay men as "stereotypically" closeted and self-hating seems to have been destined to contradict the times in which it was presented to cinema audiences. The Stonewall riots, which took place in June 1969, initiated a self-consciousness in the gay community nationwide and opened up the possibility for closeted men to assert their desires and identities in public, out of their claustrophobic spaces of privacy into the political arena. These events empowered gay men to refuse their criminalization and the moral judgment issued by the homophobic police and, by co-extension, the straight world. Friedkin's film seemed, to reviewers such as Canby, already outdated in its politics of representation. Yet his assessment merely reiterates the melodramatic mode and its tendency to reconstitute strict boundaries between surface and depth, skin and soul (Figure 1.3).

Figure 1.3 The face, skin, and soul

For our purposes, as we attempt to delineate a trajectory of Friedkin's cinema, we can understand *The Boys in the Band* as a film that, like the callers of the film's telephone game, attempts to reach out beyond the ontological boundaries that separate gay from straight, inside from outside. The film goes further than the stage play by showing how other boundaries may be critically overcome, not only between cinema and theater but also those that concern social life more generally: married/single, monogamy/polygamy, visible/invisible, explicit/implicit. The "bitch session" that comprises *The Boys in the Band* should be understood as a means of acting out within a culture where the truth of one's sexuality is constantly at issue, where judgments about inner character are made from the perception of outward signs. Moreover, the certainty of this truth is inseparable from the ontological binaries that impute a hierarchy of power relations. Alone in Michael's bedroom, Alan tells his friend, almost in a reassuring tone, that, "your private life is your own affair. I couldn't care less about what people do, as long as they don't do it in public or try to force their ways on the whole damned world." Such an assertion already relegates sexuality, and particularly homosexuality, to the private realm, while forcibly reiterating a separation between desires that may be expressed in public versus those that must remain behind closed doors. *The Boys in the Band* develops a criticality that seeks a sustained destabilization of the binaries, and by co-extension the power relations that implicitly valorize one term over another, introduced by Alan's presence at the party, precisely by presenting private discourse among gay men as a public melodrama.

THE FRENCH CONNECTION (1971)

The films I have discussed so far fall under the category of what Braudy calls the "closed" film as their narratives take place in delimited theatrical spaces, whether the burlesque theater or the dramatic stage. They provided the young filmmaker with the opportunity to come out and showcase, as I have tried to argue, his exploration into the ethics and discourse of the melodramatic mode. *The French Connection*, on the other hand, will give Friedkin the chance to work outside, in the context of New York City. We shall see that this film, his first critical and box-office success, moves between interiority and exteriority in a much more fluid manner than his previous films. In this way, Friedkin seems to be developing the politics of melodrama further by emphasizing how this fluidity illuminates a theme that the director addresses in most of his work: "the thin line between the policeman and the criminal."[29] If the films discussed in this chapter work with challenging moral norms within the popular mode of American moving pictures, *The French Connection* takes the incendiary impulse that motivates this drive toward transgression into the realm of law and justice. Appearing at a politically volatile moment in postwar American history, Friedkin's film remains ambiguous in its politics, an ambiguity that is contingent on whether or not the two main protagonists may be deemed sympathetic.

Friedkin read the 1969 book by Robin Moore, *The French Connection: A True Account of Cops, Narcotics, and International Conspiracy*, one of a number of accounts that chronicles the largest heroin bust in U.S. history. The director admittedly "couldn't get through it; it seemed dry and procedural on the page."[30] Nevertheless, he apparently saw potential in the fundamental plot of the story (flouting the interdiction against the depiction of drug trafficking by the Production Code) and sought out Eddie Egan and Salvatore "Sonny" Grosso, the two detectives around which the case revolves. For weeks Friedkin went with them on ride-alongs to the 28th and 81st precincts that introduced the director to sides of the city he had never experienced. In his memoirs, Friedkin writes of these experiences:

> They took me to bars and "shooting galleries" in Harlem and Bedford-Stuyvesant, where they were certain to find users and dealers. One night we broke into an apartment in Harlem, where a family of twelve, from young children to grandmothers, was lying around a living room floor with needles in their arms. "My God," I said to Sonny. "This is ten minutes from where I live." . . . As we entered the bars, Eddie would take out his .38 special and hand it to me. "Cover the back," he'd say under his breath. I'd be standing there with a lethal weapon, which I'd never fired, hoping the perps wouldn't bolt for the back door. Eddie and Sonny need to know that if necessary, I had their backs. They'd take control of at least fifty of the baddest dudes I've ever seen. Everyone had a record; everyone was "wrong," as Eddie would say.[31]

Friedkin would depict some of these experiences in his film, including the detectives' penchant for terrorizing "perps" by pushing them into phone booths and filling cocktail shakers with confiscated drugs. While accompanying Egan and Grosso, nicknamed "Popeye" and "Cloudy," on their stakeouts, the director cajoled them into revealing more details about how they pursued a smalltime crook with Mafia connections, a French television star, and the boss of the largest heroin network in the world.

Friedkin's film begins with a series of short scenes that depict how Popeye (Gene Hackman) and Cloudy (Roy Scheider) became embroiled in the French Connection case. The first begins in the port city of Marseille. From its narrow streets and then to the famous outdoor café, La Samaritaine, a man wearing a brown leather jacket follows and observes another man, who is elegant, well-dressed, and sports a trimmed goatee. With a baguette under his arm, the one who is being observed checks his mail in the foyer passageway to his apartment. He looks up and is violently shot in the face by another man wearing a leather trench coat, who appears for the first time in the film. The assassin is played by Marcel Bozzuffi, who also played a killer in Costa-Gavras's *Z* (1969), a film that impressed Friedkin greatly. (At the end of *Z*, coincidentally, among the modernist works that are banned in the government formed following the military *coup d'état* are the plays of Pinter.)

We then cut to the streets of Brooklyn below the tracks of an elevated subway. It is winter and two men stand outside in the cold, one dressed as Santa Claus and the other as a hot dog vendor. They are undercover cops staking out a bar full of African-American men for drug pushers. The hot dog seller abruptly enters the establishment and accosts a seated man, telling him to stand. His partner quickly pats him down and pushes him into a telephone booth. As soon as he slams the door, another man behind the bar runs out. The two policemen give chase and catch the suspected criminal in a dilapidated alleyway. Santa Claus and the hot dog vendor kick and punch him until his face is bloodied. Friedkin had some experience depicting police brutality on screen while making *The People vs. Paul Crump* in 1962, a documentary that revolves around the violent beating and incarceration of an ostensibly innocent man. As in the earlier film, in *The French Connection* a black man is threatened and aggressively interrogated with exasperating questions that are targeted only to confuse, like those I discussed in *The Birthday Party*. Popeye is particularly eager to bust the perp, demanding that he confess the last name of "Joe the Barber," which side of the street his dealer lives on, and the last time he "picked his feet" in Poughkeepsie.

The film cuts back to the goateed man, Charnier (Fernando Rey), speaking to another at the pier in Marseille. This port city is where Jean-Luc Godard's *Breathless* (1960) begins as well, a film that marks a watershed moment in cinema history for Friedkin, particularly for its improvisatory and unscripted style. The American director will adopt some of its spirit of risk-taking and jazz sensibility for his film. Other homages to French cinema will make their appearance later in *The French Connection*. Charnier states that the pier needs to be extended another hundred feet to accommodate the larger tankers he expects will be necessary for the job he has planned. "I haven't done an honest day's work since I climbed off the crane," he jokingly remarks. The Frenchman meets his mistress at her residence and they exchange gifts in preparation for his trip to America. Charnier receives a heavy coat since the weather at his destination will be very cold. Back in the police precinct building, Popeye, now dressed like a detective, tells his partner, without hesitation and without qualification, to "never trust a nigger." He is recounting an incident when he was stabbed by a black suspect. Cloudy retorts that, "he could have been white." The film does not condemn him for the utterance of this slur nor for his racist profiling of African-Americans in the Brooklyn bar.

The first ten minutes of *The French Connection* introduces us to these personas: the suave Frenchman Alain Charnier and two irascible American detectives, James "Popeye" Doyle and Buddy "Cloudy" Russo. Names are not made clear in these opening scenes. Confusion may set in for new audiences as they attempt to ascertain who will become important for the rest of the film and how these individuals are to be understood narratively. Perhaps against expectations, the sophisticated Frenchman will turn out to be a drug lord. On the other hand, the two detectives, who are typically expected to uphold the law, openly make bigoted and sexist comments, seem unpredictable and crude, and sadistically enjoy brutalizing suspects. As in *The Night They Raided Minsky's*, the appearance and behavior of these characters betray moralities that are at odds with the standards for "moral uplift" set by the Production Code. Their characterizations test the interdiction against the enticement of sympathy for criminals or by lowering the moral standards of film audiences, "when evil is made to appear attractive or alluring, and good is made to appear unattractive."[32] Moral elusiveness, of course, remains central to Friedkin's film, despite the ubiquity of the compromised cop that seems to dominate the contemporary crime film and what Paul Ramaeker, in his essay on *The French Connection*, calls the "compromised revisionist realism" of the New Hollywood *policier*.[33]

From the opening, we can discern that in both Marseille and New York, individuals pursue and are pursued, and they all commit acts of violence, sometimes with deadly consequences, against others. These disparate locations are depicted through cross-cutting, as if they were taking place at the same time, separating the French criminal from the American detectives. The cut will be a key means for the film's unfolding, creating tension between Charnier and the two detectives, as the latter pursue the former, rising in intensity as their inevitable confrontation approaches. While cross-cuts reiterate the separation between France and America, they will also construe the ideological tension between, and then the intermingling of, vice and virtue.

The film then cuts to Popeye and Cloudy sitting at the bar in the raucous Copacabana nightclub, in a scene that depicts how they began to suspect Salvatore Boca (Tony Lo Bianco) and his involvement in the inter-continental narcotics trade. The song, "Everybody Gets to Go to the Moon," performed by The Three Degrees, fades out on the soundtrack and a high-pitched, non-diegetic sound fades in, directing the attention of the audience away from the commotion in the club. Popeye looks intently at a table in the far corner of the room, as the camera shows his face in close-up, bringing the audience nearer to Popeye's inner thoughts. He tells his partner that he recognizes some of the men interacting at the table. Cloudy recognizes "a policy guy from Queens" and comments that another man is, "Jewish Lucky. He don't look the same without numbers across his chest." Notably, their hunches about Boca and his associates are based on stereotypes that link race, ethnicity, and criminality, as in the violent interrogation of an African-American man at the beginning of the film. Chuckling, Popeye quietly remarks, "that table is definitely wrong." These suspicions compel them to surveil "the greaser with the blonde" and to scope out more information about these seemingly shady characters. Cutting back and forth between shots of the detectives and their point of view, the film implicates the viewer in their interrogative look. At the same time, this look is itself placed under scrutiny, for the audience is left uncertain about whether to trust the hunches of a detective who has come off as largely unsympathetic up to this moment.

From this point onward in *The French Connection*, the look of the camera will be linked to Popeye's perspective and guide the unfolding melodrama. But this linkage remains ambivalent throughout the film. Typically, according to the expectations of the detective film genre, if the detective says they are "wrong," then the audience is compelled to pass judgment in the same manner. Todd Berliner, in his chapter on *The French Connection* in his book on narration in '70s Hollywood cinema, describes this implication of the viewer in this scene, writing that:

> The subjective cinematography and sound conform to Doyle's appraisal of the characters: Like him, we know the table is "definitely wrong"; we can feel it. Doyle appears, at least at that moment a generically suitable police detective.[34]

Berliner explains that while the audience may come to depend on Doyle's hunches, he never becomes fully sympathetic because of his many disagreeable qualities. In this, Friedkin's film may be understood as "bending," as opposed to breaking, the genre cues and conventions typically associated with the police thriller. Instead of defying Hollywood convention in order to dismantle visual pleasure and narrative cinema outright, New Hollywood genre benders like *The French Connection* lead the spectator toward false narrative conclusions in order not to fully lay bare the ideology that underpins the dominant political order but to produce the experience of spectatorial uncertainty. "Like genre breakers," Berliner writes, "[genre benders] play with genre expectations, but they are not flagrantly self-conscious and ironic, they do not encourage us to look at the form itself, and they are less likely to expose the ideologies embedded in their genres."[35] The character of Doyle fulfills what may be expected of the detective in cinema, giving insight while guiding the hermeneutic activities of the viewer. Yet as the viewer sympathizes with his perceptions, when they "feel" that the table on the other side of the Copacabana is "definitely wrong," they remain nevertheless uneasy at being guided by a character who may be characterized as racist, impetuous, and nihilistic.

For Berliner, genre bending—a renegotiating with genre conventions that nevertheless does not break from them—constitutes a key attribute of American cinema in the '70s. It describes what a new generation of filmmakers, particularly enamored with classical Hollywood, consciously brought to the legacy of genre filmmaking in their zeal to push conventions toward their breaking point. As Berliner writes:

> Genre bending can appear any time a skilled filmmaker sees an opportunity to exploit spectators' complacent acquiescence to film tradition. One would expect to see genre bending, therefore, during a period in Hollywood, such as the '70s, when audiences were both tired of conventional pictures and excited about cinema's possibilities.[36]

This generation of filmmakers, which includes auteurs such as Altman, Nichols, Scorsese, Penn, and Malick, came of age artistically during a period of transition in Hollywood. As the Production Code was dismantled in 1968, this new generation, brought up by films from classical Hollywood and the European New Wave cinemas, injected new life into a floundering industry and brought an art cinema sensibility into the mainstream. Coming off of a series of flops that resulted in tens of millions of dollars in losses, including *Dr. Dolittle*, *Star!*, and *Hello Dolly*, the industry put out films that explicitly appealed to a younger generation that looked to the cinema to reflect their more socially subversive concerns. Films like *Bonnie and Clyde*, *2001: A Space Odyssey*, and *The Graduate* seemed to speak more directly to the desires of this generation through stories and representations that would address the ideas of the counterculture and the loss of confidence in U.S. moral righteousness in the world.

Friedkin was certainly thinking of renegotiating cinematic tropes, particularly around the depiction of morality and virtue, when he directed the main protagonists in *The French Connection*. In an interview published in 1972, he makes explicit that his intention was to "mix up" these depictions:

> I felt that the only way to get into the story was not to regard Charnier as a prick, but to see him as a businessman, a man with charm and taste, devoted to his woman in France, etc. Then you have Doyle, who has no taste, no charm, he's a brutalizer of women, he lives out of his car. Charnier embodies almost all the qualities that people are brought up to think are virtuous. The intention was to mix up these elements.[37]

The opening to *The French Connection* seems largely to function to establish this blurring of the binary between virtue and vice on the level of character development. These characterizations "bend" the genre conventions of the

Figure 1.4 Men of vice meeting in front of the Capitol Building

conventional police detective film, particularly those belonging to a previous generation, and generate greater narrative drama by keeping the film viewer guessing as to how they will be resolved (Figure 1.4). "Ultimately," Berliner concludes, "the film builds its conclusion on the deviations, giving them a retrospective impact that they did not carry initially."[38] In turn, bending the cues and conventions around the Hollywood *policier* provides the discursive impetus for creating a convincing depiction of the morally compromised cop within popular cinema.

Berliner's claims about genre bending may be extended to help us think about melodrama and its relationship to space. From the interview conducted in 1972, Friedkin notes that *The French Connection* serves as a kind of culmination of his creative activity as he understood it at the time. "This film pretty much sums up most of my attitudes, abilities, and interests at this point," the director remarks.[39] If *Minsky's*, *The Birthday Party*, and *The Boys in the Band* delineate enclosed spaces where melodrama takes place and may be critiqued, *The French Connection* continues this critique by taking melodrama outdoors, out to the streets of Brooklyn, and through this enabling the interrogation of the thin line between policeman and criminal. As we have seen, the spaces of Friedkin's early films critically work with binaries—between interiority and exteriority, old and new, gay and straight—in order to show how they might be thought of as fluid and yet unresolvable. In *The French Connection*, this critical thinking focuses on the lengths, at times unvirtuous and even criminal, a policeman will go in order to pursue virtue, particularly virtue as it has been conventionally cast in the classical detective genre. And while this film is Friedkin's first to be filmed on location, these outdoor locations are nevertheless subject to the interior preoccupations of Doyle and Cloudy, whose cynical points of view subject audiences to their obsessive gaze on New York and its inhabitants. *The French Connection* is not simply about bending genre, but also about renegotiating the taking place of melodrama and its moral reasoning through the act of looking.

In *The World in a Frame*, a text whose passages on the closed film I discussed in my analysis of *The Birthday Party*, Leo Braudy explains that, starting in the late 1950s, the distinction between closed and open film styles began to break down, partly due to the introduction of lighter cameras, lamps, and sound equipment, as well as more sensitive film stock. New Wave filmmakers such as Truffaut and Godard utilized improvisatory filming techniques, broke away from Aristotelian narrative forms, and disregarded continuity editing, realizing a kind of closed cinema within an open style:

> The formal force of most important films since the late 1950s has been in the intensity of open *and* closed, the crossing of the barrier between film and the world, and, as I shall argue, between high and popular culture as well.[40]

We might say that the closed melodramas of Friedkin's earlier films come out into the wider openness of gritty New York in *The French Connection*. As a result of this coming out, his 1971 film plays out the tensions between interiority and exteriority, and specifically between the coherence of the male ego, its sovereignty over meaning, and the crime-riddled, post-sacred world outside the sovereign ego. The film seems to depict how the ostensibly virtuous detective becomes contaminated by the moral fallenness represented by a wider post-industrial, increasingly secularizing world outside it. If *The French Connection* could be said to build any sympathy for Popeye and Doyle, this is through the sense of victimization that they are subject to by the perceived immorality of 1970s New York. The openness of the city is figured throughout the film as threatening to the masculine self, permeating the closed melodrama and putting the classical system of generic signs associated with the crime film into jeopardy.

For the remainder of this chapter, I would like to elucidate this renegotiation between virtue and vice in *The French Connection*. We will look at this by continuing our analysis of key moments from the film and by focusing in particular on the intimacy of the voice and its relationship to diegetic sound. Popeye and Cloudy leave the Copacabana and wait from their car. When Boca leaves the club with a group of women, Popeye yawns from sleepiness and tells him to "go to work." From Times Square, they follow Boca to Ratner's café in Brooklyn. With day breaking, Cloudy sighs and remarks in voiceover, "Seven o'clock in the morning, I don't believe this." "Relax, you're having fun, ain't ya," his partner responds. Low, stabbing strings come on the soundtrack, indicating that the chase is to continue. Boca stops, removes a briefcase from his trunk, and somewhat conspicuously drops it off at an apartment in Brooklyn. "Man, if that's not a drop I'll open up a charge for ya at Bloomingdales," Popeye comments in voiceover. He drives to another location and switches cars. Meanwhile the jazz music rises momentarily in intensity. Boca and his blond companion drive to a modest luncheonette called "Sal and Angie's," take a stack of newspapers from the truck, and carry them inside. In order to surveil him more closely, Popeye and Cloudy rent a workshop across the street from the luncheonette. With images of Boca and Angie working, they explain, again in voiceover, who these characters are:

> Our friend's name is Boca, Salvatore Boca. B-O-C-A. They call him Sal. He's a sweetheart. He was picked up on suspicion of armed robbery. Now get this. Three years ago, he tries to hold up Tiffany's on Fifth Avenue in broad daylight. He could've got two and a half to five, but Tiffany's wouldn't prosecute. Also, downtown, they're pretty sure he pulled off a contract on a guy named de Marco.

They continue speaking about Angie, Boca's wife, in a similar manner over images of the couple serving customers. She was caught shoplifting and is nineteen years old, "nineteen going on fifty." Boca earns only $7,000 a year from the luncheonette, raising their suspicions even further as to how he is able to afford "two cars and hundred-dollar tabs at the Shay." Boca's brother Lou is spoken about as the film cuts to a shot of him working as a garbage man. They follow him to an upscale building in Manhattan, when another cut takes place, to where a character named Joel Weinstock lives. Popeye and Cloudy continue conversing and mention that Weinstock is a known narcotics trafficker.

These moments are narrated in voiceover, closely recorded in a manner that lends a kind of intimacy to the voices of the two detectives. The montage seems at once to reflect the perspectives of Popeye and Cloudy, voyeuristically observing the Bocas from a distance, while also belonging to a repertoire of images that express their inner consciousness. As in a documentary, the voices guide the viewer's attention and inform the spectator as to how each character is to be interpreted melodramatically. Indeed, the Bocas are a family of criminals, individuals who work yet seem to have little qualms about breaking the law in order to get ahead. What remains notable in this sequence, and which carries over throughout the film, is the fluidity between intimacy and distance that seems to be at issue in the films I have discussed in this chapter. If a key aim of melodrama is to make legible virtue and thus to attest to the presence of an invisible moral occult, then *The French Connection* operates by subjecting the exterior spaces of New York and Marseille to the demands of the compulsive, interior psyche. Popeye and Cloudy thus seem to speak from inside and outside the diegetic space, both participating in and observing it. They take up the position of outsiders as insiders. All of New York in 1971—its characters, clubs, streets, luncheonettes, junkyards, dilapidated warehouses, cars, and bars—becomes a series of signs that are displayed and subsequently interpreted by the melodramatic fixations of Popeye and Cloudy, which become increasingly obsessive. The film's use of natural light, hand-held camera, and force-developed footage contribute to the look of "grittiness" that is aligned with the depiction of urban blight.[41] One is presented with, as Carlo Rotella describes it in his brilliant chapter on Friedkin's film, "visual grittiness, a palette of grays and grains that came to be associated with moral and political grayness, and with a weary sense of complexity inspired by hard social facts that do not reduce to easy fiction answers."[42]

If *The French Connection* began with cross-cuts that separate Marseille and New York, the remainder of the film is occupied with bringing the villains and the virtuous into collision. This occupation is presented as an extended chase, and then intensified and accelerated in the famous and gripping sequence through the streets of Brooklyn involving a car chasing an elevated subway train. But much of the time the pursuit of Charnier, Boca, and their accomplices is tedious, involving the tailing of suspects awkwardly through empty streets, sitting in chilly cars until daybreak, and waiting outside ritzy restaurants in Manhattan in the freezing cold. (A humorous scene depicting Popeye's surreptitious chase of Charnier on the Grand Central subway platform recalls an almost identical sequence from Jean-Pierre Melville's *Le Samouraï*.) Philip D'Antoni, the producer for *The French Connection*, takes pride in the authenticity of these on-location shots of New York, remarking:

> When Gene Hackman and Roy Scheider played numerous scenes in sub-freezing temperatures where they were supposed to be tired and cold while trailing their quarry, they *were* tired and cold. This overall sense of reality communicates itself to today's perceptive audiences, who often absorb a film's authenticity rather than see it.[43]

During these episodes, shots are longer and perspectives are wider. These sequences of furtive chasing remind one of the quiet tedium that abounds in Hitchcock's *Vertigo*, when the detective played by James Stewart follows Kim Novak's character Madeleine to find out her whereabouts. Like Madeleine, Charnier is aware that he is being followed. Yet unlike in Hitchcock's cinema, *The French Connection* showcases a distinct documentary-style realism at particular moments throughout the film. With its incessant jostling, hand-held cinematography is used in shots featuring action and physical movement to escalate its chaotic thrill, such as when Popeye and Cloudy give chase on foot or in vehicles. As the film was entirely shot on location, telephoto and zoom lenses bring faces, whose accompanying bodies are embedded in real and historical contexts, within the frame.

Yet starting with their imploring the narcotics department supervisor, Walter Simonson (played by Eddie Egan, who was the detective on which Gene Hackman's character is based), to request a court order so that they can wiretap Boca's phone, Popeye and Cloudy become increasingly relentless in their chase. "We deserve this," Popeye firmly remarks. Later, on their way to a gruesome car accident, Simonson becomes impatient that they are not producing results in their investigation. They demand not to be taken off the case. Popeye argues with Simonson while shots of the bloodied driver, slumped back in his seat, and his dead girlfriend are shown. With an image of their corpses laid on the ground, Popeye and Simonson continue arguing on the soundtrack. This disregard is apparently part of what Pauline Kael finds so objectionable about *The French Connection*, the "juicy pictures of the corpses"[44] that she associates, pejoratively, with a "cinema du zap."[45] Like the man who is assassinated in Marseille in the film's opening scene, the tragedy that confronts the viewer is not given much attention by the film's narrative. This lack of ethical attention is embodied by Popeye and his disregard for loss of life as Friedkin's film unfolds, driven by his growing obsession.

A woman pushing a carriage is shot by a sniper from above, perhaps triggering memories of the University of Texas, Austin shooting of 1966. Popeye does not attend to the dead woman and even tells bystanders to, "Leave her alone! Get away! Leave her alone!" The sniper is the assassin played by Bozzuffi in the film's opening sequence. In the famous car chase set piece, Friedkin cuts quickly between Popeye's point of view as he drives the car recklessly down Stillwell Avenue in Bensonhurst and close-ups of his feet as he abruptly accelerates and brakes. Shots of the Pontiac hitting other vehicles, Popeye frantically honking the car horn, and close-ups of Hackman's frantic face are interpolated as well, as he nearly runs over another woman pushing a baby carriage and endangers countless others in his single-minded pursuit. Key shots for this chase came from a take that stunt driver Bill Hickman undertook on a whim, as Friedkin describes it: "twenty-six blocks at ninety miles an hour, through busy intersections, through red lights, with no traffic control, no permits, no safeguards of any kind, only Hickman's chutzpah, his skills behind the wheel, and 'the grace of God.'"[46] In the risks he took to get this footage, the director's fixation echoes Popeye's own. Speeding through red lights with no permits, Hickman plays out the transgressions of getting the shot, allegorized in the film through Gene Hackman's pursuit of the bad guy.

In the final moments of the film, Popeye accidentally shoots the federal agent Mulderig (played by Hickman) in an abandoned warehouse, mistaking him for Charnier. Moments earlier, he almost pulled the trigger on his partner, yet it is his resented supervisor who is shot, perhaps not coincidentally. When Cloudy remarks that he shot their superior colleague, Popeye reloads his gun and pants, "The son of a bitch is here. I saw him. I'm gonna get him." He leaves Mulderig on the ground, and with the callousness of a warlord, Popeye continues his pursuit through a decrepit area of the ruined building, with his gun pointed, and disappears into a room at the far end. The disorder of his surroundings seems to allegorize the threat to his demand for moral order, for justice within the moral melodrama. On the soundtrack, a gunshot is heard and the screen goes blank, abruptly ending the film. It remains ambiguous who pulled the trigger and at whom. The film's final sequence shows us a montage of the main protagonists: Weinstock, Angie Boca, Lou Boca, Henri Devereaux the French television star, Charnier, and Doyle and Russo. On-screen captions indicate that Charnier was never indicted and that the film's two heroes were removed from the narcotics bureau and reassigned. Doyle's shooting of Mulderig is not mentioned at all and it seems that Popeye will be free of any consequence for this action, however accidental. The cop is immune from any charges of criminality, for his motives remain narrowly righteous, moral only at the outset, and above all obsessively ego driven.

Popeye's acting with impunity throughout *The French Connection* may have triggered the memories of some viewers with knowledge of the real-life case of *Pierson vs. Ray* in 1967, which justified the need for a "qualified immunity" clause for government officials, including police officers, who are sued for civil rights violations. The case involved fifteen priests, three of them African-American, who were arrested at a bus terminal in Jackson, Mississippi while taking part in the Mississippi Freedom Rides. The spurious charges against them were dropped and the priests sued the police officers as the suit went up to the Supreme Court. Eight justices found that the judge and policemen in Jackson had absolute or qualified immunity from the charges, on the basis that the fear of potential lawsuits would hamper the ability of the police to carry out their duties. This concept of immunity from prosecution, even qualified, seems to inform how Friedkin's film treats the policemen.

Moreover, the uncertainty that concludes with the film's acousmatic gunshot expresses a deep uncertainty as to how Popeye may be morally judged within the melodramatic mode, in his relentless pursuit of Charnier. If, at the start of *The French Connection*, the spectator is compelled to identify with this detective's point of view, judging alongside him the criminality of other characters based on hunches and feelings, however ethically problematic, by the end of the film it is Popeye himself who is judged. Do his obsessions justify his disregard for, at times innocent, life? Is it possible for the viewer to sympathize with those who do not or cannot sympathize with others? To what extent does the spectator "deserve" a conclusive ending? In 1992, Friedkin himself explained that Popeye was not meant to be sympathetic:

> This guy is a racist. He's not a good guy. He's an anti-hero. I mean, take off hero . . . he's an anti. He is not meant to be glorified in this picture and when this film came out and started to turn people on, it was scary.[47]

Indeed, by making Popeye the object of moral judgment the spectator is by co-extension placed under scrutiny as well. To what extent are the fixations, fetishistic and obsessive, of the viewer complicit with the reiteration of a callous disregard for life? And to what extent does the spectator also commit acts of violence by passing judgment on characters that appear on screen? If melodrama compels moral certainty in a post-sacred world, *The French Connection* dramatizes the impossibility of realizing this certainty and underscores the fact that judgment, however discerning and virtuosic, is always already compromised. This compromise is perhaps what Friedkin means when he speaks, repeatedly in interview and in his own writings, of his interest in the thin line between policeman and criminal. In a dramatic world where good and evil are supposed to exist in Manichean opposition, the world of *The French Connection* shows us that the techniques for discerning the differences between the person of virtue and the person of vice remain the same. Again, I believe the question here is not simply whether the cops may be deemed sympathetic heroes or violent fascists, or whether the film depicts a "war on the poor" or that the city is "going to hell." The critical power of *The French Connection* derives from its capacity to interrogate precisely these kinds of politically engaged judgments, judgments that are themselves grounded in the melodramatic mode.

Friedkin's film was released to theaters in October 1971 and about a year later, on December 27, 1972, the Knapp Commission released its final, 264-page report detailing widespread corruption in the New York Police Department. The report concluded a two-and-a-half-year investigation into collusion between plain-clothes police officers and gambling pads and narcotics peddlers, as well as after-hours bars, cab drivers, prostitutes, and accused defendants who wanted their cases dropped. Payouts, sometimes in the tens of thousands of dollars, were made to these police officers to turn a blind eye. The commission report detailed incidents of police brutality during shakedowns as well as corrupt deals with the criminals they were incarcerating. New York police were widely thought to be untrustworthy by the public during the years of the investigation, as the report states:

> At the present time, a citizen wishing to complain about a policeman knows that his complaint will ultimately be investigated by other policemen. This discourages complaints, because many New Yorkers just don't trust policemen to investigate each other.[48]

The most well-known whistleblower on the case was Frank Serpico, an undercover cop whose story was depicted in Sidney Lumet's *Serpico*. Public hearings were held and broadcast on television, besmirching the reputations of New York policemen in the eyes of those who still held them in high regard and saw the NYPD shield as an emblem of virtue. According to Carlo Rotella, "Sonny" Grosso was deeply offended by Lumet's film and believed that such stories damaged the reputation and morale of the already besieged police. "He does not deny that there was corruption," Rotella writes, who spent time with Grosso, "he just does not see why anybody would want to make or see a movie about it, although he does have a theory: 'I guess Lumet, [Budd] Schulberg, people like that, Elia Kazan, they're informers, and they make movies about heroic informers.'"[49]

The parallel between *The French Connection* and its historical context is even more remarkable in another story that unfolded after the release of the film. At the time the Knapp Report was released, the *New York Times* reported that $10 million of heroin, about fifty-five pounds, had been stolen from the French Connection supply stored as evidence since 1962.[50] The article indicated that Eddie Egan would also be questioned as part of the ongoing investigations. Later it would be revealed that, between 1969 and 1972, New York policemen removed hundreds of pounds of heroin from the Property Clerk's Office on 400 Broome St. and replaced it with parcels of flour.[51] The morally questionable methods utilized by Popeye and Cloudy in their pursuit of criminals, acting out under the shield of qualified immunity that typically protects figures of law enforcement, seemed to anticipate the dishonest and illicit activities of the NYPD, linking film and history. As a *New York Daily News* article from 2012 put it, "The heroin was being pilfered and replaced at the same time that 'The French Connection,' the film based on its original confiscation in 1962, was winning Academy Awards."[52] It is as if Friedkin's film had prepared its viewers for the revelations to come, merging fiction and documentary, the play of light and shadows inside the cinema with the gray, morally ambiguous world of New York City outside.

NOTES

1. Ralph Rosenblum and Robert Karen, *When the Shooting Stops . . . the Cutting Begins: A Film Editor's Story* (New York: Viking Press, 1979), 14–15.
2. Roger Ebert, "Review: *The Night They Raided Minsky's*," *Chicago Sun-Times*, December 23, 1968, accessed February 2, 2021, <https://www.rogerebert.com/reviews/the-night-they-raided-minskys-1968>
3. Renata Adler, "Screen: 'Night They Raided Minsky's':1920's Film Directed by William Friedkin Starts Run at 86th St. East and at Victoria," *New York Times*, December 23, 1968, accessed February 2, 2021, <https://www.nytimes.com/1968/12/23/archives/screen-night-they-raided-minskys1920s-film-directed-by-william.html>
4. William Friedkin, *The Friedkin Connection* (New York: Harper, 2013), 118.
5. Leonard J. Leff and Jerold L. Simmons, *The Dame in the Kimono: Hollywood, Censorship, and the Production Code from the 1920s to the 1960s* (New York: Grove Weidenfeld, 1990), 290.
6. Friedkin, *The Friedkin Connection*, 118.

7. Friedkin, *The Friedkin Connection*, 118.
8. *Harold Pinter: Plays One* (London: Faber and Faber, 1996), 44.
9. From the Friedkin papers at the Margaret Herrick Library archives.
10. *Pinter: Plays One*, xiii.
11. Vincent Canby, "Screen: Unsettling World of 'The Birthday Party': Pinter's Adaptation of His Play Arrives Film Playing at Coronet Directed by Friedkin," *New York Times*, December 10, 1968, accessed February 2, 2021, <https://www.nytimes.com/1968/12/10/archives/screen-unsettling-world-of-the-birthday-partypinters-adaptation-of.html>
12. Peter Brooks, *The Melodramatic Imagination: Balzac, Henry James, Melodrama, and the Mode of Excess* (New Haven: Yale University Press, 1995), 12.
13. Brooks, *The Melodramatic Imagination*, 21.
14. Brooks, *The Melodramatic Imagination*, 125.
15. Linda Williams, *Playing the Race Card: Melodramas of Black and White from Uncle Tom to O. J. Simpson* (Princeton: Princeton University Press, 2002), 17.
16. Williams, *Playing the Race Card*, 29.
17. Christian Metz reminds us that the cinema "was born in the midst of the capitalist epoch in a largely antagonistic and fragmented society, based on individualism and the restricted family (= father-mother-children), in an especially super-egotistic bourgeois society." Christian Metz, *The Imaginary Signifier: Psychoanalysis and the Cinema*, trans. Ben Brewster (Bloomington: Indiana University Press, 1982), 64.
18. Francis Gillen, "Harold Pinter's *The Birthday Party*: Menace Reconsidered," in *Harold Pinter: Critical Approaches*, ed. Steven H. Gale (London: Associated University Presses, 1986), 42.
19. James R. Hollis, *Harold Pinter: The Poetics of Silence* (Carbondale: South Illinois University Press, 1970), 38–9.
20. Lucina Paquet Gabbard, *The Dream Structure of Pinter's Plays: A Psychoanalytic Approach* (London: Associated University Presses, 1976), 55.
21. Brooks, *The Melodramatic Imagination*, 80.
22. Leo Braudy, *The World in a Frame: What We See in Films* (Chicago: University of Chicago Press, 2002), 46–7.
23. Braudy, *The World in a Frame*, 65. In a number of ways, what Braudy describes as a closed film may be compared to Gilles Deleuze's concept of a closed set (elaborated in his first book on cinema), which is tethered by only a fine thread to other possible sets.
24. See Vito Russo, *The Celluloid Closet: Homosexuality in the Movies* (New York: Harper & Row, 1987), 163.
25. Ramzi Fawaz, "'Beware the Hostile Fag': Acidic Intimacies and Gay Male Consciousness-Raising in *The Boys in the Band*," in *The Boys in the Band: Flashpoints of Cinema, History and Queer Politics*, ed. Matt Bell (Detroit: Wayne State University Press, 2016), 220.
26. Fawaz, "'Beware the Hostile Fag,'" 231.
27. Lauren Berlant, *The Female Complaint: The Unfinished Business of Sentimentality in American Culture* (Durham, NC: Duke University Press, 2008), 9.
28. Vincent Canby, "Screen: 'Boys in the Band': Crowley Study of Male Homosexuality Opens," *New York Times*, March 18, 1970, accessed February 13, 2021, <https://www.nytimes.com/1970/03/18/archives/screen-boys-in-the-bandcrowley-study-of-male-homosexuality-opens.html>
29. Friedkin, *The Friedkin Connection*, 147.
30. Friedkin, *The Friedkin Connection*, 143.
31. Friedkin, *The Friedkin Connection*, 147–8.
32. Leff and Simmons, *The Dame in the Kimono*, 289.

33. Paul Ramaeker, "Realism, Revisionism and Visual Style: *The French Connection* and the New Hollywood *policier*," *New Review of Film and Television Studies* 8, no. 2 (June 2010), 149.
34. Todd Berliner, *Hollywood Incoherent: Narration in Seventies Cinema* (Austin: University of Texas Press, 2010), 106.
35. Berliner, *Hollywood Incoherent*, 94.
36. Berliner, *Hollywood Incoherent*, 100.
37. Michael Shedlin, "Police Oscar: 'The French Connection': And an Interview with William Friedkin," *Film Quarterly* 25, no. 4 (Summer 1972), 7.
38. Berliner, *Hollywood Incoherent*, 108.
39. Shedlin, "Police Oscar," 6.
40. Braudy, *The World in a Frame*, 103.
41. This is elaborated in the interview with the film's cinematographer, Owen Roizman. See Herb Lightman, "Photographing The French Connection," *American Cinematogapher* 53, no. 2 (February 1972).
42. Carlo Rotella, *Good with Their Hands: Boxers, Bluesmen, and Other Characters from the Rust Belt* (Berkeley: University of California Press, 2002), 129.
43. Quoted from Lightman, "Photographing The French Connection," 159.
44. Pauline Kael, "Urban Gothic," in *Deeper Into Movies* (Boston: Little, Brown, and Company, 1973), 318.
45. Kael, "Urban Gothic," 315.
46. Friedkin, *The Friedkin Connection*, 179.
47. Transcript of the Harold Lloyd Master Seminar, AFI, September 2, 1992. From the Friedkin papers at the Margaret Herrick Library archives.
48. *The Knapp Commission Report on Police Corruption* (New York: George Braziller, 1973), 14.
49. Rotella, *Good with Their Hands*, 110.
50. David Burnham, "$10-Million Heroin Stolen from a Police Office Vault," *New York Times*, December 15, 1972.
51. David J. Krajicek, "Justice Story: How 'French Connection' heroin went missing from NYPD Property Clerk's Office," *New York Daily News*, January 1, 2012.
52. Krajicek, "Justice Story."

CHAPTER 2

Policing the Police

TO LIVE AND DIE IN L.A. (1985)

A scene that occurs about twenty-seven minutes into *To Live and Die in L.A.* quickly takes us to the most important theme of the film. An undercover federal officer named Richard Chance (William Peterson) pursues Carl Cody (John Turturro) through LAX. Cody is a "mule" whose job is to transport counterfeit U.S. currency for the artist and criminal Eric Masters (Willem Dafoe). Openly brandishing his handgun while running through crowds of travelers, the officer's hostile presence creates fear and confusion in the busy airport. This chase sequence echoes the one featured at the beginning of *The French Connection*, where Santa Claus and his partner run after an African-American suspect. Instead of featuring hand-held camerawork, however, as in the 1971 film, here it is filmed with a Steadicam mount, lending the actors' movement a smooth fluidity as they run unrestrained through the pre-9/11 airport terminal. Chance gives chase until they reach the men's restroom. With his gun pointed, the federal officer kicks down the door to one of the stalls and violently pulls Cody out. The suspect almost gets away but Chance impulsively shoots a bullet above Cody's head, stopping him in his tracks. The plain-clothes officer aggressively forces Cody's body against the tiled wall and proceeds to restrain him with handcuffs. As he does so, an airport policeman barges in with his gun pointed at Chance and yells, "Stop it, asshole! I'll blow your head off!" Attempting to clear up the confusion, Chance announces himself as a member of the "U.S. Secret Service" while presenting his badge. "I'm arresting this guy for counterfeiting," he explains. And then, the very next moment, Chance's partner John Vukovich (John Pankow) bursts into the restroom, melodramatically in the nick of time, with his gun aimed at the airport policeman. Vukovich identifies himself as Secret Service to the airport officer as well. The tension

POLICING THE POLICE 53

Figure 2.1 Accusing the accusers

between the three men, guns pointed at each other, is broken up with a bit of humor as a civilian sheepishly walks in to the restroom. "I just came in to take a leak," he remarks while cautiously stepping back (Figure 2.1).

When performed by the one who enforces the law, the act of pointing a gun at another is tantamount to accusing the one who is targeted of wrongdoing, while also condemning the accused as morally compromised. In this brief scene from *To Live and Die in L.A.* we have a series of such performances, one circumscribing another, inducing a momentary crisis of judgment as accusers are accused of legal transgression. As Chance exercises his power to accuse and arrest Cody, his legal legitimacy is momentarily placed under scrutiny when the airport officer barges in and points his gun at him. Vukovich then accuses the latter of committing a crime against a federal officer in a similar manner. The cramped men's restroom becomes a space where moral individuals confront each other and employ their power of judgment, perhaps like those delineated by the stage of Minsky's theater, Meg Bowles's boarding house, or Michael's New York apartment—claustrophobic spaces where the moral underpinnings of the melodramatic mode are exposed through their critique. The one who points their weapon and the one pointed at, policeman and criminal—any clear distinctions between these roles, and the Manichean moral conflicts that underpin them, are placed under scrutiny in this scene.

We thus find ourselves returning to some key themes that Friedkin has repeatedly articulated about his films. Legal transgression and the thin line between policeman and criminal constitute the central problem not only of *The French Connection* and *To Live and Die in L.A.*, as we shall see, but are also obsessions for the director that started early on with the depiction of the Chicago police in *The People Vs. Paul Crump* (1962) and which continue through to Samuel L. Jackson's Childers in *Rules of Engagement* (2000) as well as Matthew McConaughey's Joe Cooper in *Killer Joe* (2011). These figures of law enforcement exercise brutal methods and exploit legal loopholes, acting with impunity, in their desperate pursuit of the bad guy. These are cops who feel emboldened to do bad things in order to become good cops. In other films, such as *Cruising* and *Jade*, sanctioned criminality is linked to sexual transgression, a connection whose aesthetic and political implications we will explore in the next chapter. In all of them, legal judgment is continuous with the moral judgment associated with the popular melodrama mode, suggesting that they are actually not concerned with the logic of law per se, but with the manifestation of virtue that legal discourse makes visible. These films also associate violence with sexuality and sexual desire, associations that are typically organized around constructions of masculinity and homosexual panic.

Phillip Lopate has called *To Live and Die in L.A.* "one of the best, and most underrated, American films of the 1980s."[1] The film appeared in a watershed decade when Hollywood was breaking from vertically structured modes of production, distribution, marketing, and exhibition associated with the classical period. Temporary contracts between studios, agencies, and talent, constituting networks of horizontally organized agglomerations between the film industry and a wide array of non-film business operations, indicated that Hollywood was moving in new directions. While ticket sales remained flat, the industry enjoyed rising box-office revenues throughout the 1980s due to new ancillary markets and distribution platforms, including cable, pay-per-view, and home video. Stephen Prince notes that Hollywood survived the decade primarily because of the opening up of global markets and through mergers between the majors and electronics, music and book publishing, television and cable, financial services, and retail and mail-order industries. "Instead of making films," he writes, "the industry shifted to the production of filmed entertainment."[2] As the costs for filmed entertainment soared, particularly as resources were refocused along the lines of the blockbuster, Hollywood entered into crisis and radically restructured to accommodate a panoply of business concerns, with cinema becoming only one form of "software" among new entertainment platforms. These changes are registered in *To Live and Die in L.A.* through its radical problematization of the moral underpinnings of American subjectivity that are brought to crisis in the 1980s. Commenting on the transformation of Hollywood and its incorporation of a wide range of non-cinema interests, Prince notes that "the Hollywood industry bought time in the 1980s, but the economics of its operation remained wasteful and counterproductive to its long-term health."[3] Through its depiction of legal and moral compromise, *To Live and Die in L.A.* may be read as an allegory of the compensatory efforts of Hollywood narrative form, manifest through the film's obsessive attempts to shore up moral virtue, during this phase of transformation.

If Popeye's obsession takes us to the limits of the moral metaphysics that underpin the melodramatic mode in *The French Connection*, Richard Chance is similarly driven to a fatal end through the exploitation of his grievance and the desire for retribution after his partner Jimmy Hart (Michael Greene) is murdered by Eric Masters.[4] And like Gene Hackman's character, Chance repeatedly flouts the rule of law in his pursuit to bring Masters to justice. In another scene from *To Live and Die in L.A.*, he and Vukovich surveil the house belonging to the counterfeiter's lawyer, Max Waxman (Christopher Allport), from a small parish across the street (reminding us of the stakeout location Popeye and Cloudy rent out across from Sal and Angie's in *The French Connection*). Later that night, Masters arrives at the house and a struggle ensues between the artist and Waxman, ending with a man dead from a bullet. The police arrive and enter the home, but Chance and Vukovich have fallen asleep when they are supposed to be maintaining their observation. They quickly awaken and rush into the house with their guns raised. Friedkin does not show the infiltration and search of Waxman's house, but quickly cuts to their return back to police headquarters. Chance reveals that he has removed a small book from Waxman's office that details dates and dollar amounts of forged money. His partner responds uneasily, "It's a crime scene. The book is evidence. What if the cop remembers it's missing?" The federal agent brushes off Vukovich's concerns, making it clear that he does not plan to place the book into police custody. Apparently justified by his self-righteous pursuit of wrongdoing, Chance will keep the book and in doing so grant himself the authority to take the law into his own hands. An argument between the two federal officers ensues, as Chance questions Vukovich's loyalty to his partner and wonders out loud whether he would be willing to "take heat" while catching criminals.

In a later scene, Chance aggressively demands a federal judge that he sign a legal writ to pardon Cody, who was captured in the scene described above at LAX and later incarcerated. The mule still awaits arraignment. Chance tells the judge that Masters killed his partner, as if his grievance is reason enough to compel the overturning of legal protocols around who may be pardoned and by whom. This compulsion is ironically emboldened through his own position as the one who ostensibly enforces the law. In Chance's relationship with Ruth Lanier (Darlanne Fluegel), a woman with a questionable past and who serves as both his informant and lover, he exploits this position to maintain control over her. When she expresses a desire to discontinue this unequal power relationship, he claims the right to access all her criminal connections (as well as her body) by threatening to revoke her parole and send her back to prison. The power of blackmail reasserts the policeman's legitimacy to accuse another of crime.

In another scene Chance belligerently pleads with his supervisor to approve the release of $30,000 in government funds to purchase one million dollars of counterfeit money. His plan is to apprehend Masters while undercover at the moment they make the purchase. The supervisor refuses, stating that the amount is against policy, and then he reminds Chance that he and Vukovich violated "section 302.5." He goes on to cite this section of police procedure, remarking that, "[t]he agents must notify the agents in charge of all ongoing investigations." By now, it goes without saying that Chance has repeatedly disregarded this policy and he says not one word about his activities or the progress of the investigation. Acting outside the scope of law, he is unflagging in his attempts to build evidence that will prove the guilt of the guy he thinks is wrong, beyond a reasonable doubt.

Yet in the most egregious scene to depict the crossing of the thin line between the policeman and criminal, Chance and Vukovich rob a man from San Francisco who is carrying $50,000 to Los Angeles. Thomas Ling (Michael Chong), repeatedly referred to as a "Chinaman" by many of the film's characters, has brought this money in a metal suitcase, ostensibly to buy stolen diamonds. Chance apprehends him in Union Station, pushing Ling into a car driven by Vukovich. As he does so, two plain-clothes policemen, sitting in the waiting room of the station and whose identities are unknown to the viewer, rise and begin chasing after the three men. In the back seat of the car, Chance points his gun at Ling and, like a man who has kidnapped another for money, demands the key for the suitcase. They reach a concrete-lined location near the Los Angeles River and aggressively pull the "Chinaman" from the car. The two officers demand that Ling hand over the money. While Vukovich draws his gun, Chance breaks open the suitcase and, instead of money, a phone book falls out. Angrily insisting on only real money, the two men accuse Ling of hiding it somewhere on his person and force him to strip. "Get your pants down," Chance commands. The money is indeed attached to his belt.

Meanwhile, the unknown men from Union Station appear on a bridge spanning the river and, watching the interaction below, aim their rifles at Chance and Ling. For a moment, the scene recalls the sniper who shoots at Popeye in *The French Connection*, but here it is policemen shooting at other policemen impersonating criminals. This situation also recalls one described in an earlier scene at the beginning of this chapter: multiple accusations, one circumscribing another, each constituting a gesture that polices the police. In both situations, accusers who enforce the law are judged while the raised weapon indexes the accused. Here, as in the bathroom scene in LAX, confusion arises as to who is policeman and who is criminal, and about who deserves to live and who to die.

The men on the bridge start shooting at Chance, Vukovich, and Ling below. These three men scatter from the scene. Suddenly, the parked car that was driven by the shooters, which has taken up an entire lane in the highway, is rear-ended. Somehow this causes one of the men to inadvertently discharge their rifle, hitting Ling in the back and killing him. Vukovich peers incredulously at the motionless body with a growing awareness of his own moral and legal wrongdoing. He then rushes back to the car, where Chance has taken the driver's seat. Recalling *The French Connection* once more, a thrilling chase sequence ensues, one that takes them along the Los Angeles River and into the Terminal Island Freeway. As they are being chased, weaving between cars and even driving against dense Los Angeles traffic, confusion quickly sets in as to who is pursuing and who is being pursued, and about which car moves in accordance with or against the law. At the end of the sequence, Chance joyfully celebrates his evasion of the policemen who chased them while Vukovich remains clearly disturbed by their criminality. Adding to the confusion, they are notified that Ling was also an undercover cop who arrived in L.A. to take part in a sting operation sponsored by the FBI. His death deepens the criminal culpability of Chance and Vukovich further.

In these and other moments, Chance is shameless, not only in his dereliction of duty to uphold the law, but also in his infringement of the norms that underpin the Manichean dualism between good and evil. While the opening scenes of the film depict him as a heroic agent of Reagan's secret service, his character is quickly corrupted as the narrative of *To Live and Die in L.A.* unfolds and as he is drawn into the underworld of lawlessness and crime. The violent methods typically associated with criminality—theft, the exploitation of others, murder—are those utilized by the federal agent throughout Friedkin's film, methods that muddle the relationship between melodrama and the law. Chance's obsessiveness, which seems to supersede his moral compass, compels uncertainty as to how his actions should be judged while obscuring the line between justice and revenge.

Yet the protagonists featured in these films are not detectives who had initially upheld the law and gradually became corrupted over time, but men who perceive themselves to have been victimized and who thus feel empowered to disregard the law in the name of righteous justice. They resist legal actions that threaten their moral entitlements while acting out against a world that is perceived to upend their sovereign judgment, a world that is increasingly diversifying and one allegorized perhaps by a Hollywood that is increasingly underwritten by global capital. With consideration of these shifts, Michael S. Shapiro contextualizes the acts of policing in *To Live and Die in L.A.* as revolving around the policing of masculinity and the shoring up of borders that separate men from that which is perceived to threaten them. Sexual, class, and racial differences threaten to overcome this besieged masculinity:

> It is the "police", a group of detectives in pursuit of a counterfeiter, who engage in active homosocial male bonding rituals, which include a continual use of phallic imagery and a preoccupation with showing that one has "balls". At the same time, it is the police who maintain rigidly heterosexual *personae*, while the object of their investigation, an artist/counterfeiter, has a relationship with a bisexual and androgynous appearing woman, and moves about in venues that are ambiguously gender-coded.[5]

As in *The Boys in the Band*, where distinctions between straight and gay are developed in order to critique them, *To Live and Die in L.A.* proceeds along similar lines. Chance and Vukovich are thrown into a world, set in Los Angeles, where generic boundaries that delineate sexual difference seem fluid, where masculinity takes on feminine signs and vice versa. In this, it continues to work with themes around sexuality and criminality introduced in *Cruising*. And as in the films we have discussed so far, such distinctions are underpinned by the production and obsessive shoring up of moral virtue. While playing out and radicalizing the ethics of the melodramatic mode, Chance exploits the sense of grievance claimed by the loss of his partner to justify his acting out, to stand his ground as an arbiter of straight, masculine virtue. Yet as the film unfolds, his increasingly violent behavior becomes also incommensurate with the ethics that delineates victim from victimizer, masculinity from femininity, heterosexuality from homosexuality.

The depictions of recursive judgment I discussed above, where the legality and morality of the actions of the police are placed under scrutiny, point us toward the problem of what legitimizes the law, a problem many of Friedkin's films seem repeatedly to seek out. Cops in Friedkin's cinema are not bound by their moral duty to enforce legal imperatives, but are emboldened by the legitimacy these imperatives grant them to exercise extralegal acts of violence. And while such performances are part and parcel of the exercise of moral decision that political beings enact in everyday life, Chance is clearly invested in the testing of moral boundaries, at times gleefully so. Brushing up against their limits, he recklessly aims his gun at civilians, steals $50,000 from an undercover detective, and brutalizes informants. By asserting the right to judge the legality of another, he also asserts a kind of sadistic sovereign power over them. Blurring the boundary between the policeman and criminal, *To Live and Die in L.A.* reveals the performative assertion that underpins the legitimacy of both. In the face of this moral uncertainty, as well as a profound anxiety produced in response to the illegibility of the legitimacy of paper money, Chance violently reasserts this sovereign power over his impulse to recuperate a normative moral universe. His character critically reveals the relationship between suffering and retaliatory violence and shows how the latter emerges through an intolerance to moral doubt.

The critical discourse of sovereign judgment is brought into relief as the act of judgment is framed and itself interrogated. Yet through this, the discourse of masculinity, as constituted through the reiteration of that which separates sameness from difference, undergoes critical interrogation as well. When Chance is reproached in the LAX restroom by the airport police and when he and Vukovich are shot at while harassing Ling, these instances raise the issue of how the problematization of moral virtue may be linked to the crisis of his masculinity as well as to the interrogation of its discursive conditions.

Throughout the film, Chance's resentment grows as his pursuit of Masters is repeatedly stymied by police protocol and legal procedure. His seething rage seems perpetually inscribed in his facial expressions and is barely contained by the volatility of his body. Lashing out through moments of police brutality and the obsession that drives it, Chance seems to retaliate against forces outside himself that he perceives as delegitimizing his authority as a man of justice. Clearly, Masters's sexual ambiguity, depicted in one of the first shots we see of him at the dance performance, from behind, only exacerbates the sense of frustration felt by the sovereign look, for the one who demands certainty—sexual, moral, and otherwise—in the other.

Friedkin notes that he intended the car chase in *To Live and Die in L.A.* to serve as the centerpiece of the film while explicitly comparing it to the much-touted parallel sequence in *The French Connection* involving a car and an elevated train. "I thought for many years," he writes, "about what I might do to surpass the chase in *The French Connection*."[6] After calling the chase sequence "the purest form of cinema,"[7] the director recalls that he was thinking of the earlier film and believed that with the help of stuntman Buddy Joe Hooker they could "top" the famous chase sequence from 1971. Friedkin remarks that:

> I didn't want the film to be a clone of *The French Connection*. I would abandon the gritty macho look of that film for something in the unisex style of Los Angeles in the 1980s. [. . .] I had seen *Paris, Texas* by the German director Wim Wenders, photographed by an Austrian cinematographer, Robbie Muller. His films were beautifully lit and composed, with long uninterrupted takes. This was the style I wanted for *To Live and Die in L.A.*, in which the city would be portrayed as a violent, cynical wasteland under a burning sun.[8]

The later noir film indeed showcases Los Angeles as a brightly lit city, with working areas filled with large anonymous warehouses and factories, highways teeming with car and truck traffic, palm trees, and unspecified offices and living spaces. The clothing of the characters certainly fulfills the unisex style Friedkin was going for, but it also seems to have no historical specificity of its own. Brooklyn in *The French Connection* is gritty, dense, and seems devoid of light, even during the daytime. The upbeat songs and new wave soundtrack by Wang Chung in the later film contrast sharply with the jazz score composed by Don Ellis in Friedkin's earlier one. Before filming, Friedkin went on ridealongs in New York that enabled him to witness real crimes taking place, while in his research before filming started in Los Angeles he took on the retired Secret Service agent who wrote the book on which the film is based as a consultant. *To Live and Die in L.A.* enframes key narrative and visual elements of *The French Connection*, like the scenes in the LAX restroom and Ling's shooting, that self-consciously enframe the question of police authority and the legitimacy of their judgment.

To consider the aesthetics of *The French Connection* and *To Live and Die in L.A.* together, to look from 1971 to 1985, inspires comparisons that help us understand key features of both. Despite the stories of both films taking place in December and January, the contrast in the depictions of the bitter chill of New York and the temperate sunniness of L.A. remains striking. Both films feature male protagonists, accompanied by a skeptical, yet nevertheless complicit partner, who will stop at nothing to shore up their moral certainty. Cloudy may be compared to Vukovich in their roles as conflicted spectators of their respective partners, roles that align them with the moral conflicts of the films' spectators. On the other hand, Chance remains arguably more violent and licentious in his interrogation methods compared to Popeye. Yet Friedkin seems to have sensed that the protagonist's behavior in *To Live and Die in L.A.* could not go with impunity. He writes:

> Halfway through production, it occurred to me that Petersen's character, Chance, had to die. This was not in the script or the novel, but I thought it was unexpected and justified, given that he lived constantly on the edge. He wasn't a superhero immune to danger.[9]

In contrast, Popeye in *The French Connection* does not get Charnier in the end and is reassigned, all but ensuring his mythification as a figure of law enforcement who heroically gave it his all.

Nevertheless, from New York to Los Angeles, Friedkin clearly attempts to model key elements of the later film upon the earlier. The disparities between *The French Connection* and *To Live and Die in L.A.* reflect differences, not of kind, but of degree. The obsession embodied by Popeye's character is ramped up in that of Chance, becoming more unbridled and volatile, almost hysterical. In this, Friedkin's film puts the legitimacy of Chance's violence into greater jeopardy, encouraging sharper judgment of his villainy. Moreover, the moral ambiguity embodied by Popeye's character suffuses the diegetic world of Friedkin's film from 1985, expanding beyond the body and contaminating the film's *mise-en-scène*, and spilling over into its narrative form and content. Los Angeles is not simply an urban wasteland but is depicted as anonymous, decontextualized, and emptied of history. Protagonists, antagonists, and supporting characters, all generic types in the classic film noir, here become morally ambiguous; their politics are not simply hidden behind surfaces, but remain unspecified.

We may thus think of the later film as expressing an attitude of nostalgia in relation to the earlier. In 1984, one year before Friedkin's film was released in theaters, Frederic Jameson published his well-known essay, "Postmodernism, or The Cultural Logic of Late Capitalism," where he discusses how an "omnipresent, omnivorous and well-nigh libidinal historicism" gives rise to a nostalgia for a past that is perceived to have been more coherent and seemingly more virtuous.[10] The past becomes referent as signifiers of an ostensible golden age reappear as stylistic connotation. On the one hand, this helps us understand how nostalgia and loss underpin the relationship of *The French Connection* to the *policier* and the classical film noir. *To Live and Die in L.A.* could be understood in a similar manner in its expression of nostalgia for Friedkin's much more financially successful 1971 film. The morally compromised policeman and his complicit partner, the foregrounding of the interlocking acts of moral and legal judgment, the long sequences depicting the validity of heroin and the validity of fake money, and the thrilling car chase sequences: both films cover similar ground and raise comparable problematics. The later film is constituted as a nostalgic pastiche of elements from the earlier. On the other hand, the multiplication of ambiguity throughout the form and content of *To Live and Die in L.A.* takes the critique of Manichean morality into the realm of cinematic signification itself. For not only are Vukovich, Thomas Ling, Carl Cody, and Chance's girlfriend Ruth ambiguous in their alliances, but this uncertainty spills over into the tortured logic of the film's editing and its rendering of continuity. In its introduction of seemingly unimportant characters and unrelated locations, *To Live and Die in L.A.* manifests what Jameson calls the "breakdown of the signifying chain,"[11] as its montage seems less to obey the demands of causality and becomes constitutive of something like "a series of pure and unrelated presents in time."[12] As the film unfolds, confusion arises as to what is happening where, an experience that is perhaps akin to Jameson's famous phenomenological description of dislocation while navigating the Bonaventura Hotel in Los Angeles. As he notes, the Bonaventura may be interpreted as an allegory for the city in which it is situated and which surrounds it.

Above all, if the viewer does indeed become confused as to who may or may not be trusted in *To Live and Die in L.A.*, about how the space of Los Angeles is constructed in the film, or how cross-cut scenes relate to each other, this is a result of the failure of cognitive mapping, or an inability of the film to present the postmodern city as a coherent space. In this city without center, where locations seem historically and ontologically disconnected from each other, the film's editing expresses this lack of continuity in that cuts do not facilitate continuity of movement and time, but rather induce confusion as to how we get from point A to point B. If anything, this style seems to induce a moment-by-moment anticipation of the next shot, the next unexpected place that is to be represented. For some viewers, of course, this demand for continuity may not matter so much, betraying what Steven Shapiro calls "post-continuity."[13] After Chance gleefully announces that he knows about Masters's whereabouts from

Waxman's address book, the film cuts not to the location ostensibly indicated in the book but to Ruth's small apartment. Vukovich is told, by an art collector we see only once in the film, that Masters's studio has a Chinese character (which ironically means "to combine" or "bring together appropriately") on its exterior. But when he arrives at the location and checks out the building, the film cuts away and introduces a new character, Jeff Rice (Steve James), playing basketball in a location somewhere that has not yet been shown to the viewer. In her seminal essay on Friedkin's film, Sharon Willis writes that Los Angeles is depicted as having a "fragmented topography, where spaces seem not to communicate, much less interlock, because one can only circulate through them by driving."[14] The timestamps that appear throughout the film, each in a different font, indicate the passing of time but are contradicted by the perpetual sun of southern California. Clock time seems not to matter much for telling the story of *To Live and Die in L.A.* anyway. Los Angeles is depicted in Friedkin's film not as a topography that can be schematized according to principles of time and space, but ideologically, through categories of identity and assumptions around gender, race, and class. "Space remains implicitly social," Willis notes, implying with this claim about Friedkin's film that space is known to have been traversed only when difference is encountered, such as the industrial part of Los Angeles where the strip club of Chance's girlfriend is situated or Rice's largely African-American neighborhood.[15]

Perhaps the most important allegory of this postmodern condition is the presence of counterfeit money, of illegal currency, around which the entirety of the film revolves and which remains unbearable to the rule of law. Indeed, the fluidity between legal and illegal tender allegorizes the moral and ideological confusions produced by the film—between friend and enemy, between truth and dissimulation. When Chance exchanges real money for counterfeit money, the distinctions between the two break down, giving rise to a crisis of legitimacy, unbinding it from the law that authenticates it. Somewhat ironically, Friedkin expresses some pride in the scenes from the film that depict Masters's counterfeiting process, introduced to him by former Secret Service agent Gerry Petievich, particularly in the ease by which the illicit currency is passed:

> The counterfeiting scene was filmed in an abandoned warehouse in the desert outside Bakersfield, California. We shot it in loving detail. One of the special effects men took home some of the bills, all twenties, printed on one side only. His teenage son grabbed a handful off his father's bedroom dresser and with a friend bought some candy at a local supermarket. Within minutes, Secret Service agents were on the scene. They arrested the boys and asked where they got the money. The boy confessed: "From my dad." The boy's father was interrogated and said the bills were made for a movie.[16]

Friedkin explains that the special effects man later rebuffed requests to be questioned by the Central District of California. But this anecdote raises provocative questions around what legitimates the power of legitimization and the force of law. Like the performative accusations I addressed earlier, one nested within the other, this question reveals that the validity of money is constituted through a kind of performance as well. Its legitimization takes place through an act of visual perception in Friedkin's film, as paper bills are passed off and imbued with the possession of authentic exchange-value. The irony here is of course that the exchange-value itself remains groundless in its relationship to things, accruing value solely in its function of placing commodities in relation to each other. Real money had to be stolen and procured from Ling, an illicit diamond dealer who is really an undercover federal officer, so that it might be exchanged for counterfeit money. "As his partner points out," Willis writes,

> they've had to steal thirty thousand dollars of real money, taxpayer's money at that, to buy counterfeit. So it is the simulacrum that turns the law into an outlaw. There is no difference between the pose and the reality: to impersonate outlaws, they must become outlaws.[17]

Characters, the viewer comes to learn as the film unfolds, are never what they seem. They move fluidly between law and lawlessness, like the paper bills that are circulated between them.

But the circulation of Masters's imitation bills, visually indistinguishable from "real" money in the film, draws one's attention to the key aspect of this performative: the mystical foundations that ground it. Authentication takes place at the moment of giving and receiving the paper bills, not in the state and legal body whose name is printed on it. The passing of the inauthentic, of the copy, from one to another calls the one who judges into question and interrogates the performance of judgment undertaken by the sovereign subject. This is the critique that Robert Arnett, in his article on noir cinema from the 1980s, calls the "dissenting voice in Reagan's America."[18] In addition to productions such as *Manhunter*, *Blue Velvet*, and the first season of *Miami Vice*, Arnett argues that while *To Live and Die in L.A.* does not simply reiterate postmodern tropes of nostalgia and pastiche, it also does not return "to the status quo of Reagan's America because the viewer understands the masks worn by the characters."[19] This critical interrogation, in turn, places the passing of judgment itself into jeopardy. In the light of this critique, one may perhaps understand both Masters's impulse to burn his completed paintings as well as the scene depicting his immolation at the end of the film. The counterfeit cash he produces threatens his status as a bourgeois artist, reminding one perhaps of the art forger Elmyr de Hory from Orson Welles's 1973 film, *F for Fake*, who is nevertheless committed to the production of original art. It is not simply that what he produces is commodified; Masters's creations are, first and foremost, pure commodities whose value inheres solely in their exchange-value. He cannot lay claim to his currency, even as it passes between individuals as authentic, for it is owned by no single individual, yet its legality is manifest through the ritual of exchange itself. The dissolution of the unique work of art signals, in this, the "'death' of the subject itself = the end of the autonomous bourgeois monad or ego or individual," as Jameson puts it.[20] Embodying the compulsion toward lawlessness and chaos, Masters seems to be aware that the morality that produces this compulsion remains without foundation. He becomes master of nothing at all (Figure 2.2).

In a text called *Given Time: 1. Counterfeit Money*, Jacques Derrida critically considers the ontology of the gift through the giving of counterfeit currency. Ontologically speaking, gift-giving betrays its own name, for when a gift is given to another, it implicates a reciprocal economy, one that inaugurates the everyday politics concomitant with exchange, credit, debt, and the expectation of return. Within this economy, the gift is annulled at the moment it is exchanged between individuals (the individual constituted as *homo economicus*). Indeed, the very act of giving reinscribes the mundane metaphysics that underpins the politics of sovereign power, of elevated and besmirched reputations, and of moral actors engaged in the give-and-take not only of things but also of the political emotions that underpin ethical concepts such as guilt, obligation, revenge, and forgiveness. Such a logic of the gift buttresses the *quid pro quo* of intercourse between political beings in public life. On the other hand, when counterfeit money is given between these actors, it maintains its status as an exchangeable commodity

Figure 2.2 An exchange of counterfeit currency

by being recognized as legal tender at the same time as its critical illegitimacy is maintained, a status that is nevertheless secretive and unknowable. Counterfeit money guides us to deconstruct the exchange-value of money as well as the nature of exchange itself, as Derrida writes:

> Counterfeit money is never, *as such*, counterfeit money. As soon as it is what it is, recognized *as such*, it ceases to act as and to be worth counterfeit money. It only is by being able to be, *perhaps*, what it is. This irreducible modality taken into account, and inasmuch as the title may belong to it, it obligates you. It obligates you first of all to wonder what money is: true money, false money, the falsely true and the truly false—and non-money which is neither true nor false, and so forth.[21]

There are thus two implications that Derrida brings to bear on his reading of a short story by Baudelaire called "Counterfeit Money": one, that the content of the story addresses this critical thought and, two, that the story itself constitutes a kind of counterfeit money, one exchanged between Baudelaire and his readers. It is a simulacrum given by the author, told by a fictive narrator who produces a narrative that nevertheless has true discursive effects on the reader. Considered in this manner, the gift of literature both requires and annuls the possibility of narrative as well as the gift of language itself.

Derrida's thoughts help us to appreciate the radicality of Masters, an artist who produces counterfeit money, and his allegorical relationship to Friedkin's film. Based on experiences narrated by Petievich, who eventually came to serve as the "technical advisor" for the film, the script for *To Live and Die in L.A.* was written in three weeks. Friedkin's film can thus be thought of as a "counterfeit" adaptation of genuine experiences remembered by a real Secret Service agent that are passed off to the film viewer through a moving image medium that counterfeits reality. Taking this into account, we might thus read the director's use of counterfeit money in the film in a new way. Continuing the anecdote introduced above, Friedkin expresses delight that the banknotes used for the film convinced others of their authenticity as he himself impersonates a criminal:

> When the film came out, there were news stories about people trying to make counterfeit money after seeing the step-by-step process in our film. I took some of the twenties, those printed on both sides of course, put them in my wallet, and spent them, in restaurants, shoe-shine parlors, and elsewhere. The money was that good.[22]

The heroin in *The French Connection* was authentic, while the money in *To Live and Die in L.A.* is an authentic counterfeit—another instance, perhaps, of postmodern nostalgia. Here Friedkin enjoys a bit of perverse delight in the mundane passing of fake money and the lack of scrutiny that enables it. We might think of Masters as the allegorical stand-in for Friedkin, both figures who are producing simulacrums of art, within a culture industry that is concerned above all with the production of "real" profit. The neo-expressionist paintings featured in *To Live and Die in L.A.* were produced by real-life artist Rainer Fetting, who makes a brief appearance in the film, specifically during Chance Vukovich's stakeout, as a fake Catholic priest. Moreover, one could also mention, in this regard, that *The French Connection* includes the real policemen, Eddie Egan and Sonny Grosso, on which the story is based, while the real Gerry Petievich plays a special agent in *To Live and Die in L.A.* in a very minor role in a film that otherwise features only actors playing policemen. Despite Friedkin's perverse and cynical joy in making the latter, moral and legal judgment ultimately do not inhere in the sovereign self, for the phenomenological power of the counterfeit inheres in its capacity to upend, and thus put into relief, the reciprocal *quid pro quo* that is constitutive of the political animal in everyday life.

RULES OF ENGAGEMENT (2000)

In his review of *Rules of Engagement* for the *New York Times*, Elvis Mitchell compares its plot, about a "bitter veteran looking to gain a shot at long-lost glory," with the career trajectory of the then sixty-five-year-old director up to this point: Friedkin, the film critic disparagingly writes, "whose seminal genre films *The French Connection* and *The Exorcist* put him on Sugar Mountain in the 1970s and who has been trying to rekindle the legend ever since."[23] While Mitchell does point out an inconvenient truth regarding the director's career trajectory, this film starring Samuel L. Jackson and Tommy Lee Jones continues Friedkin's obsessive concern with issues of law and lawlessness and it is here where we can start again. Around the same time that *Rules of Engagement* was released, a longer cut of *The Exorcist*, "The Version You've Never Seen," also appeared in theaters. This new version has a number of changes from the 1973 theatrical cut: more notable among them are some new scenes depicting Regan receiving a physical, the "spider walk" shots, a key conversation between Karras and Merrin that takes place during a moment of respite from the exorcism, and a recut and slightly changed ending. The re-release of Friedkin's most successful film, twenty-seven years later, brought back good reviews and audiences, reviving the "legend" of the New Hollywood director.

Rules of Engagement is like the production immediately preceding it, Friedkin's *12 Angry Men*, a remake of the well-known 1957 courtroom drama directed by Sidney Lumet. The success of this television film seemed to provide momentum for *Rules of Engagement*, a legal drama/war film based on a script by Jim Webb. Webb is a Vietnam veteran who was awarded a Navy Cross for heroism and served as U.S. senator for the state of Virginia from 2007 to 2013. In addition to his public service, Webb has been a fairly prolific writer, having penned several novels, screenplays, and articles for major news outlets including the *New York Times* and *The Washington Post*. He ran for president as a Democrat in the 2016 elections but withdrew in October 2015 after the first round of debates. The script for *Rules of Engagement*, like much of Webb's fictional work, draws from his own experiences on the front and addresses themes of loyalty and the morality of war. According to Friedkin's account, the film

> tells of the clash between American relations in the Persian Gulf and military justice for one man. The rules of engagement are flexible guidelines devised by the U.S. military to minimize excessive violence in combat. But combat *is* excessive violence, soldiers are sent into battle to kill people and blow things up. Webb's script asks the question, "What constitutes murder in a military action?"[24]

In the following, we will look at how *Rules of Engagement* poses this question and see how it asks about the definition of murder within the context of war, particularly as the film foregrounds how the justification for killing another human being is judged within the scope of the popular melodramatic mode. By elucidating these conditions for judgment, which I have begun to raise in my analysis of *To Live and Die in L.A.* above, I hope to show how *Rules of Engagement* provides us with a more precise look at how masculinity, empowered by moral righteousness, disavows the ambiguity between law and lawlessness.

Rules of Engagement begins with an episode that takes place in South Vietnam in 1968. Two marine regiment leaders, Hayes Hodges (Tommy Lee Jones) and Terry Childers (Samuel L. Jackson), are leading their small platoons toward an American combat base in Ca Lu. Because a direct path through the dense jungle will prove dangerous, they flip a coin to decide who will flank up the hill and who will traverse the swamp. This moment recalls a similar situation from Friedkin's *Sorcerer*, where two trucks delivering explosives split up to traverse a hazardous jungle somewhere in Latin America. *Rules of Engagement* cross-cuts between Hodges and Childers as they go their separate ways. Images of Viet Cong soldiers are interpolated, signaling that a firefight is imminent. Shots break out and both American battalions are attacked, but only Childers's squad manages to overtake their enemies. He pulls Vietnamese soldiers from their camouflaged hiding places and aggressively questions them about the number and locations of their units. The Viet Cong do not answer, either in English or Vietnamese, and look impassively at the American commander's livid face.

Meanwhile, Hodges and his men have been taken by surprise and are attacked in the swamp. They fall one by one. Hearing the gunshots from a distance, Childers demands that a Viet Cong commanding officer, Bin Le Cao

(Tuan Tran), call off the attacks on his colleague. Becoming increasingly frustrated, the U.S. colonel puts a gun to the head of another Vietnamese soldier (Peter Tran), demanding that the attack on Hodges be called off or, as he remarks, "this motherfucker's dead and you're next." This tense moment recalls one of the most iconic photographs of the war taken by Eddie Adams in 1968 called "Saigon Execution," depicting the moment before a Viet Cong prisoner is shot in the head by a South Vietnamese general. The violent and shocking image was published in national newspapers and appeared on American televisions, playing a key role in turning public opinion against the war. After a moment passes with no response from the soldier, Childers pulls the trigger, killing the man instantly. He turns the gun back to the Vietnamese commander and tells him once more to halt the attack. Another intense pause follows. The film cuts back to Hodges and his soldiers, taking cover from the continuing onslaught by their enemies. And as soon as the attack began, it is called off. Over the radio transceiver, Childers tells Hodges that, "You got a reprieve, you hear me? You don't get to die today. You got your Hail Mary."

The opening set piece of Friedkin's film raises the problem of what constitutes "ethical" murder when confronted with the possibility of the death of one's friend. Although this scene from *Rules of Engagement* does not yet delve into the legal complications of Childers's decision to shoot another human at point blank range, it nevertheless invites moral judgment and reasoning within the melodramatic mode. One is led to wonder whether his violent means outweigh the ends and is asked to evaluate how the value of human life may be represented when deciding between friends and enemies. Do the deaths of the many justify the shooting of a single villain? What is the line between legitimate and illegitimate murder during times of modern warfare? How do the reasons for killing affect the determination of this moral line? And how does the method of killing inform where this line is drawn? The opening scene raises these questions, while the decision to kill the Viet Cong soldier defies moral norms, raising the question of the relevant "rules of engagement" that apply to this tense and uncertain situation.

In the end, however, these questions and irregularities are papered over in the name of male camaraderie and loyalty among fellow soldiers. Following the film's opening segment, Friedkin cuts to the present day, to a well-attended party celebrating Colonel Hodges's retirement after thirty-two years of service. As his colleagues call for a speech, he is presented with a surprise. Childers's smiling face emerges from the multitude gathered in the crowded room. His old friend presents Hodges with the U.S. Marine Corps Mameluke sword: "The symbol of a warrior," Childers remarks, "and you are a warrior. The best I ever served with." Later we learn that after he was relieved of his duties as a military soldier, Hodges became a JAG (Judge Advocate General) officer and served in this demoted capacity, "riding a desk for the past twenty-eight years," and was thus barred from serving in a more active role. The two men have not forgotten what happened in Vietnam as their bond is secured through the collective memory of a traumatic experience as well as by the shared culpability in the violent assassination of another human being.

Childers is reassigned to command the 24th Marine Expeditionary Unit. In a new scene the two men walk through a forest together. Hodges reminisces on how past events have come to affect, seemingly inexplicably, present circumstances: "One guy walks out through a swamp, he gets to come home to a desk. Another guy drives up a hill and he gets to still be doing it, all over the flip of a goddamn coin." Congratulating each other, they reflect on all that they have accomplished. However, the memory of what happened in Vietnam will soon repeat, like a compulsion, despite all attempts to repress it through their tacit agreement that whatever happened in the past remains ultimately justified and just, buried in their narratives of the glories of war.

Rules of Engagement cuts to another military mission involving Childers taking place in the present day. He has been assigned to provide "extra security" for the American embassy in Yemen. The embassy building is surrounded by local demonstrators who have become increasingly unruly. When Childers is ordered to provide support for this escalating situation by his commanding officer, in an aircraft carrier somewhere on the Indian Ocean, no reason is provided as to why the Yemenis are protesting—no historical context, just the understanding that America is under attack by non-American, Muslim enemies. Popular melodramatic fiction typically extracts from history only what can serve its reductive aim of recognizing victims and its need for making virtue legible. Childers and his platoon are helicoptered onto the roof of the embassy building and, on the way, their aircraft is shot at by snipers and machine guns from the ground. The demonstrators become increasingly agitated by the presence of American soldiers and begin throwing rocks and Molotov cocktails. Childers's helicopter touches down behind the building and as soon as it does so, men disembark and rush in to evacuate the U.S. ambassador (Ben Kingsley) and his family. They are shot at by armed Yemeni protestors but the American soldiers do not return fire.

After securing the ambassador and his family in a helicopter and flying them to safety, Childers and his soldiers continue to be targeted by gunfire on the roof of the embassy. He sees that his men are falling to unseen snipers and makes a crucial decision to retaliate, a decision that reiterates the moral dilemma raised in Vietnam and will be consequential for the remainder of the film's plot. Taking cover from enemy fire, Childers indignantly commands his subordinate officer and his men to return fire at the protestors, despite the presence of women and children among them, and "waste the motherfuckers." With some hesitation, Captain Lee (Blair Underwood) orders his platoon to shoot into the crowd gathered outside the embassy. Countless Yemeni bodies fall, most of whom did not wield weapons but were there only to peacefully protest. At the end of the encounter, the area is strewn with dozens of bloody corpses. A few women wail to mourn their loved ones.

The remainder of the film depicts the juridical litigation of Childers's decision while simultaneously inviting the viewer's litigation of his character. These discursive lines of judgment become intertwined in *Rules of Engagement* in its popular mode of address. When Hodges agrees to represent his old friend as his lawyer, the film's melodramatic stakes become clarified and raised even further, for they revolve around Hodges's disposition and the conflict between his professional duty to justify the questionable actions of Childers and his allegiance to his comrade. Under scrutiny is the legality of his decision to fire upon protestors and the question of whether the American soldiers had just cause to retaliate against a crowd of mostly unarmed protestors. In the courtroom sequences to follow, the legality of whether this decision to murder civilians will be debated while consideration of its morality will underpin the underlying narrative stakes and solicit viewers to consider whether Childers's command to kill may be felt as a moral good. The claim of who fired first is questioned repeatedly throughout in order to definitively determine victims and victimizers. While Friedkin depicts Childers as initiating the attack first, the security cam footage that would have corroborated this is destroyed by the National Security Advisor, Bill Sokal (Bruce Greenwood). Sokal, in despair at the negative publicity and besmirched reputation this case will bring to the U.S. military, conspires to pin blame solely on Childers. As the film shifts registers and becomes a courtroom drama, replicating many plot points featured in *A Few Good Men* (1992), judgment is rendered on Childers's judgment. As in the nested acts of judgment depicted in *To Live in Die and L.A.*, where we saw how the police are policed through the force of accusation and the pointed gun, the legitimacy of Childers's sovereign decision, one that takes power over the lives of others, enters into a realm of moral confusion and juridical indeterminacy.

We can clarify the terms of this confusion by trying to understand the conditions under which the assertion of a legal decision, particularly in times of anomic social and moral instability, grounds the assertion of political power. In his text from 1922, *Political Theology*, Carl Schmitt famously asserts that the "sovereign is he who decides on the exception."[25] This claim has been understood to describe how sovereignty is grounded through a speech act that declares the distinction between legality and illegality, and which is carried out through a rhetorical circumvention of law. In an exercise of pure power, one that aspires to transgress the norms of law, the speech act itself legitimizes its own declaration. Schmitt suggests that sovereign power is defined through its own power to judge and deem any political action or any person as falling within or outside the law's binding force. Indeed, according to his claim, power is consolidated at the moment judgment is rendered, in the very performative of the decision that deems another to be criminal. Considered in this manner, the performative, not law, grounds sovereignty, allowing the sovereign to act without impunity, to make decisions as if they were not being policed by the other. "After all," Schmitt writes, "every legal order is based on a decision, and also the concept of the legal order, which is applied as something self-evident, contains within it the contrast of the two distinct elements of the juristic—norm and decision. Like every other order, the legal order rests on a decision and not on a norm."[26] For our purposes, one may think of the enactment of a decision as an assertion that aims to elude democratic norms and circumvent the checks and balances of power. The definition of the nature of sovereign power and the decision it carries out become particularly urgent in determining the legitimacy of the use of violent force. How does the use of violence stand in relation to the law? What kinds of violent action fall within the jurisdiction of the law and what are the limits of this jurisdiction? When violence is judged according to law in this manner, who decides where the line between the permissible and impermissible (and by co-extension between the policeman and criminal) may be drawn?

These are ways of critically restating Friedkin's question, "What constitutes murder in a military action?" In *Rules of Engagement*, this question is put into motion by Childers and the decisions he makes about killing his enemy, both in Vietnam and in Yemen. With both the Viet Cong soldier and the protesting Yemenis, he makes the decision to kill in order to preserve the lives of the American military. Killing the enemy is, ostensibly, to be expected in a time of war, yet Friedkin's film asks about the very legitimacy of this violent act and its legal limits during wartime. As a commanding officer, it is Childers's obligation to make these difficult decisions and to protect his troops while serving his country. On the other hand, his carrying out of these decisions is what manifests his sovereign power in a circular movement between power and speech, such that his rank legitimizes the command to kill and vice versa. His crude order to "waste the motherfuckers" both legitimates and is legitimized by the right to protect the sovereign territory of the U.S. and the exercise of authority over the marines in his regiment. The contradiction here, of course, is that Childers, a soldier whose violent means are apparently circumscribed by law and the rules of engagement, is put on trial for instigating extra-judicial violence, for authorizing violence that cannot be sanctioned by the norms of the law. This contradiction is papered over in Friedkin's film, shored up to prop up the discourse of sovereignty.

From this, another split quickly emerges, one that is narrativized and drives the development of the plot for the last half of the *Rules of Engagement*. This split arises between the logic of law and the logic of melodramatic sympathy, presenting viewers with another contradiction that aims for resolution and whose positions are embodied in the positions of the lawyers. In his opening argument, the federal state prosecutor, Major Biggs (Guy Pearce), articulates the chief accusation against Childers, while clearly indicating that his decision to retaliate in Yemen stepped over the boundary of his sanctioned authority:

> Why did a well-trained fighting unit have to slaughter unarmed men, women, and children when their orders were simply to protect and if necessary, evacuate the embassy? The answer is, they didn't. They were ordered to open fire, and that order came from one man, Colonel Terry Childers, who stands trial here today, a day of sadness, a day when America has to accept responsibility for its failures and its mistakes as well as its glories. We will show you that the accused, through his mindset and actions, ignored the rules of engagement and went far beyond the scope of his authority to intentionally order the murder of eighty-three innocent people.

Biggs accuses Childers of acting extra-judicially, of exploiting his status as a soldier to commit an illegitimate act of violence by "ignoring" the rules of engagement and disregarding the normative boundary between law and lawlessness. One may be reminded here of Giorgio Agamben, who in commenting on Schmitt's elucidation of the sovereign connects such an act of exceptional decision with the ecstatic experience of power:

> *Being-outside, and yet belonging*: this is the topological structure of the state of exception, and only because the sovereign, who decides on the exception, is, in truth, logically defined in his being by the exception, can he too be defined by the oxymoron *ecstacy-belonging*.[27]

The men who actually pulled the trigger are not put on trial here, only the one who made the decision, the one who performs an act of speech that demarcates who or what will be considered an exception to law. In the heat of war, the camera showed us the resolve on Childers's face and the way he barked his furious demands, signs expressing emotions that may be considered extra-legal yet nevertheless dovetail with the rules of engagement in popular cinema concerning the act of moral judgment. Melodrama is thus instrumental here, providing the film spectator with the opportunity to assign intent to Childers's character.

In tension with this Schmittian logic of sovereignty, another mode comes to the fore, one that appeals to the sense of unconditional allegiance among soldiers, nostalgia for a shared traumatic past, and the belief in authentic virtue that is somehow beyond the reach of law. This position, one that values the friendship and loyalty of fellow comrades, is elaborated in Hodges's opening statement to the trial. In contrast to the impersonal logic of law, he will mobilize a melodramatic force that recognizes virtue and the "felt good" produced by it to exonerate his personal friend:

> I took this case because Terry Childers told me I would have done the same thing he did if I'd been in his shoes. I took the case because I know Terry Childers. His word is his bond. He told me he did what he had to do. Now, I hope I don't let him down. We sent Terry Childers out on a very touchy mission. And when it went bad, and he did everything he could to save the lives of his marines, save the lives of the embassy people, you turn around now and want to blame the whole mess on him, send him to prison possibly for the rest of his life. That's not fair. It's not right.

As the prosecution and defense pursue their lines of argument, legal judgment splits away from moral judgment for the remainder of Friedkin's film. Hodges appeals to the sympathies of the jury, citing Childers's sentimental fidelity to his word and to his vaunted duty to protect Americans at all costs. Accusations against his friend should ultimately be deemed "not fair" and "not right," according to this logic: he is not guilty of murder because he represents the virtuous friend of all Americans. Ironically but also fittingly, Hodges's appeal to the sympathies of the jury is itself an appeal to a logic of exception, that is, melodramatic feeling as exception to the force of law.

As the film continues, the Yemeni ambassador, Captain Lee, a Yemeni doctor (Amidou, who played "Martinez" in *Sorcerer*), Sokal, Childers himself, and finally Colonel Bin Le Cao from Vietnam are called to the witness stand to testify. They are questioned about a series of key details regarding the encounter in Yemen: who shot first, the level of danger felt by soldiers on the roof of the embassy, if there were any weapons on the dead bodies that were recovered, the current location of the closed-circuit camera footage, whether the protesting Yemenis could be identified as Islamic Jihadists. Throughout the courtroom scenes, Friedkin interpolates scenes that either have already taken place or are unfolding in between them, illustrating and contextualizing them for the film viewer. While on the witness stand, Childers is asked to recite the rules of engagement governing military ground conflict in urban areas:

> One, if possible, the enemy will be warned first then asked to surrender. Two, deadly force is the last resort. Three, when possible try to arrange for the evacuation of civilians prior to any U.S. attack.

The marine commander concedes that his actions violated these rules and he becomes increasingly agitated as his intentions are scrutinized. Finally,

Childers exclaims that, "I was not going to stand by and see another marine die just to live by those fucking rules!" Biggs's line of questioning, on the other hand, is answered by Hodges's urge to cast Childers as a beset hero. "Under the rules of engagement," his longtime friend maintains, "a civilian pointing a weapon is no longer a civilian, and the use of deadly force is authorized in order to save lives. It's not murder, it's combat." Moreover, Hodges himself is cast as sympathetic, as a character who puts his reputation at stake by defending his former war comrade (Figure 2.3). *Rules of Engagement* creates a bit of dramatic irony by allowing the viewer some information that remains unknown to the jury: Childers's call to cease fire that went unheard in Yemen, the lies told by the ambassador Mourain to the jury testifying to his lack of patriotism, and Sokol's burning of the closed-circuit camera footage that definitively shows the Yemenis attacking first.

Perhaps the film's most egregious attempt to create melodramatic feeling as a way to justify the legality of murder is through the appearance and testimony of Colonel Bin Le Cao, the Viet Cong commander who called off the attack on Hodges's regiment years ago. In his case against Childers, Biggs poses questions that draw parallels between the sovereign decisions the U.S. soldier made in 1968 and those of 2000. Hodges then pursues another line of questioning, one that remains reductive and ahistorical in its politics, and asks if Colonel Cao would "have done the same thing Colonel Childers did if the situation had been reversed?" Echoing his opening statement where he states that he took Childers's case because "I would have done the same thing he did if I'd been in his shoes," Hodges once more appeals to the sympathies of the jury as well as the viewer of the film who remembers its opening sequence set in Vietnam, but also to his former enemy in war. Colonel Cao answers affirmatively, agreeing that he would have done the same if he were in Childers's position. With this affirmation, a former enemy of war allies himself with all soldiers who are bound to serve their respective nations, implicitly producing a kind of universal

Figure 2.3 Sentimental fidelity justifies the flouting of the law

comradery among those who must fight, who have memories of shared victimization in war, and whose authenticity is beyond reproach. Distinctions between friends and enemies are dissolved within the melodramatic mode. Vietnamese and American soldiers are all rendered beset because of the difficult decisions they made in the past.

At the end of the trial, Childers is found not guilty of murder and evades court-martial as the politics of sentimentality wins out over the punitive force of law. His military credentials and the sympathetic feelings aligned with patriotism are found to be more convincing than the charge of his exercise of excessive force that violates the legal rules of engagement. Childers leaves the courthouse and is met by a throng of media outside. He looks in disdain but turns to see Colonel Cao approaching his car in the parking lot. Cao turns as well and the eyes of the formerly adversarial soldiers meet. Mustering resolve, the Vietnamese veteran suddenly stiffens and salutes the American soldier. Childers's face relaxes slightly and the acquitted man salutes in return. Their acknowledgment of their shared memory is underpinned by their shared status as soldiers. This mutual acknowledgment confirms that which underpinned Childers's acquittal, which enabled his legal prosecution through the logic of exception constituted by the appeal to sentimental virtue.

Rules of Engagement shores up Childers's moral righteousness in the end. Like the many men in Friedkin's films whose actions skirt the line between law and lawlessness, this character plays out this reactionary response to corrupt politicians like Sokal and the lying U.S. ambassador to Yemen. In response to Childers's authentic experience of war, and the memories of it he shares with Hodges and Colonel Cao, these are enemy outsiders who ostensibly cannot understand the reasons for how and why he decided to murder in wartime. Moreover, Childers and Hodges fought in Vietnam but they continue the war, by other means, in the court of public opinion as well as in the courtroom. And so like many of the men in Friedkin's films, they are placed under siege by discursive and ideological forces that are perceived to threaten their authority. From 1968 to 2000 and in the films he made in the intervening years, Friedkin's men seems to be obsessed with doing the right thing, beyond any adherence to moral and legal norms, in increasingly litigious contexts. Yet by depicting characters who exploit their victimization and act out, these films foreground the discursive limits of these norms, revealing the very conditions that legitimate the assertion of sovereign power. Childers and Hodges reiterate Friedkin's fascination with the thin line between law and lawlessness by appealing to a nostalgia for a time when the rules did not constrain men's obsessive pursuit for moral authority, when their acts of civil disobedience were not deemed as violations of the law, all while garnering the sympathy of the viewer for their putative victimization by their times. Yet in doing so, they provide some viewers with the opportunity to critique this logic. What happened in 1968 was not litigated in court, but the violence committed then somehow became justified over time, became myth, and returned to redeem the righteousness of their decisions in the present. When Elvis Mitchell wrote that Friedkin "has been trying to rekindle the legend" since the successes of his earlier work from the late '60s and early '70s, this claim seems equally to apply to the morally compromised men of his films.

THE HUNTED (2003)

The Hunted was produced immediately following *Rules of Engagement* and showcases Friedkin's interest in the chase as constitutive of narrative cinema. Earlier I quoted the director calling the chase the purest form of cinema. Working with aspects that made the car chase set pieces in *The French Connection* and *To Live and Die in L.A.* so appealing to audiences, he takes its basic structure and linear form and extends it over the duration of a feature-length film. But Friedkin seems to have taken up an attitude of faith in terms of where the chase would go while directing *The Hunted*, as many of its formal and narrative elements were realized on the spot. In an interview conducted in 2003, he describes his process:

> You open yourself to what the film is telling you, about its rhythms, about its subject matter, about where the cuts should come, and it really is a process where, if you can attach yourself to it, the film speaks to you. I had no idea about many elements in *The Hunted*, or in any of my films, how they would finally evolve, and we can get into more specifics, how they would evolve until I heard the film in the cutting room, and so a lot of things were changed, including the beginning and the end was never scripted. It was almost a completely different movie that I set out to do.[28]

The Hunted is a chase film whose formal and narrative elements were realized at the time of production. It seems that Friedkin left these elements to fate, as this description of opening oneself to what the film is "telling you" suggests that he let them develop through his attunement to the materials that immediately confronted him. His role as director seems to have been less of an overseer and more of an interlocutor, one whose job was to unlock possibilities—especially those that are unforeseen—in the footage and the sound design organically. These possibilities would dictate the course of the chase in *The Hunted* while allowing a number of moments of narrative excess to emerge. The following analysis of Friedkin's film will take note of some of these moments. In a later chapter, I will also address what the director has called the "mystery of fate," which I see as aligned with this attitude of open acquiescence, more explicitly.

At the same time, the plot of *The Hunted*, like the other works I have addressed in this chapter, revolves around men of law enforcement who run up against the limits of the law. Their narrow self-righteousness is recuperated through their right to sovereign power and their claim to suspend law. FBI Special Agent L. T. Bonham (Tommy Lee Jones, once more) is a master tracker who has trained scores of soldiers to become highly skilled killers. Now retired, he discovers that a string of murders that took place around the Portland area were committed by one of his best students, Army Sergeant Aaron Hallam (Benicio del Toro). Hearing about two men who were ritualistically murdered in a forest situated in the Pacific Northwest ("the dead men were both dressed and quartered the way you'd quarter a deer," he is told), Bonham notices footprints in the mud, debris caught in moss, a rope tied to a tree, and a hole in a tree trunk, apparently produced by a hunting knife. "He used a knife with a serrated edge on one side," the Special Agent explains, "and a filet blade on the other." Bonham continues his analysis of the environment and remarks that the killer wore a size ten shoe with no tread and that he worked alone. Friedkin shows what the FBI agent examines through close-ups and point-of-view shots, showcasing his ability for observation. This and other scenes that depict Bonham's tracking skills tell us much about how he and Hallam interact with the natural world. The FBI agent is a master of reading signs in nature and the world around him, and his skills will help guide the melodramatically inclined viewer who also reads these signs in order to ascertain and assign character intention. And in so doing, Bonham models the act of observation in order to mobilize the momentum of the film's plot.

Bonham eventually encounters Hallam in the forest and they engage in a brief melee. The vigilante soldier is subdued with a tranquilizer dart and taken into custody by the Portland police. Colleagues of the special forces arrive and attempt to take control of the case by challenging the authority of the city police, explaining that Hallam fought in Kosovo and was engaged in classified assignments after he returned to the U.S. These colleagues comment that Hallam has become a shameless killer due to his PTSD. They take the young veteran away and, while being transported in a prisoner van, he manages to escape. The vehicle crashes as a result of a stupendously ill-aimed gun that kills the driver. While drinking a glass of water at an airport bar, Bonham sees a live news report on television that shows the crashed van. With this, the chase is back on.

Hallam makes a brief stop at his home, where his girlfriend Irene (Leslie Stefanson) and their young daughter live. An awkward homecoming scene ensues as del Toro makes an unconvincing father figure. Bonham also arrives at the house with his partner Abby Durrell (Connie Nielsen) and while she questions Irene, he continues searching for clues as to Hallam's presence in the home. Bonham looks around the house carefully, scanning the daughter's bedroom and glancing at the cat on her bed. He enters the bathroom and sees the facial hair caught in globules of shaving foam. Again, through close-ups and point-of-view shots, Friedkin aligns Bonham's tracking skills with the viewer's capacity to detect traces of the escaped soldier. The two men meet once more in one of the bedrooms of the house, but Hallam quickly escapes and steals a car. Unlike in *The French Connection* and *To Live and Die in L.A.*, this car chase sequence is relatively short and stymied by Portland's traffic congestion, forcing both men to continue the chase on foot. Bonham exits the car and runs through the busy streets of the city, through underground sewers, over bridges, and, in an exciting set-piece sequence, on a speeding tram going over the famous Hawthorne Bridge. "Here the whole movie is a chase," Roger Ebert writes in his review of *The Hunted*, "sometimes at a crawl, as when Hallam drives a stolen car directly into a traffic jam. What makes the movie fresh is that it doesn't stand back and regard its pursuit as an exercise, but stays very close to the characters and focuses on the actual physical reality of their experience."[29]

While Ebert viewed the film positively, most reviewers were quite critical. More than a few noted its resemblance to another action film franchise set in the Pacific Northwest starring Sylvester Stallone. "The film is just a *Rambo* rehash," notes Peter Travers of *Rolling Stone*.[30] Michael Atkinson of *The Village Voice* writes that, "William Friedkin's *The Hunted* is essentially a reheating of 1982's *First Blood*—a psychologically wounded warrior-vet pits himself against civilized America—but the fallout this time is simultaneously more ruthless, less emotional, and duller."[31] It is ironic, perhaps, that one of the writers of the film, Art Monterastelli, would come to work on the *Rambo* reboot from 2008. While Friedkin's film may be thought of as a kind of counterfeit *Rambo*, a film whose plotting is also intimately linked with the chase, *The Hunted* will nevertheless revisit the aesthetics of this form in order to pursue other more philosophical concerns.

Echoing Friedkin's claim about the chase and cinema, Tom Gunning notes that, "the chase had been the original truly narrative genre of the cinema."[32] This is because, according to the film scholar, it sutures together moments of attraction with film plotting while bestowing these moments with a discernable narrative destiny. Gunning writes that the chase film, since about 1903–1906, enabled early cinema to evolve from an aesthetics comprised solely of attractions by providing "a model for causality and linearity as well as a basic editing continuity."[33] Moments of spectacle such as cars ramming into each other, the brutal assassination of the Portland police chief, a fearful man held hostage in the tram, and Hallam diving into Willamette River from atop the vertical lift are strung together through the forward plot movement generated in Bonham's chase. Each of these moments showcases the thrill of the stunt and, by co-extension, the thrill of the cinema itself. And in the shot-to-shot movement of one man running after another, such moments heighten the drama by interrupting and slowing the narrative flow, teasing the viewer as to whether the tracker will finally catch up to his vigilante student. As Gunning puts it, in another context but still relevant here, "they encounter some slight obstacle (a fence, a steep slope, a stream) that slows them down for the spectator, providing a mini-spectacle pause in the unfolding of the narrative."[34] This dialectic of unfolding and interruption toys with the expectation for cathartic conclusion, moving between forward movement and delay, creating the dialectic of pathos and action that is integral to the melodramatic mode.

And yet the chase is nevertheless constituted by two men who occupy some relationship to the law, even if it is at the limits of its jurisdiction. Victims are pursued by victimizers, and vice versa. When, in the scene from the Portland police station, a special forces officer (Mark Pellegrino) explains the nature of Hallam's special assignments after he returned from Kosovo, he describes the experience of war trauma and Hallam's status as a non-person in the eyes of the law:

> Hallam's battle stress has become so deep, it is a part of his personality, and it's impossible to reverse. He's a killing machine. There is no way he can be indicted or tried in open court, or any court. He cannot be processed, interviewed, charged with a crime, or copped out as a psycho. His picture cannot appear in any newspaper. As far as the world is concerned, sir, Aaron Hallam doesn't exist.

Aaron Hallam exists as an exception to law's binding force, there where he "doesn't exist," akin to the figure of Roman law, *homo sacer*, that has been critically delineated by Agamben. Schmitt's formulation seems to be relevant here once more, as with the morally compromised men that appear in Friedkin's other films. In the opening scene of *The Hunted*, Hallam is depicted infiltrating an Albanian village that has been taken over by Serbs, and, after passively observing men being slaughtered, he deftly murders their commanding officer. His suffering, stemming from the emotional aftermath wrought by his engagement in Kosovo and the sympathy this is intended to elicit, trumps the rule of law in the film. Hallam has been endowed with a kind of qualified immunity that renders him exceptional. And in this, because he has been deemed the exception by the sovereign power of the U.S. government, he can act with legal impunity and have recourse not to juridical law but to the sense of righteousness made possible by the melodramatic mode. Like Childers in *Rules of Engagement*, he is a figure that has been allowed to occupy a space beyond law's binding force, a status that is paradoxically sanctioned by the sovereignty of law itself.

Moreover, the source of Hallam's grievance revolves around his perception of having been slighted by Bonham following his experience of the

Kosovo War. He learned his skills from the older man, skills that were utilized toward morally questionable ends in Kosovo and in Portland. On the other hand, like a son who perceives that he has been unloved, Hallam demands approval from the older man. "How come you didn't answer my letters," Hallam asks during their first melee encounter. Later Bonham finds one of these letters, addressed to him, which in part reads: "L.T., those guys you trained to come and kill me: they're not soldiers, they're robots." The hunted was once the hunter, the subordinate who sought his teacher for guidance. Bonham taught his students how to dispatch enemies quickly and efficiently, but he did not teach them the ethics of killing or how to critique the epistemological grounds that underpin the decision to kill. A flashback sequence depicts this deadly art, which includes Sayoc Kali, a Filipino martial art involving the use of hand knives. Bonham demonstrates how to target specific locations on the body and swiftly sever connective tissue, puncture a lung, slice through a femoral artery, and bring down a man using only a small knife. In a 2003 interview about his film, Friedkin remarked that,

> They're both "the Hunted," there's also a father-and-son overlay to all of this that sort of hangs in the background of the story. Tommy Lee is probably the only father figure Bennie's character has ever had, and he taught him all of these skills and then abandoned him.[35]

The teacher perhaps feels some sense of guilt and responsibility—although this is not made explicit in the film's narrative or acting—for having produced such a skilled student who has become a "killing machine."

The nature of the relationship is made even more explicit in the film's appropriation of the story of Abraham from the Old Testament. Throughout *The Hunted*, the relationship of teacher to student is analogous to that of father and son. At the very beginning of the film, as the credits roll, the deep voice of Johnny Cash intones with the following words:

> God said to Abraham, "Kill me a son." Abe says, "Man, you must be puttin' me on." God say, "no"; Abe say, "what?" God say, "You can do what you want, Abe, but the next time you see me comin', you better run." Abe says, "Where do you want this killin' done?" God says, "Out on Highway 61."

These lyrics to the first stanza of Bob Dylan's 1965 song, "Highway 61 Revisited," retell the well-known parable of faith with obvious differences. In the original account from the book of Genesis, Abraham obeys God's command to offer his son Isaac up as a sacrifice. The father raises his knife and, just as he is about to kill the boy, an angel of God appears, melodramatically "in the nick of time," replacing Isaac with a ram. Dylan's version here features a much more skeptical Abraham who refuses to commit this ethically heinous act and thus refuses to submit to the divine sovereign. As an epigraph to *The Hunted*, the words spoken by Cash seem to prepare viewers for a story revolving around a deadly chase—"you better run," Bonham seems to be telling his student. The lyrics tell us that it takes place between God and man, the "holy father" and his son, but in Friedkin's film the pursuit is between teacher and student. In citing this biblical reference, *The Hunted* seems also to be implying that the chase between Bonham and Hallam is as old as time.

And yet, despite Dylan's reconfiguration of the story of Abraham, somewhat inexplicably read by an aging country singer, there is another reference to the parable, one that cites the biblical text directly. When Bonham searches through the Pacific Northwest forest, he looks inside a hollow tree trunk (visually echoing the cut moments before), and finds Hallam's copy of the Bible, bookmarked to the book of Genesis. From chapter 22, verses 5 to 7 are displayed within the frame of the screen. They recount the moments when Abraham took his son up Mount Moriah with a knife and the wood of a burnt offering to make the sacrifice. Bonham turns the page and finds a postcard reproduction of a painting by Rembrandt, *Sacrifice of Isaac* from 1635, which depicts the scene from the passage stuck within the pages (Figure 2.4). Hallam had apparently imagined his relationship with his teacher in terms of the biblical story as well. Underneath this postcard is a photograph of Irene and her daughter, signaling the space of innocence and family life that was lost by Hallam's exceptional status.

Figure 2.4 Rembrandt's *Sacrifice of Isaac* (1635)

This citation points us toward the many interpretations of the story, beyond the scope of the chase in *The Hunted*, and allows us to think this "original truly narrative genre of the cinema" in relation to a key issue that centers on Abraham's trial of faith. Ostensibly, this film is an allegory about the father chasing his son who has lost his way. But these citations also allow us to understand how the mystery of faith is constituted through the narrative logic of *The Hunted*. It was faith that compelled Abraham to undertake what Søren Kierkegaard, in his reading of the parable in *Fear and Trembling*, calls the "teleological suspension of the ethical."[36] Not conforming to the ethical law, Abraham suspends it by deciding to murder his son Isaac, thus placing himself above the "universal," and this in the name of his sacrifice to God. For Kierkegaard, this act is not only fundamentally unethical and immoral, but it is also wholly "absurd." He explains that the biblical father must have experienced intense anguish for three days as he climbed the mountain, heavy with the thought of killing his son. To sacrifice one's son is a sinful act, to take the life of another, and yet Abraham goes forward with it, transcending the universal ethical good so that "the single individual as the single individual stands in an absolute relation to the absolute."[37] On the face of it, one ought to be ethically compelled, by what Kierkegaard identifies as the legacy of "Greek philosophy," to love one's son more than oneself. And yet, Abraham's profoundly paradoxical position as a single individual above the universal cannot be made into object of theoretical reflection, resolved in a dialectic, or reduced to a theory of Oedipal drives. This contradiction comprises the core of the problem of the ethics of filicide, embodied in the question of what constitutes the conditions that allow for this heinous act. For Kierkegaard, the resolution to this problem inheres in faith, defined as exceptional in relation to prevailing legal and moral norms.

In the penultimate final scene from *The Hunted*, Bonham engages Hallam in a hand-to-hand melee with hand knives. Friedkin depicts the preparatory moments leading up to it. In the biblical story, Abraham prepared and took time to "to chop the firewood, to bind Isaac, and to sharpen the knife."[38] In *The Hunted*, both men take time to whittle and forge sharp weapons from metal and stone. They meet in a mountainous region, on a flat, stone area surrounded by loud waterfalls. The scene was filmed around the Elwha Dam in Port Angeles, Washington, a region that perhaps bears some resemblance to the geography of Mount Moriah. After a prolonged fight scene showcasing their prodigious knife skills, Bonham sinks his sharp weapon into Hallam's chest. He undertakes, in other words, the absurd, singular, sinful act that Abraham did not. As the younger man slumps to the ground, FBI agent Abby Durrell and three accompanying officers arrive on the scene with their guns pointed. Bloodied and covered with mud, Bonham looks down at his student who remains motionless on his back. Physically pained, he caresses the head of the dead man with a look of emotional anguish.

The Hunted then cuts to Bonham taking refuge in the remote cabin in British Columbia featured in its opening shots. He is reading the letters sent to him by Hallam. Walking over to the fireplace, he throws them into the fire, concluding the narrative. Bonham steps out and spots a white wolf wandering through the snowy forest landscape. Underscoring the connection to the biblical sacrifice, Johnny Cash's voice intones once more: "God said to Abraham, kill me a son." *The Hunted* then ends.

In his *Political Theology*, Schmitt quotes a passage from Kierkegaard that underscores the importance of the place of the exception in perceiving the general or the universal ethical, noting that the exception "thinks the general with intense passion."[39] For the Protestant theologian, intense passion motivates the state of exception. It inspires faith despite the interdictions given over by the moral law and sustains the ethical paradox that constitutes the very unintelligibility of faith. At the end of *The Hunted*, Bonham is not explicitly censured for his act of murder and is allowed to return to his isolated cabin. This act is unfortunate but somehow necessary in order to eliminate the outlaw Hallam and to restore order once again. His murder takes us back to that which circumscribes acts of moral judgment and which compels questioning into what grounds judgment itself. The place of exception overlaps here with the legitimization of judgment within melodrama, putting into relief how those who enforce law must transgress law in order to bring the lawless "to justice." Within the regime of this popular mode, we can think of this place as aligned with what Kierkegaard calls the "tragic hero," the one who knows that his actions violate the universal yet is compelled, for reasons of self-aggrandizement or self-pity, to carry them out anyway. In the biblical story of Abraham, Isaac is spared and returned to his father. "He gets Isaac back again," Kierkegaard writes, "by virtue of the absurd. Therefore, Abraham is at no time a tragic hero but is something entirely different, either a murderer or a man of faith."[40] Whether Bonham is a man of faith or a murderer remains an open question, as the ambivalence at the end of Friedkin's film is produced precisely due to the uncertainty surrounding his status. Yet if the viewer comes to admire his character, it is because this FBI detective evidences features of the tragic hero, a vigilante detective who is somehow also deemed a man of virtue.

Friedkin begins a chapter entitled "The Mystery of Faith" from *The Friedkin Connection* with an epigraph from the biblical book of Hebrews: "Faith is the substance of things hoped for, the evidence of things not seen."[41] This chapter from his memoirs recounts the filmmaker's experience of producing *The Exorcist*, but seems also to resonate with the parable of Abraham in *The Hunted*. In the later sections of this book, we will continue to think about what Friedkin calls the "mystery of faith," about contradictions that challenge viewers to believe in things in which there is no scientific evidence and consider the extent to which the question of faith informs the experience of his cinema more generally. The morally ambiguous men in Friedkin's films, who are unmoored from ethical norms and from melodramatic expectations of what constitutes right and wrong, elicit this mystery through their actions and take us to the paradoxes that Kierkegaard believes are at the heart of faith. So far, we have seen how problems of morality raised by the actions of men such as Chance in *To Live and Die in L.A.*, Childers in *Rules of Engagement*, and Bonham in *The Hunted* have compelled us to ask questions of political theology and moral ambiguity within popular cinema. In this chapter, I have tried to forge these connections to the logics of sovereignty that are played out through the narrative logic of Friedkin's films. In the subsequent chapters we shall see how his films address the mystery of faith in other ways, specifically centering around the experience of the cinema itself. These are questions I have already begun to address: Who or what legitimizes law? How does one come to believe in what one sees and hears? Who or what legitimizes the credibility of visual representation, of what counts as real or fake? What is the role of faith, as a critical and secular concept, in the cinema?

NOTES

1. Phillip Lopate, *Totally, Tenderly, Tragically: Essays and Criticism from a Lifelong Love Affair with the Movies* (New York: Anchor, 1998), 135.
2. Stephen Prince, *A New Pot of Gold: Hollywood under the Electronic Rainbow, 1980–1989* (Berkeley: University of California Press, 2000), xi.
3. Prince, *A New Pot of Gold*, xxi.
4. The unusual name "Chance" may remind viewers of John T. Chance, the tough but virtuous sheriff played by John Wayne in *Rio Bravo* (1959).
5. Michael S. Shapiro, "Value Eruptions and Modalities: White Male Rage in the '80s and '90s," *Cultural Values* 1 (1997), 64.
6. William Friedkin, *The Friedkin Connection* (New York: Harper, 2013), 388.
7. Friedkin, *The Friedkin Connection*, 388.
8. Friedkin, *The Friedkin Connection*, 384.
9. Friedkin, *The Friedkin Connection*, 391.
10. Frederic Jameson, "Postmodernism, or The Cultural Logic of Late Capitalism," *New Left Review* 146 (July-August 1984), 66.
11. Jameson, "Postmodernism," 71.
12. Jameson, "Postmodernism," 72.
13. See Steven Shapiro, "Post-Continuity: An Introduction," in *Post-Cinema: Theorizing 21st-Century Film*, eds. Shane Denson and Julia Leyda (Falmer: REFRAME Books, 2016).
14. Sharon Willis, "Disputed Territories: Masculinity and Social Space," in *Male Trouble*, eds. Constance Penley and Sharon Willis (Minneapolis: University of Minnesota Press, 1993), 264.
15. Willis, "Disputed Territories," 272.
16. Friedkin, *The Friedkin Connection*, 392.
17. Willis, "Disputed Territories," 270.
18. See Robert Arnett, "Eighties Noir: The Dissenting Voice in Reagan's America," *Journal of Popular Film and Television* 34, no. 3 (2006).

19. Arnett, "Eighties Noir," 125.
20. Jameson, "Postmodernism," 63.
21. Jacques Derrida, *Given Time: 1. Counterfeit Money*, trans. Peggy Kamuf (Chicago: University of Chicago Press, 1992), 87.
22. Friedkin, *The Friedkin Connection*, 393.
23. Elvis Mitchell, "'Rules of Engagement': It's a War Out There, Soldier, and the Uniform is Made of Cynicism and Pain," *New York Times*, April 7, 2000.
24. Friedkin, *The Friedkin Connection*, 430.
25. Carl Schmitt, *Political Theology: Four Chapters on the Concept of Sovereignty*, trans. George Schwab (Chicago: University of Chicago Press, 2005), 5.
26. Schmitt, *Political Theology*, 10.
27. Giorgio Agamben, *State of Exception*, trans. Kevin Atell (Chicago: University of Chicago Press, 2005), 35.
28. Christopher Lane, ed., *William Friedkin: Interviews*, Conversations with Filmmakers Series (Jackson: University of Mississippi Press, 2020), 81.
29. Roger Ebert, "The Hunted," *Chicago Sun Times*, March 14, 2003.
30. Peter Travers, "The Hunted," *Rolling Stone*, March 14, 2003, accessed February 13, 2021, <https://www.rollingstone.com/movies/movie-reviews/the-hunted-255683>
31. Michael Atkinson, "Man's Pest Friend," *The Village Voice*, March 18, 2003.
32. Tom Gunning, "The Cinema of Attractions: Early Film, Its Spectator and the Avant-Garde," *Wide Angle* 8, no. 3/4 (Fall 1986), 68.
33. Gunning, "The Cinema of Attractions," 68.
34. Gunning, "The Cinema of Attractions," 68.
35. Scott B., "An Interview with William Friedkin," last updated May 20, 2012, accessed February 13, 2021, <https://www.ign.com/articles/2003/03/11/an-interview-with-william-friedkin>
36. Søren Kierkegaard, *Fear and Trembling* and *Repetition*, ed. and trans. Howard V. Hong and Edna H. Hong (Princeton: Princeton University Press, 1983), 54.
37. Kierkegaard, *Fear and Trembling*, 56.
38. Kierkegaard, *Fear and Trembling*, 52.
39. Schmitt, *Political Theology*, 15.
40. Kierkegaard, *Fear and Trembling*, 57.
41. Friedkin, *The Friedkin Connection*, 220.

CHAPTER 3

Criminal Desires

CRUISING (1980)

Friedkin's most maligned film at the time of its release, *Cruising* tells the story of an ostensibly heterosexual rookie cop who goes undercover in New York's gay, S&M underground scene. Its themes were bound to attract vilification, particularly in its sensationalistic and voyeuristic look at this relatively unknown world, one to which Friedkin does not belong. When the production schedule was announced in *The Village Voice* by writer Arthur Bell, *Cruising* brought death threats by mail and phone calls to United Artists before filming even began. Copies of the script were leaked, provoking outrage for its exploitative depictions of gay men linked to violent criminality and deviant desire. Detractors predicted that the film would reinforce homophobic myths and encourage violence against the gay community as a consequence. When shooting began, local New Yorkers shouted, whistled, and threw bottles into locations in Greenwich Village, while people who lived near them blasted their stereos to undermine the production. Friedkin said that he threw the bottles back at the protestors.[1] In an article published in summer 1979, Bell, whose descriptions of unsolved killings in New York's gay community in fact informed Friedkin's film, implores "readers—gay, straight, liberal, radical, atheist, communist, or whatever—to give Friedkin and his production crew a terrible time if you spot them in your neighborhood."[2] LGBT groups petitioned mayor Ed Koch to revoke the permits that were already granted to *Cruising*. All but one of the bars that were slated to be featured in the film withdrew from the production. When *Cruising* was released to theaters in February 1980, activists picketed in New York and San Francisco, and renewed calls for a boycott of the film.

Friedkin has maintained that his intentions for *Cruising* were simply to tell a story of murder mystery set against an "exotic background that mainstream audiences had not seen."³ In 1980, he remarked with some defensiveness that, "*Cruising* is no more about gays than Woody Allen's *Manhattan* is about New Yorkers."⁴ But it remains difficult to determine whether his obliviousness to the film's controversy are willful or disingenuous. "If anything," he continues, "the film will alleviate the violence against gays in the country. I feel also that *Cruising*, in its portrayal of sexuality, will turn a lot of people on."⁵ Despite the controversy, Friedkin still contends that his film was not intended as a depiction of the gay community in general but as only one of its subcultural segments. Yet, as Alexander Wilson has argued in an article published in 1981, while the film does reveal contradictions about the political strategies of the gay community immediately following Stonewall,

> any film that so insistently blurs it meaning, trades on ignorance about homosexuality, and refuses to treat in any but the most shallow way the links among violence, desire, and authority, must of necessity distort the character of even that "segment" of gay society it purports to address.⁶

Vito Russo, in his seminal history of queer cinema, describes the protests and controversies raised by Friedkin's film while also commenting that, "many gay people correctly perceived [*Cruising*] to be homophobic at the conceptual level."⁷ Indeed, much of the outrage revolves around the political correctness of the film's representations and the extent to which its depictions of homosexuality debilitate the interests of gay men and gay politics in public life.

Despite being a moderately budgeted Hollywood film, *Cruising* and its film historical legacy seems on the one hand to occupy a place somewhere between Kenneth Anger's experimental work, which eventually gained legitimacy in the "straight world," and the rise of adult film theaters throughout the 1970s. On the other hand, however, critics have long acknowledged Friedkin's film as being complicit with the reiteration of representations of the "killer queer" that appeared in a number of generic slasher films, like *Windows*, *Prom Night*, *Dressed to Kill*, and *Deathtrap*, in the year and throughout the decade *Cruising* was released. In addition to the "Bell Tells" articles, the genesis of Friedkin's film can be traced to a few other sources. Its plot is derived from the book of the same name by *New York Times* journalist Gerald Walker, while narrative details come from the director's interactions with Randy Jurgensen, a former cop who did undercover work in the S&M scene, and an interview with Paul Bateson, who was arrested for killing eight gay men in New York. Jurgensen played small roles in a couple of Friedkin's films, including a figure of law enforcement in *The French Connection*, but also Scanlon's betraying friend Vinnie in *Sorcerer*. His real-life "fieldwork" experience in the S&M world would be instrumental for Friedkin in his depiction of the film's central protagonist. Bateson, Friedkin was stunned to learn, played a nurse in *The Exorcist* in the scene depicting Regan's arteriogram. When he asked his former acting collaborator if he had indeed committed the crimes, Bateson remarked that remembered only the first murder, Addison Verrill, a journalist who wrote for *Variety*. He was apparently too high on drugs to remember the others. According to New York police, the body parts of the slain men that were found in and around the East River were definitively linked to Bateson. Verrill was also a friend of Bell and his death was commemorated in a 1977 article in *The Village Voice* where Bell lamented the lack of media coverage for murdered gay men.

Considering the chorus of disapproval around Friedkin's film, it is perhaps surprising that *Cruising* has nevertheless enjoyed a strange longevity, attaining an almost cult-film status among some viewers precisely for its gritty sexuality and subversive atmosphere. Robin Wood's essay on "the incoherent text" of '70s cinema, one of the first serious considerations of *Cruising*, remains generative in its appreciation of the film's peculiar "negativity."[8] Wood is adamant in showing that "positive" images of gay men in cinema do not always empower gay male subjectivity, nor do they typically provide any explicit positive alternatives for countering homophobia. Despite all this, in comparison to *American Gigolo* (1980), which came out the same year as *Cruising*, Wood finds the social effect of this Paul Schrader-directed film "far more harmful" in that its homophobia is "covert and insidious."[9] Guy Davidson, D. A. Miller, David Greven, and Damon Young have, more recently, offered reappraisals of *Cruising* in the spirit of Wood's article in their acknowledgment of this particular film's anomalous status in the history of queer cinema. Davidson writes that *Cruising* has enjoyed renewed interest

> mainly by a younger gay audience, for which the film's allegedly lurid depiction of Manhattan's gay S/M underworld is a compelling and historically valuable envisioning of the libidinal intensities of the 1970s New York leather scene that is scarcely available elsewhere on celluloid.[10]

With its scenes set in seedy bars and lurid porno theaters, depictions of men in leather, anonymous hookups in crowded parks, punk rock soundtrack, and explicit scenes of gay sex, Friedkin's film flouts homonormative films about homosexual men that seem to dominate queer film history. Critics and scholars have taken up *Cruising* once again, not to only to judge whether its representations are positive or negative, but to revisit its epistemological contradictions and, in doing so, renew its subversive aesthetics and politics. In his insightful analysis of *Cruising*, Greven notes that negative images of gay men, while at times pernicious, can also be understood as "attempts to get at something in the nature of homoerotic identity and experience."[11] It is along this line of inquiry that I will engage with Friedkin's film and, indeed, the ideas I will present here fall into the legacy of scholarship inspired by Wood's essay and its articulation of the film's "incoherence." In this section we will continue our analysis into how criminality in the cinema, particularly its system of signs that makes morality legible, is problematized in *Cruising*. In Friedkin's film, this problematization will have ramifications for the visual and auditory regime within the context of sexual identity and desire.

Earlier we have seen how Friedkin's films engage a number of key epistemological binaries that underpin their moral universes: gay/straight, legibility/illegibility, masculinity/femininity, victim/perpetrator, inside/outside the closet. Toward the end of my reading of *The Boys in the Band*, I mentioned how this film from 1970 gestures toward fluidity between boundaries, allegorized in the traversal between interiority and exteriority. *Cruising* will bring this transgressive fluidity into sharper focus, which will suffuse its narrative and form. Through a series of close readings, Eve Kosofsky Sedgwick, in *Epistemology of the Closet*, shows how the homo/heterosexual definition underpins a series of key epistemological oppositions that have formed the basis of modern Western social organizations since the nineteenth century: "secrecy/disclosure, knowledge/ignorance, private/public, masculine/feminine, majority/minority, innocence/initiation, natural/artificial," and so on.[12] For Sedgwick, these oppositions intersect with more traditional axes of gender, class, and race in the narration of the self. By isolating moments where distinctions between gay and straight are elucidated and by performing a deconstructive critique that takes these distinctions to crisis, Sedgwick reveals how these binarisms constitute and are constituted through the legacy of the homo/heterosexual division while destabilizing their legitimacy. Moreover, as we have seen already, these oppositions are integral to the melodramatic mode and specifically to its aim of exteriorizing and making visible invisible, interiorized virtue. *Cruising*, as Stephen Snyder writes, participates in this mode through its elucidation of "the urge of 'authority' to possess everything, to make the world *readable*."[13] Friedkin's film takes the melodramatic mode and the politics of violence that typically constitute these binaries to their discursive limits, allowing us to critically think the legal and moral distinctions that separate the policeman from the criminal as well.

Cruising opens with a scene that takes place in New York's Hudson River, with the discovery of a severed arm floating on the water, rotted and discolored green. The fingers are misshaped and the fingernails overgrown, as if the hand belonged to an alien being. In the morgue, the coroner Dr. Rifkin (Barton Heyman, who played Dr. Klein in *The Exorcist*) impassively tells Detective Lefransky (Randy Jurgensen) that, "we got a hand here—we can get a fingerprint and call it a homicide." Because the cause of death cannot be determined, Lefransky remarks that the case will be categorized as unsolved, or "Circumstances Undetermined Pending Police Investigation" (CUPPI), and will not be linked to a crime until the entire body is recovered. He motions to leave and Dr. Rifkin cynically comments that the detective's refusal to prosecute the case as a homicide means that police work is "just a numbers game, huh? Body count? That's all it is to you guys!" The arm is laid out on the CUPPI drawer for storage, along with other real human remains that coroner Michael Baden allowed Friedkin to film. Delighted in getting this access, already legally and ethically questionable, the director has maintained his demand for authentic props in this work and others throughout his career. "When word of this leaked out," Friedkin recollects, "Mayor Koch fired Baden. It became a public scandal, on the front page of the New York newspapers."[14]

With the film's initial plot quickly presented, *Cruising* cuts to night patrolmen DiSimone (Joe Spinell, who played a friend of Dominguez in *Sorcerer*) and Desher (Mike Starr) watching the night beat in their squad car, uttering misogynistic slurs about the former's runaway wife and disgust at the crowds of gay men walking the streets. As the camera tracks a busy street full of prowling men, their dialogue recalls a well-known scene from Scorsese's *Taxi Driver* when De Niro sits in his cab while his voiceover insists that the rain "wash all the scum off the streets." In a similar shot, DiSimone drives his cop car and cynically remarks that, "One day this whole city's gonna explode. Used to be able to play stick ball on these streets. Look at these guys. Christ, what's happening . . ." These words refer to no one in particular, but to everyone they see. The contemptuous cops stop two transvestite prostitutes and start threatening the pair, demanding sexual favors from them. From the dialogue, one can deduce that this is not the first time they solicited their services. Their grim voices are heard close-up, likely recorded in post-production, allowing the film viewer to hear their vulgar timbre. This acoustic moment evokes a scene from the Copacabana in *The French Connection*, when the viewer gains an intimacy with the interiorities of Popeye and Cloudy through their voiceover. In *Cruising*, however, this intimacy is presented as discomfortingly close, forcing the listener to experience a kind of acoustic claustrophobia with these boorish policemen.

Friedkin then takes the viewer to the Cockpit, a gay bar where men cruise for other men. As with the spaces of melodrama I discussed in previous chapters, these gay bars function as spaces of exception, where normative legal and moral protocols are suspended. A man wearing a black leather jacket and dark sunglasses (Larry Atlas) descends the concrete stairs to the crowded and confined club. "Lump" by the funk band Mutiny plays loudly over the speakers. In tight medium shots, sweaty men in black leather jackets and jockstraps, showing bare buttocks and concealing their faces with dark aviators—such as those worn by the cop in Hitchcock's *Psycho*—drink, kiss, dance, and fuck. Men pack the bar, appearing in the foreground, middle ground, and background of the image, and as the camera pans through the space, male bodies continue to fill the frame of the screen (Figure 3.1). These shots recall the black leather scenes in Anger's *Scorpio Rising* (1963), sharing with the earlier

Figure 3.1 Male bodies fill the frame

film a penchant for the brazen and profane. As a Hollywood film, however, *Cruising* remains unprecedented for its unflinching depictions of homosexual desire—eleven years after Stonewall and before the AIDS crisis of the 1980s. Sexual desire and the possibility of death will soon be inextricably linked.

The sunglasses-wearing man cruises Loren Lukas (Arnaldo Santana) and, as quickly as he arrived, departs with him. Cutting to a room in the St. James Hotel near Times Square, where wrestling magazines are strewn on the floor, the men have sex. Later Lukas awakens to find the other man, still wearing sunglasses, rifling through his belongings. He turns and asks Lukas if he is afraid and puts a knife to Lukas's neck, quietly singing, "Who's here? I'm here. You're here." With leather straps, he binds the consenting but terrified man face down on the bed. Lucas is stabbed three times. "You made me do that," the murderous man quietly remarks with the camera close up on his moving lips. Creating an association between sex, death, and penetration that is perhaps too on the nose, Friedkin intercuts the next knife thrust with a quick pornographic shot of anal sex.

In these first ten minutes of *Cruising* and throughout the film Friedkin maintains these closely recorded voices set against quiet backgrounds. This particular sound design was necessitated by the director's attempts to deal with on-set sounds and noises made by protestors at the time of filming. He recounts in an interview with Linda Ruth Williams:

> There's one shot in the movie when you see Pacino walking down a street late at night coming away from one of the clubs, and it's dead silent. We filmed it at three in the morning, and all you can hear are his footsteps

on the street. But at the time we filmed it there were thousands of gay men out of shot shouting "Pacino you little faggot! You little cocksucker! You motherfucker!" And he has to walk down the street as if there was nobody there. He really freaked out during the making of the film.[15]

As a result, what the spectator hears in *Cruising* is "eight percent looped. And the sound effects and Foley are just this side of one hundred perfect reproduced," according to the supervising sound effects editor.[16] As in *The Boys in the Band* and *The Birthday Party*, diegetic sounds are sourced from events that take place within enclosed spaces, while noises outside these rooms are silenced, underscoring the conditions of a sound stage but also disavowing their very existence from the world of the film. In *Cruising*, moreover, outdoor sounds that originate on the streets of New York have a dry timbre, as if to make explicit their sounding from within a Foley-studio and thus foregrounding their artificiality. New York in 1980 is brought close to the body of the listener. The sound of bootsteps, clinking belt chains, and squeaking leather seem to call attention to themselves through their rendering in post-production, as if spotlit within a silent, black background. They evince what Béla Balázs calls the "sound close-up," bringing to consciousness the "undertones, the minor events of the acoustic world that slip unawares into the unconscious" in order to raise the opportunity for film audiences to critically think their phenomenology.[17] A set of keys, attached to the killer's hip, seems to jingle with a particular intensity when he dances in the Cockpit and as he follows his next victim. These focused sounds are in turn linked to the body of the sunglasses-wearing murderer. The non-synchronized voices of all the characters in *Cruising* bring a clarity to what they say, even as they whisper in loud contexts, but their timbre also creates a mood of uneasy intimacy with the spectator, bringing at the same time the gentle voice of the killer close to the ear.

We are later taken to a scene featuring rookie cop Steve Burns (Al Pacino). He enters the office of Captain Edelson (Paul Sorvino) and is asked, "Ever been porked? Or had a man smoke your pole?" The naive officer laughs somewhat uncomfortably and responds in the negative. The line of questioning and innuendo recalls that pursued by DiSimone and Desher earlier in the film when the cops extorted sexual favors from two transvestite prostitutes. Earlier the captain grumbled about civilians increasingly impersonating the police and the inability of the police in distinguishing the guilty from the innocent. Edelson believes Lukas was the victim of a killer who likes to hunt men that look like Burns ("late twenties, hundred forty, hundred fifty pounds, dark hair, dark eyes. . .," according to Edelson) and that these murders might be connected to the CUPPIs, including the severed arm found in the Hudson Bay. He makes Burns an offer: go undercover into the gay S&M sex clubs as bait, catch the killer, and he will be promoted to detective. Burns accepts and remarks, with a slight smile, "yeah, I love it."

Cruising cuts to a short scene with Burns and his girlfriend, Nancy (Karen Allen), both lying naked in bed. She asks about the "new thing" that is his assignment. Burns responds that, "I can't talk about that, Nance, I told you." The exchange underscores his orientation as straight through the closeting of any signs of homosexual desire, in work and in pleasure, and his effort to reinstate the heterosexual contract. He seems to know that his consent to go undercover has already brought his professional aspirations into contact with sexual desires, conflating his public life as a policeman with the realm of private, and perhaps unknown, longings. As the film's story unfolds, the viewer will be challenged to ascertain what motivates his investigation. And as we have seen with Friedkin's other films, the boundaries between these roles, and the binaries that underpin them, dissolve over the course of the narrative, revealing the discursive modalities of morality they share. Policeman/criminal, gay/straight, public/private: the clear delineation of these roles and categories is the discursive mission set out for Burns's character. And this challenge is inextricably linked to judgment within the melodramatic mode. The viewer will thus be tasked with making clear discursive delineations that constitute the epistemology of the straight mind, and thus of distinguishing the killer, the straight man, the virtuous policeman, all by setting out to restore certainty around the truth of the moral and sexual self.

Epistemological binaries are progressively deconstructed as Burns's character becomes increasingly implicated through multiple acts of cruising. Friedkin's film highlights how the bodies of cruiser and cruised are brought into proximity, and this before the internet took cruising online through social media. The undercover cop patrols the Meatpacking District but avoids making eye contact with others, indicating his discomfort in being watched. *Cruising* cuts to his first-person perspective, with men looking directly into the camera, as if to give the lens itself a once-over as they size up Burns and contemplate cruising him. The scene replicates several shots in the prologue of *The Boys in the Band*, where Emory cruises two men on a busy New York street. And like the gaze issuing from Lacan's sardine can, the aggressive gazes of these men displace the straight undercover cop and, by co-extension, the straight male film spectator. Narrative developments underscore that Burns does not belong in this scene. He wanders into a small shop and asks the clerk about the various hankies for sale. They belong to a system of signs that signify desire: light blue indicates blowjobs, yellow for golden showers, green for hustlers, and the pockets in which they are placed, either left or right, indicate receiving or giving. The clerk asks Burns if he sees anything that he "wants." "I'm gonna go home and think about it," the undercover cop responds as he sheepishly walks out the door.

At a later moment, Burns is in the Wolf's Den, another underground bar. Friedkin again switches to Burns's point of view through close-ups of sweaty men looking directly into the camera, this time with more determined desire. He has already become more familiar to the scene. Willy DeVille's hard rock song, "It's So Easy," plays throughout this sequence. Returning the gazes of these men but not yet responding to their desire, Burns sits with his arms crossed, observing his observers, including Stuart Richards (Richard Cox), the man on whom Burns will eventually pin the murders. One of the men who checks out Burns is the acne-scarred policeman DiSimone wearing the same shirt and jacket as Richards. If the viewer recognizes him from this fleeting appearance, they may be shocked to realize that he is the same contemptuous uniformed man of the law who demanded oral sex from a transvestite prostitute in the opening scene of the film. Here, in the underground Wolf's Den, he wears leather and conforms to the style of the men around him. Strangely, when he looks at Burns and into the camera, there seems to be no flash of recognition in his eyes, no sense that he acknowledges a colleague of the NYPD. As the film's narrative unfolds, the identity of who is seen by the undercover policeman will remain fluid and this anonymity will remain significant; we learn that the leather jacket can indeed signify both the hustler and the cop. A shirtless man approaches Burns in the bar and sees a yellow handkerchief in his back pocket. He is asked if he is into water sports. The undercover policeman replies, however, "I kinda like to just watch." Annoyed at this misunderstanding, the man who cruised him yells, "If you like to watch, take that hanky out of your pocket, asshole!" Burns only cruises but does not partake, at least not yet.

As the cop learns the codes of cruising, Friedkin's film implicates the viewer and their acts of looking even further. On the one hand, *Cruising* clearly links these acts with libidinal desire. And yet, this form of scopophilic looking does not merely reiterate the fetishistic viewer that desires the fantasy of plentitude offered up by the imaginary signifier. It is more anticipatory and temporally forward-looking in that it looks toward a desire that will be consummated in physical pleasure. Narcissistic aggressions that are typically displaced from the voyeur back onto the narrative are explicitly depicted in *Cruising*, rerouting the drive toward sex to impending death. But above all, cruising in Friedkin's film reveals the extent to which looking at others desirously also means looking at others within the ethical norms set out by the melodramatic mode. Cruising and the work of criminal detection overlap in Friedkin's film and often it is not clear what motivates Burns's scopophilia—individual desire or the act of judging as a policeman. These acts of looking survey the empirical signs that indicate intent: the color of a handkerchief and its location in the back pocket, the sound of jingling keys or of the body moving under a leather jacket, the movement and expressivity of the face, the way another man looks at Burns, and the legitimacy or illegitimacy of the role one plays.

The film reveals this form of overdetermined looking not by confirming the viewer's own expectations around morality and virtue but by troubling them and bringing the inextricable alliance of scopophilia and moral judgment to the fore. As Burns becomes acclimatized to the gay S&M scene, the virtues he holds as a straight cop become "contaminated," not only by the values and virtues of this world, but by the hermeneutic incoherence that this contamination instigates. Elaborating on the homophobic metaphors of contamination and contagion, Davidson argues that *Cruising* critically replicates this figuration of gay identity as a process of anonymized cloning, one that undermines the cult of individuality in popular cinema through its insistence on "mimetic or replicative *proliferation*."[18] Indeed, in many ways, the politics of *Cruising* pivots around the panic induced by the fears of contagion that repeat throughout the film. While in Nancy's apartment, Burns still does not disclose the details of his special assignment, but wearily remarks that, "What I'm doing is affecting me." While he is still wearing his leather, she asks him why he does not desire her. In the following scene, Burns meets with Edelson in a subway station and they discuss their use of brutal interrogation methods. "I don't think I can do the job," Burns protests, "I don't think I can handle it, that's all . . . It's just, things happening to me." While he thinks that his task is to "just watch," he quickly comes to realize that the cost of engaging with this world through scopophilic surveillance involves his own objectification by the desiring gaze of other men.

On the other hand, it is also clear that what has affected him began much earlier. Burns does not explicitly become homosexual, but, as D. A. Miller notes, is "queered" through his experience and contact with other men in the scene.[19] His face-to-face encounters with unabashed homosexuality incite a profound challenge not only to his identity but also to that which grounds the capacity of moral judgment itself. We see this at work most explicitly in a scene that takes place during "Precinct Night" at the Cockpit. Countless patrons in this bacchanal sequence have arrived wearing wear police accoutrements—leather jackets, officer's shirts and caps, aviators—symbols of straight authority. Burns was apparently not made aware of the event and arrives in regular blue jeans and leather. He watches, while breathing heavily, as nipples are pinched, backs whipped, and batons are fellated. "You a police officer?", a bouncer asks the undercover cop, "This is Precinct Night. You got the wrong attitude. I'm afraid I'm gonna have to ask you to leave." The once-separated spaces of homosexual club patron and heterosexual police officer overlap and clash, leaving Burns as confused as the bouncer is assured that something about him is not right. Here, as I discussed in the previous chapter, the policeman is policed, the one cruising is cruised and is deemed an illegitimate fake cop by another fake cop. His role as decoy becomes confused—does he entrap others or is he entrapped? (Notably, the epigraph to Gerald Walker's original novel is "Each is pursuer, each pursued."[20]) That he is profoundly affected by this interaction is indicated in an abrupt cut. Friedkin seems to deny Burns time to secure some sense of himself when the film quickly cuts to him having sex with Nancy. She kisses his chest, and as her head moves lower and leaves the frame, his face grows blank.

While the character of Burns and the methods used by the New York police modify as the film unfolds, the identity of the killer himself also constantly shifts. His face is never revealed, although he perhaps resembles Richards. And in each of the killings depicted in the film, a different actor plays him, each moving differently and having different visual profiles, thus confounding the determination of his identity further. What is more, the post-synchronized sound allows Friedkin the opportunity to dub in a voice that does not belong to the body who utters his words. Called the "Voice of Jack" in the script for *Cruising*, it is performed by James Sutorius, whose disembodied voice marks his only presence in the film. Each time the killer cruises, setting out to kill, Sutorius's voice unnervingly recites his lullaby: "Who's here? I'm here. You're here." These words are ironic given the constantly shifting identity of the killer. Friedkin had already experimented with voice and produced the monstrous through the mismatch between it and the body in *The Exorcist* (Mercedes McCambridge as the demon Pazuzu).

Two additional murders illustrate the progressive troubling of the killer's identity and the inability of visual and auditory perception to definitively ascertain it. In the second one, we pick up on the moment Burns is cruising in Central Park at night, where he makes eye contact with DiSimone, again without any sign that they recognize each other as fellow policemen. (DiSimone will appear once more, toward the end of *Cruising*, back again in uniform and consulting Edelson.) Burns instead follows another man played by Larry Atlas, who played the killer in the film's first murder. The film then abruptly cuts away to Burns checking in with Edelson at a dive bar during the day. Here, as in many moments in the film, Friedkin organizes images not along strict lines of cause-effect continuity but in a manner that forces viewers to make connections between them. What happened between Burns and the man in Central Park? What was the nature of their interaction? The film then cuts back to the park at night and, this time, does not take Burns's point of view. The camera follows the man played by Atlas walking through a parade of faces, cruising the available men. He talks to someone shrouded in the shadows. We recognize Atlas's face, his nose and cheekbones, and when he speaks his voice is seemingly his own. But the shadowed man he cruises possesses (or is possessed by) the Voice of Jack. As they walk off into a secluded area where other men are hooking up, the soundtrack shifts from orgasmic moans to the voice of the killer as he softly sings, "Who's here? I'm here. You're here." The man played by Atlas looks around and asks, "Where are you?" But before he finds the answer to his question, the killer rushes him from behind and stabs him in the back. The question of "who is here" gains in reflexive meaning as the killer in the film's first murder becomes the victim in the second. Like a cop who becomes a john, or a straight man who cruises and is cruised, perpetrators of sexual violence become victims in *Cruising*.

In the film's third murder, the killer's visual and auditory identity once again defies melodramatic expectations, expectations that are geared toward isolating his identity through the cinematic signs that have been gleaned up to this point. A well-dressed man named Martino (Steve Inwood) is closing his women's clothing shop while his friend, Joey (Keith Prentice, who played Larry in *The Boys in the Band*), helps him load his car with packages. Martino drives off and goes to a busy porno theater. There he cruises the many men hanging around the booths and picks up one of them who is wearing leather and a police cap. His features remain largely illegible. Although the shot of this man is very brief, he is played by Arnaldo Santana, who played Loren Lukas, the very first murder victim in the St. James Hotel. The two men enter a booth and start watching a film. Martino drops to his knees in front of the man he just cruised. Friedkin cuts in a shot of Lukas to underscore the connection to the film's opening sequence, foreshadowing the murder that is about to take place but also the fact that the illegible man was once a murdered victim. Now a perpetrator of violence, he stabs Martino multiple times in the back. His raised knife casts a dark shadow on the pornography projected in the booth while blood splatters on the screen. Quick cuts to another pornographic film are interpolated into the sequence, doubling the film playing in the booth. "You made me do that," the Voice of Jack intones, in another reference to the film's first murder. The film's leader appears on the screen, indicating the end of the show.

With the visual and aural referents to the killer's face and voice isolated on the soundtrack, Friedkin invites the viewer to gather evidence about the man who Burns is ostensibly pursuing, but then confuses these cues. Juxtaposing known voices, sounds, and images, these scenes lead spectators to believe that they might know the face and movements of the serial murderer but are quickly left unsure. The killer could be a single individual or multiple people. Adrian Martin notes these discrepancies and writes that, "indeed, we are led to suspect, in one way or another, that virtually every character in the film could be the killer, potentially or actually, in the past, present, or future of the narrative."[21] This interchangeability between potential killers draws attention to the real killers and cops playing roles in Friedkin's films, including Paul Bateson, Randy Jurgensen, and Sonny Grosso, but also to the repetition of actors from earlier films by Friedkin, for example Keith Prentice, Barton Heyman, Joe Spinell. In *Cruising*, character and moral disposition are not wedded to individual bodies, but reconstituted at each moment through each appearance, performed through gesture and dialogue that bring the body into legibility.

Moreover, this multiplicity, of criminal identities cloning and possessing other identities, resonates with serial murder cases that terrified Americans in the 1970s. There were the Son of Sam murders that terrorized New Yorkers in the summer of 1976 and galvanized fears of skyrocketing crime as the city was in economic decline. During this period, New Yorkers were sent into a frenzy of fear as David Berkowitz repeatedly eluded and taunted the police. His seemingly ubiquitous presence in the media compelled the State Legislature to devise a "Son of Sam law" that would prevent criminals from profiting from the publicity of their crimes. Berkowitz was apparently offered substantial sums of money by publishers and film producers for his story. There was also the "Hillside Strangler"—these nicknames already indicate the sensationalism such cases generated in the news media—who raped, tortured, and murdered ten young women in the hills surrounding Los Angeles and in Washington State between 1977 and 1978. The apparently lone strangler turned out to be two, Kenneth Bianchi and Angelo Buono Jr. In an even more unusual case involving serial murder and multiple identities, Henry Lee Lucas committed multiple killings over a span of almost twenty-five years, starting with his mother in 1960. After he was caught, Lucas bizarrely claimed to have committed hundreds more and his testimonies at first provided resolution to countless cold cases. Following some rudimentary fact-checking, it was found that these claims were false.

As a film that abounds in the signification of desire, *Cruising* remains obstinate in its refusal to provide definitive signs indexing the murderer as single individual. Contagious relations make symptomatic reading increasingly difficult and the signs of criminality increasingly obscure. In its most provocative move, Friedkin's film eventually suggests a collusion between the killer and Burns himself. Immediately following the latest murder, the film cuts to Burns wearing the leather regalia of the killer, suggesting that he may in fact have been the Voice of Jack. After the murder in Central Park, he is shown walking to Nancy's apartment. And after the murder in the porno theater, we see him returning to his own apartment. Linking shots of Burns immediately following murderous actions, *Cruising* suggests criminal culpability through montage. The possibility that Burns himself may be the serial killer and has thus crossed the line between policeman and criminal (and by co-extension from straight to bisexual or gay), is turned into a certainty when he stabs Richards in Central Park. "I want to see the world," the undercover cop remarks, after having cruised Richards. Burns then recites the killer's lullaby, "Who's here? I'm here. You're here," as he takes the taller man's leather cap and puts it on his head (Figure 3.2). Later Burns will be cleared of having stabbed the suspected killer. Edelson tells his subordinate that the grand jury will deem his actions, however murderous, as "necessary force" and that he will be granted legal immunity. Like Popeye in *The French Connection*, like Richard Chance in *To Live and Die in L.A.*, the police break the law with impunity and walk away from murder.

CRIMINAL DESIRES 99

Figure 3.2 "Who's here? I'm here. You're here."

Significantly, the sovereign and its fundamental role in liberal equality serves as the culmination to Damon Young's far-reaching reading of *Cruising*. For Young, Friedkin's film manifests this structure in the "fraternal social contract" that makes visible the ontological contradiction around which sovereign agency revolves, namely the tension in the figuration of policemen but also in that of fathers. In a sequence instigated by Richards looking through a box of unsent letters to his father, which anticipates the letters of help sent by Hallam to Bonham in *The Hunted*, he is seen speaking to his disapproving father. "I wish just once you'd say something positive to me," he remarks, as if reading one of his letters aloud, "I've tried to do everything you wanted, but it's never good enough." Friedkin cuts in quick shots from the murders we have already seen, as the father remarks, "You know what you have to do." This father figure, in addition to the policemen and other figures of paternal law, manifests a space of legal exception through his directive to kill. And because of its visibility in Friedkin's film, this figuration "exposes sadomasochistic relations or domination as the underside of the system of liberal equality."[22] In doing so, *Cruising*, particularly in its explicit depictions of homoerotic desire, offers "a queer theory of the social contract," one that is sustained by the logic of the exception delineated by Schmitt.[23]

As the signifiers for identifying the murderer shift and mutate, the capacity for assigning culpability for these crimes becomes progressively tenuous in *Cruising*. This difficulty pivots around the disintegration of the human body as a unified field of visual and auditory signs, and which signifies the evidence of interior virtue (or more specifically the lack of it) within the melodramatic mode. As if to underscore this problematic, the film shows a close-up of the cover of a book by the psychoanalyst C. G. Jung, *Word and Image*, as Burns illegally breaks and enters into Richards's Columbia University dorm room. This construction of the human being demands the synchronization of the voice and body, not merely as a mechanical process involving the image track and soundtracks of film, but as an ideological one that sutures sound and image together. Moreover, within the bourgeois concept of character within the melodramatic mode, normative distinctions between victim and perpetrator, male and female, criminal and policeman, must also be maintained. Within these norms of popular cinema, the figure of criminality often infiltrates the detective's home or family but in *Cruising*, criminality, that which radicalizes these norms, suffuses the realm of word and image constituted by the cinema medium. Elaborating broadly on this breaking point between sound and image, Michel Chion writes:

> Of course, via the operation called synchronization, cinema seeks to reunify the body and voice that have been dissociated by their inscription onto separate surfaces (the celluloid image and the soundtrack). But the more you think about synchronization, the more aware you can become, as Marguerite Duras did, of the arbitrariness of this convention, which tries to present as a unity something that from the outset *doesn't stick together*.[24]

The unified, singular body of the serial murderer in Friedkin's film should sound like no other body, have a particular identifiable identity—male, gay, leather wearing, jingling keys—and must utter "Who's here? I'm here. You're here" with an immediately identifiable cadence. Yet *Cruising* dissects this unity, compelling viewers precisely to think about synchronization in the cinema, the way it arbitrarily constructs humanity, and in so doing to consider critically the desire of the spectator who demands a unified construction of word and image in the cinema. The disturbing non-coincidence of both, on the other hand, inspires questioning into the ideological binaries that underpin the very legibility of the killer's profile. The inability of the voice to find its "proper" body is what Chion calls the "impossible anacousmêtre," which he explicates by drawing from the examples of the mother's voice dubbed over Norman's body in Hitchcock's *Psycho*, a film that has obsessed Friedkin, as well as the guttural voice that haunts Regan in *The Exorcist*.[25] These instances of improper embodiments, when a female voice is embodied by a male body or an evil demon speaks through the body of an innocent girl, induce an uncanniness that also points to the process of reintegration that is integral to the sound film. At stake is the very concept of an originating personality, or soul, who may be named as the cause of some action in the world. When these images are experienced as uncanny, this experience points to the sense of dislocation when epistemological binaries between male and female, virtuous and not, are transgressed in these improper bodies, giving one pause as to who or what possesses them.

The voice and image of the killer in *Cruising* coincide in the film's first murder, but as the film progresses, this voice becomes dislocated and becomes a "voice from nowhere" as the murderer's seen corporeality becomes dislodged from his identity.[26] Like a spirit that leaves its body following the body's physical demise, the sounds and image of the murderer leave his identity and haunt the surfaces of Friedkin's film, troubling the very concept of the speaking human being, the figure constructed by the cinema and who solicits judgment by the spectator. One may be reminded of James Lastra's insistence on the inseparability of sound and its origin within the cinema technology, a regime that he calls a theory of "nonidentity."[27] There is no origin of the voice, no original or copy, when it is always already "deformed" through recording, editing, re-recording, and playback. The readable surfaces of the film remain fractured, obscuring its ultimate denouement. Through acoustic estrangement, *Cruising* dismantles the concept of assigning guilt, showing how judgment is endemic not to a single individual but to the diegetic world of the film and the environments that surround the human characters. In this, criminal guilt is unlocatable outside the space of the cinema theater; not in the script, or in Arthur Bell's accounts, Gerald Walker's novel, or in the gay men who are ostensibly represented in *Cruising*. The repetition of the Voice of Jack upends the expectation that a singular culprit, body, or identity may be identified by the end of the film. Indeed, one might borrow a formulation by Stephen Heath from his description of the use of sound in films by Straub and Huillet: sound in *Cruising* is no longer subservient to the image but "*gives space*, not as coherence but as contradiction, heterogeneity, outside."[28] That it remains unclear not only why the killer kills but also whether this perpetrator of violence was also a victim of it, one who typically breaks the law or one who enforces it, or whether the killer identifies as gay or straight, is due to the disassociating regime of the cinema technology. If, as Michel Foucault has argued, it is through sex "that each individual has to pass in order to have access to his own intelligibility," *Cruising* repeatedly refuses to grant the viewer this intelligibility, this identity that seeks discernment along lines of sexuality, criminality, and otherwise.[29] The impossibility of assigning guilt within the narrative space of the film brings greater meaning to the image of the dismembered arm found floating in the Hudson Bay and Lefransky's inability to identify it as a signifier of homicide. If there is a culprit that may be identified, one may point to the homunculus that is the cinema, an inorganic form of life that, in Friedkin's film, foregrounds its uncanny inhumanity.

Cruising ends with Burns back in Nancy's apartment, however this seeming return to a space of innocence does not re-establish the heterosexual coupling. Moreover, as D. A. Miller writes, the film fails to definitely restore the mutual exclusivity of gay and straight desire by its conclusion.[30] Burns shaves in the bathroom while Nancy is in the living room. She spots Burns's undercover costume, his aviator sunglasses, police cap, and leather jacket, and tries them on herself. Cutting back to Burns, he looks at himself in the mirror and then turns his eyes to look directly into the camera and, by co-extension, at the spectator.

Burns's look at the camera serves as the culminating moment of *Cruising*, bringing the dissection of the killer's identity to a critique of the cinema situation itself. The returned gaze repeats those that featured shots of cruising throughout the film, of men looking at Burns. Here his face expresses the bored look worn by men looking for a quick sexual encounter. And with the possibility that Burns might be the underground killer, the shot also places the viewer in the position of being his next possible victim. The impulse toward murder spreads like a contagion in Friedkin's film, migrating between actors and characters, victims and perpetrators, and actors from the director's other films. This final shot from *Cruising* seems also to indicate that this impulse will pass from the bodies in the film who committed acts of violence to the bodies sitting in the theater. It collapses the binary between the diegesis and the world of the voyeuristic viewer, between film and reality, by aggressively demanding that the viewer engage with the critique of their relationship with the cinema apparatus. Indeed, in the end one is left with the insight, derived through the film's manifestation of the fraternal social contract, of a sovereign power that paradoxically legitimizes the discourse of liberal humanism. For the breakdown of the discursive boundary that typically separates screen and spectator may itself be considered a form of violence made possible through the logic of the exception. Between the victim and perpetrator, the one who sees and is seen, and the one who hears and is heard, this moment highlights the reversibility of these terms, collapsing all these actions into the ambivalent practice of cruising.

JADE (1995)

Continuing to disembody the voice from the speaking body, *Jade* begins with a murder that is not seen, only heard. The opening scene introduces themes of dissimulation and disavowal that will come to dominate the film as a whole. Several tracking shots take the viewer into a San Francisco mansion at night, extravagantly furnished with paintings, tapestries, vases, and sculptures associated with European and Asian high culture. The house here functions as a museum where objects are placed on fetishistic display. A section from Part Two of Stravinsky's *Rite of Spring*, the "Ritual Actions of the Ancestors," plays on the soundtrack as the camera glides through the house's foyer, lavish rooms, and hallway while the film's credits appear on screen. The mobile camera draws attention momentarily to several photographs on various embellished tables: Ronald Reagan, Margaret Thatcher, and Richard Nixon. Each of these images, featuring key figures of 1970s and 1980s conservativism, also contains a distinguished-looking, yet unidentified man wearing a dark suit. While the music builds in intensity, a man's voice can be heard off screen saying, "No! No, don't!" The camera turns a corner and ascends a staircase as the music suddenly blares with brass and wind instruments. At the top, we pause momentarily to come face-to-face with an African tribal mask. As the camera continues to explore the rooms of the second floor and its collection of art and anthropological artifacts, more indecipherable shouts can be heard. The disturbing sounds of chopping come on the soundtrack. Another chop, and then two more as a man screams in pain. Finally, the sound of an object, presumably the instrument of murder, dropping on the floor, and then momentary silence. The camera drifts close to a mirror hanging above a fireplace but turns away before it reveals itself and moves back to an ornate three-part dressing screen. Bright, ruby-red blood seeps from underneath the screen as the scene ends.

This murder takes place entirely off screen, disavowing the viewer's desire to see and judge its gratuitousness while positing the presence of a corpse that, for the remainder of the film, remains always unseen. The series of photos, each including an unidentified man, featured in the tracking shots suggests that he is the one being victimized, however it is unclear who is victimizing him and why. This man will later turn out to be prominent businessman Kyle Medford. For the remainder of the film's narrative, this unseen character will pique the viewer's curiosity to know how this Medford, seemingly with some political clout among political conservatives, was killed.

Appropriately, when *Jade* continues following this scene, it cuts to a shot of an empty, disembodied suit suspended in the air by balloons. They are decorations for a lavish gala being held at the Palace Hotel in San Francisco. Here we are introduced to the film's three protagonists: Assistant District Attorney David Corelli (David Caruso), his unrequited love interest the psychologist Trina Gavin (Linda Fiorentino), and Trina's husband, Matt Gavin (Chazz Palminteri). The plot to *Jade* will involve this love triangle but center on the role Trina played in the murder of Medford and her secret life working in the sex trade.

Jade takes up problems around the relationship between sound, image, and criminality I introduced in the previous section while also sharing with Friedkin's *Cruising* an atmosphere of cynicism and depravity. Its scriptwriter, Joe Eszterhas, had experienced meteoric success with his script for *Basic Instinct* and went on to write *Sliver* and *Showgirls*, the latter now considered somewhat of a "cult" film. These "erotic thrillers" preceded *Jade* and feature neo-noir plots revolving around highly sexualized femme fatales. Notably, Linda Ruth Williams has called *Cruising* "arguably the erotic thriller's clearest starting point," a genre that would come into fruition through the work of Paul Verhoeven, actor Michael

Douglas, and Eszterhas's scripts throughout the 1980s and 1990s.[31] When *Jade* was released in October of 1995, critics panned it, complaining of its sleaziness and narrative incoherence while also noting that Friedkin seemed "jaded" in light of his heyday in the early 1970s.[32] Barbara Schulgasser of the *San Francisco Examiner* asserts that, "Eszterhas, the several million-dollar author of the laughable 'Showgirls,' but also previously responsible for watchable trash ('Basic Instinct'), isn't even trying anymore."[33] While remarking that *Jade* shamelessly recycles the plot to *Basic Instinct*, Kenneth Turan finds that the film's representation of gender remains limited:

> With its pseudo-raunchy dialogue and slimy situations, "Jade" retreads familiar territory for both director William Friedkin and Eszterhas. And despite the writer's recent public protestations that his women are strong masters of their own fate, he once again hasn't been able to come up with female protagonists who aren't victims or hookers or, more likely, both.[34]

Following the critical and commercial failures of *Sorcerer* and *Cruising*, Friedkin entered a dark phase of his career. In March 1981, the forty-six-year-old director, while driving his car, experienced a shooting pain starting in his left arm that quickly escalated into a full-blown heart attack. "When I was dying of a heart attack on the Warner Bros. lot in the infirmary [in 1981]," he remarks in an interview, "I heard one paramedic say when he was using a defibrillator, 'I'm not getting anything.' And I remember thinking, Oh my God, I'm dying and I've accomplished nothing in my life."[35] After weeks of recovery and regaining the strength to walk and be active again, Friedkin was determined to return to filmmaking. He directed the comedy, *Deal of the Century*, in 1983, starring Chevy Chase and Gregory Hines, and then *To Live and Die in L.A.* in 1985. In addition to some productions made for television (an episode of *The Twilight Zone* in 1985 and the television movie *C.A.T. Squad* in 1986), he made the drama-thriller, *Rampage*, which I will discuss in greater detail in the next chapter, as well as the horror film, *The Guardian* from 1990, whose plot revolves around a killer tree and a druidic babysitter. Most of these were financial failures at the box office. This was a period that he describes as "an uphill climb to the bottom."[36] It was only when he met Sherry Lansing in 1991 that some stability was brought into Friedkin's life. Both working-class Chicagoans, the couple had arrived in Los Angeles around the same time, yet were at different phases in their career when they met at an Oscar party. While Friedkin was struggling with *Cruising* and its poor reception in 1980, Lansing, thirty-five at the time, became president of Twentieth Century Fox, the first woman to achieve this position at a major Hollywood studio. They married three months after meeting in Bel Air and the following year Lansing became the chairperson of Paramount Pictures.

Shortly after taking control of Paramount in 1992, she bought a script treatment written by Eszterhas for *Jade* for $2.5 million, then the highest amount ever paid for an outline.[37] Meanwhile in 1993, Paramount's president and Lansing's former producing partner, Stanley Jaffe, offered Friedkin the chance to direct a film that exposes corruption in the college basketball recruiting process called *Blue Chips*. The result reminded viewers of the kind of filmmaking that made Friedkin's career, particularly in its characterization of the obsessive coach played by Nick Nolte, its quick cutting, and the energetic depiction of basketball play. Unlike many of his other films, *Blue Chips* ends with the redemption of its protagonist while conforming to the narrative trajectory of popular melodrama. It did not do well at the box office, however, and served to prolong Friedkin's professional and creative malaise. When Lansing proposed that Friedkin direct Eszterhas's script, the screenwriter at first expressed enthusiastic approval. "What [Friedkin] brings to the party is a kind of spooky, dark energy, which fits perfectly into *Jade*," he remembers thinking.[38] For the director's part, Friedkin seemed eager to take up the themes of sex and crime that were part of Eszterhas's trademark and to reassert himself with a story that, according to him, is kind of a "rip-off" of Luis Buñuel's *Belle de Jour* from 1967. Both films feature a female protagonist, a married woman who keeps secrets, and whose allure is embodied in the dichotomy between sophistication and smut.[39] At the time, many had suspected that Friedkin had been contracted as director on the project because of his partner, although Lansing claims that she had recused herself from the decision.[40]

Despite Friedkin's retrospective claim that *Jade* "contained some of my best work," he painfully acknowledged its failure at the time of its release.[41] "I felt I had let down the actors, the studio, and most of all, Sherry," the director reflects, "I went into a deep funk."[42] Meanwhile, Eszterhas blamed the negative reception of the film to the changes Friedkin made to the script, after the scriptwriter was promised that it would be filmed without alteration. Apparently, Friedkin interpolated dialogue and actions throughout *Jade* that were intended to raise moral questions about its characters and thus stage the filmmaker's fixation with law and lawlessness. Following the violent murder of Medford depicted in the film's opening scene, for example, Corelli finds a cufflink at the scene and does not submit it as official evidence. Not in the original script, this moment recalls a similar one from *To Live and Die in L.A.* when Chance refuses to submit Waxman's ledger into the official record, circumventing police protocol.

Eszterhas took particular umbrage at the charges of misogyny launched by critics who disapproved of the highly sexualized depictions of the women that dominate his scripts—"victims or hookers, or more likely, both," as Turan put it above. In a letter he wrote to the *Los Angeles Times* after *Jade* was released, Eszterhas explains that his aim has always been to depict strong women:

> The central tenet of *Jade* is that a wife whose husband cheats on her decides to cheat on him. She doesn't want to fall in love with anyone, so she cheats with a series of men, once with each man.
>
> The central tenet of *Showgirls* is that a young woman turns her back on stardom rather than be spiritually destroyed by the corruption of the male-dominated world that she is in. She turns her back on the money, the glamour, the ambition—and goes back out on the road. Alone.
>
> In both movies, the women, Trina and Nomi, take action as a result of what men have done to them: Trina's husband betrays her; Nomi's male-oriented Vegas world betrays her. They refuse to be victimized and, strong women, they do what they have to do to control their destinies.[43]

Later in his memoirs he remarks, seemingly with sincere incredulity, that he finds it ironic that some critics have called his previous screenplays "feminist" while others have accused him of misogyny. The victimized women in his scripts represent, for Eszterhas, female entertainers who are harassed and abused in reality, "women in the world who, discovering that their husbands have betrayed them, decide to cheat themselves, to get even."[44] While rejecting the symptomatic reading that has been deployed to ascertain whether the women in *Jade* and *Showgirls* are victims or hookers, he reiterates his aim to tell stories that reflect the struggles of women working as Vegas showgirls. Indeed, at stake for both Eszterhas and his critics is the question of what constitutes a "positive," and therefore sympathetic, representation of women and the extent to which this representation may be judged in relation to ideologies of feminine virtue and to real women "in the world."

I believe that the problem of virtue is indeed at stake in *Jade*, a problem that brings sexuality into the scope of criminality. In order to elaborate this, let us undertake a close analysis of Friedkin's film. Following the murder of Kyle Medford in the opening sequence, we return to his San Francisco mansion and see it through Corelli's investigative eyes, revisiting it as a crime scene. Medford was apparently quite the fetishist. He collected the pubic hair of individuals he desired sexually and was in possession of photographs showing powerful men sleeping with high-class prostitutes. Moreover, his vast collection of exotic artifacts, many of which seem to have erotic or transgressive purposes, also seems to reflect an intensely fetishistic attitude toward the display of these many "exotic" objects. We may remember that, according to psychoanalysis, fetishism is a response, typical to male heterosexuality, to the experience of difference. It imbues an inanimate object with erotic power, holding it up as a substitute for a desired object that is perceived to have been lost. The fetishistic object commemorates this absence while taking on its libidinal charge. Such an object, as Freud puts it, "has taken its place, has been appointed its substitute, as it were, and now inherits the interest which was formerly directed to its predecessor."[45] On the one hand, Medford's collection of artifacts and pubic hair seems to reflect this tendency to fetishize objects that at once serve as reminders of past pleasures and as substitutes for the physical act of sex itself. That he has surrounded himself with commemorative objects attests to an urge to memorialize past desires.

On the other hand, Medford's own absence in these opening scenes induces an additional layer of meaning to the film; another fetishism is produced around the desire to confirm the event of his death. Since the viewer only hears and does not see this event, it must be imagined, while it simultaneously sets up a desire to know. The tracking shots leading into Medford's mansion show his still image only briefly in the photographs, taken with well-known heads of state, while his live-action image will remain disavowed from the spectator for the entirety of the film. Like Medford's fetishistic objects strewn about his home, his absence, and the numerous ways in which it is signified in the narrative, will persist throughout Friedkin's *Jade*, like the absent sovereign in *Cruising*. The objects and clues seen throughout the film, moreover, stand in for the dead man himself, as if memorializing his loss while signaling their continued relevance to the living for film's plot. His murder will propel the film's narrative forward and the presence of his absence, like an imaginary signifier, will haunt the events that unfold.

The logic of the fetish continues to determine what is revealed and concealed throughout *Jade* as the impulse toward forensic investigation converges with fetishistic desire. Other objects, other signs, point back to Medford's murder while also conforming to the erotic logic of substitution. The small tin container inscribed with the Chinese character for "Jade" contains the pubic hair of the woman Friedkin's film sets out to find. When Corelli confirms its provenance, the film cuts to Trina boarding a private jet to Los Angeles. She is due to give a talk on the etiology of aggressive impulses and the experience of "hysterical blindness" that accompanies acts of extreme violence. As she boards the plane, Trina looks at the front page of a newspaper reporting on the murder of Medford, goading the viewer to associate her character with this event. Later in *Jade*, another murder takes place, this time in Medford's Pacifica seaside home. Detective Vasko (Ken King) and Corelli enter the bedroom, another crime scene, where objects such as fetishistic masks seemingly from Africa and Asia have been found among sex toys and bottles of massage oils. Vasko holds up a "harmony" pillow and reads aloud a label that is attached to it: "This pillow allows deeper penetration by positioning both partners most advantageously. It raises the female hips facilitating male entry." Continuing to search for clues, he opens the nightstand drawer, revealing many little bags containing pills and vitamins, a sex toy, and a mirror with a small amount of cocaine. Meanwhile, Corelli opens a small refrigerator next to the bed and identifies a few high-end food brands inside—Cristal, Beluga, Wolfgang Puck—then concludes, with humorous sincerity, that "it's a fuck house." Everything in the room has become a means toward excessive sexual and criminal ends. Objects are read as brazen traces of sexual debauchery and appear as signs of moral transgression. Later Detective Heller recovers a damaged tape in the burnt fireplace. Apparently Medford was using his Pacifica house to lure and videotape San Francisco's powerful men to have sex with prostitutes. These tapes would be used as blackmail.

Corelli and the San Francisco police search for the killer and look for someone to blame, someone who entertains sexual and murderous pleasures simultaneously, a femme fatale perhaps, someone who has been given the name "Jade." That her namesake evokes a vague Asian backdrop heightens the insistence on the logic of fetishism in its mild evocation of both orientalist fascination and erotic anxiety. The numerous appropriations of Chinese culture—the Chinatown parade, the Chinese theater, appropriations of the exotic in James Horner's score, the film's title itself—infuse the verisimilitude with nothing specific about that which it references. Other than the extras at the parade, there are only three Asian actors in *Jade*, each given only one sentence to speak. Like the artifacts scattered around Medford's mansion, the Asian items throughout are expensive orientalist decorations with no significance beyond that of their owner showcasing his capacity to possess them. Associated with anxieties of "yellow peril" fantasies, they recall fears of foreign commodities coming to flood the U.S. market. At the same time, *Jade* and its criminal characters allay these anxieties by fixating on them further, linking them to the realm of transgression and associating them with a series of signs that are required for triggering sexual desire.

As in *The Hunted*, the cinematic chase, with its linearity and goal-oriented action, organizes and channels the movement toward the pursuit of criminal culpability and the search for the fetishized woman. Corelli and Vasko locate the woman identified in the photos sleeping with the governor as, somewhat improbably, working as a manicurist at a Chinatown nail salon. They chase Patrice (Angie Everhart) through the neighborhood's alleyways and into a Chinese theater, through the sets of empty seats. She is apprehended and in the station house tells the officers that some of the men did not choose to sleep with her, but another woman named Jade, who was apparently known for her unbridled skills. When Patrice begins talking, she speaks solely to Corelli, but through sleight-of-hand editing, Friedkin inserts Vasko and Hargrove into the room, listening intently as well.

Corelli finds himself caught between conflicting forces—he is threatened by the governor to keep him out of the investigation, while the mounting clues point to Trina, the woman he still desires. Nevertheless, he is obsessed with pursuing the killer to such a degree that he puts himself and others in harm's way. As with Popeye in *The French Connection*, Friedkin realizes this self-righteous attitude through a car chase. Patrice wants to see Corelli to talk about Jade. On her way to the Italian restaurant where they are to meet, she is violently run down by a black car with darkened windows. It turns back to drive over her head. Corelli watches incredulously, then rushes out of the restaurant to pursue the vehicle through the hilly streets of San Francisco. In place of the spontaneous recklessness of *The French Connection*, *Jade* features tightly controlled, well-choreographed interactions between the car and its urban environment. The pursuit starts, stops, and starts again, leading to a bizarre anti-chase through a street choked by a parade, with flamboyant dancers and a Chinese dragon, slowly moving its way up Chinatown's busy Grant Avenue.

Moreover, as with *Cruising*, the conflation of fetishism and criminality in *Jade* takes on an increasingly obsessive, increasingly pollutive status through the film's narrative. The *mise-en-scène* of Medford's home, the foreignness of Chinatown, women who work as manicurists by day and high-class escorts by night: this world repeatedly betrays itself as corrupt, seemingly without morals, covetous, and sexually unrestrained. As the film unfolds, the spectator is made privy to the corruption of Matt Gavin while Corelli undergoes a process of contamination by a fallen world, one that has been corrupted over time. The film seems to revel in what has become of San Francisco and its counterculture of sexual liberation, now over-priced and populated by overly affluent men who make their money in high-stakes careers. In the place of the street-smart thugs of *The French Connection* and *To Live and Die in L.A.* is a lawyer wearing a tuxedo to a crime scene. In this, Matt is equally ambitious, but does not think twice about his constant infidelity or his clients' white-collar crimes. "There's only three fun things in life, paisan," he tells Corelli. "Money, sex, and power." Evidently morally bankrupt, Matt's lack of compassion applies to each of his victims, including his wife. Yet *Jade* eventually shows us that morally compromised men must continue to obsessively find blame and pass judgment in order to shore up their masculinity in this post-sacred world. "I do the fucking," the lascivious Governor Edwards (Richard Crenna) remarks, "I never get fucked." Their masculinity is reiterated through wanton acts of criminal and sexual licentiousness, acts that pass with legal and moral impunity, while its coherence is maintained through a sovereign power that repeatedly pardons itself from all culpability. Part of this effort to shore up masculinity's own contaminated subjectivity is to "outsource" this moral debasement, to expunge that which has been deemed foreign from the self, and to find the other guilty of crime or of sexual transgression through an act of violent projection. Everything and everyone can be fetishized and therefore corrupted, by this moralizing gaze. Medford's death haunts the objects and clues of the film while also inducing this corrupting look, tainting the film's characters and *mise-en-scène* with a transgressive, libidinous evil eye. This outward directed, moralizing gaze is most emphatic in the judgment and characterization of Trina by the men of the film and by Friedkin's narrative. Their condemnatory, sexualizing look reiterates their putative certainty about her guilt. They project monstrous sexuality onto Trina, effectuating a moral violence, the corruption of fetishistic criminality, of moral fallenness and deceit that is inextricably linked to the fact of her sexual difference. Here Friedkin's film reveals how the guilt of the femme fatale, a paradoxical characterization seen in *Belle de Jour*, is produced through the male gaze.

Woman is thus deemed in *Jade* as both fetish and criminal—the latter corresponds to just one strategy by which men may react to the distress generated by the encounter with sexual difference. Through this, difference is disavowed through the devaluation of her gender. According to psychoanalysis, this reaction can take either one or the other form—woman is typically seen as either fetish or criminal. Yet Trina, like many women who appear in the erotic thriller film, is both, embodying an ambivalence that puts her decisively within the orbit of the femme fatale. Perhaps this ambivalence explains Linda Ruth Williams's observation that the erotic thriller remains "ideologically confused" and that "they wear this confusion on their sleeves in a way that blockbusters don't."[46] Trina as both "victim and hooker," to cite Turan's binary once more, remains an incarnation of an ambivalent male fantasy that in Friedkin's *Jade* renders any distinctions between the two irrelevant to her character.

This act of male projection continues most disturbingly in the final scene of *Jade*. In it a series of photographs depicting Trina's sexual exploits are displayed across her dresser, forcing her to confront her own promiscuity once again while shaming her for it. She cries as Matt suddenly acknowledges that he killed Medford to protect them both. "I don't remember any of it," he remarks, recalling Bateson's explanation to Friedkin while the director worked on *Cruising*. Matt's admission that he is the murderer comes without any fanfare, as if the viewer were supposed to know of his secret identity all along (Figure 3.3). When he looks for his cufflinks, he finds only one in his drawer. The other was taken by Corelli in Medford's mansion, disturbingly suggesting that the district attorney refused to submit them as evidence at the time out of loyalty to his old friend (out of the kind of male comradery I discussed in *Rules of Engagement*). This refusal, of course, raises the question of whether Corelli knew of Matt's culpability all along.

Moving toward her while the photographs are doubled by her dresser mirror, Matt remarks, "You know what I think it is? Hysterical blindness. Do me a favor, Trina. Next time we make love, you introduce me to Jade." Matt shames Trina for her participation in the sex trade and then taunts her to reveal herself as a high-class hooker, whose pubic hair Medford fetishized

Figure 3.3 Matt reveals his knowledge of Trina's exploits

and stored in a tin container. As Linda Ruth Williams puts it, "the woman's guilt pervades *Jade*, and even though in this case she isn't actually guilty, she is somehow guilty anyway."[47] This guilt—her innocence somehow seems impossible here—is constituted by the sovereign judgment performed by all the men of Friedkin's film. With a close-up of Trina's frowning face, the film ends abruptly, cutting to black, the abrupt ending recalling *The French Connection*, where the viewer is left with their own thoughts and invited to reconsider the key narrative details of the film.

The camera roaming through Medford's home at the beginning of *Jade* denied the audience a look into the mirror, yet by the end, Trina's vanity mirror forces her to accept her own judgment by the fetishizing male gaze. (In an earlier scene, Trina sees herself, while wearing a stocking over her face, in a mirror while having sex with one of her clients. When she recognizes her image, and sees herself as an object of judgment, she immediately demands that her partner stop.) In *Cruising*, Pacino's character looks in the mirror not to look at himself, but at the viewer, confronting them with their own act of moral judgment. In a taped interview on the Dick Cavett Show, Friedkin remarks that *Jade* is about "the secrets that husbands and wives have from each other."[48] In these final shots, Friedkin seems to be suggesting that once the masks are off, once the logic of the fetish and its collusion with criminality are exposed, Trina nevertheless remains trapped within Matt's judgmental gaze. When the masks are removed, all are revealed to be sinners, including those who were thought to be innocent of crime.

KILLER JOE (2011)

As in *Jade*, the plot elements of *Killer Joe* revolve around an unseen dead person. In Friedkin's 1995 film, the murdered Medford leaves behind a myriad of fetishistic objects and criminal relationships that reflect the desires of the wealthy San Francisco businessman. And in Friedkin's 2011 film, a poor woman from rural Texas is murdered by a hitman cop hired by her son and ex-husband. Her death sets a series of transactions into motion that will come to a head at the end of *Killer Joe*. The characters in this film interact with each other in accordance with the ethics of reciprocity, an ethics that motivates their pursuit of old testament justice, such that money and virtue become exchangeable as individuals act and react according to the logic of *quid pro quo*. The violent murders of these characters take place off screen, hidden from the view of the spectator. *Jade* and *Killer Joe* place greater emphasis on the physical and psychic brutality that is committed by and between the living. Moreover, these films depict worlds that are fundamentally compromised morally, where policemen transgress the law they are supposed to uphold and become cold-blooded murderers.

In this, *Killer Joe* returns us to Friedkin's thematic obsessions. Yet it also brings an unprecedented degree of terror to the corrupted cop in the character of Joe Cooper. In her essay on the film, Christina Marie Newland contextualizes this character within the literary legacy of the Southern Gothic, including work by William Faulkner, Charles Laughton's 1955 film *The Night of the Hunter*, as well as the legacy of slavery, sex, and violence in the South.[49] Played by Matthew McConaughey, Joe's entrance is signaled by the clicking sound of his Zippo lighter, triggering fear and dread each time it is heard on the soundtrack. The final scene, when Joe takes stock of the moral and financial debts incurred by the dysfunctional Smith family, will be difficult to watch for most viewers in its explosive violence and exploitative brutality. Shots depicting Sharla (Gina Gershon) fellating a fried chicken leg and the sadistic beating of Chris (Emile Hirsch) with a tin can were among those that earned *Killer Joe* an NC-17 rating.

Much of *Killer Joe* will take place in the enclosed space of the Smith trailer home. As with Friedkin's early films, this film is based on a theater script and works with the constraints set by the delimited space of a theater stage. The scriptwriter, Tracy Letts, was born and raised in Oklahoma and has written three plays, all set in the South. "I love the material," Friedkin writes, "and I believe Tracy's work is a direct line from Harold Pinter's, which had so profound an effect on me."[50] Earlier, we saw how Friedkin's use of space allowed him to exploit the dichotomy between inside and outside, one that is fundamental to the expressive discourse of the melodramatic mode. We also saw how enclosed spaces in Friedkin's films are key to producing narrative tension, which builds toward their explosive climaxes by undermining essential elements of the melodramatic from within. He returns to the cinematic and ethical conditions imposed by enclosed spaces in *Killer Joe* with the depiction of the Smith trailer home. Here the small living room and dingy kitchen, lit by drab fluorescent lighting, are connected to each other, while Dottie's bedroom is at the end of a short hallway. The walls of the trailer home are paper thin: conversations and any violent movements can be heard clearly from one end to the other. "I find *Killer Joe* very cinematic," Friedkin remarks, in an interview conducted in 2014, "in that it's about action and character. The action is sometimes weird, you might think, and the characters are all bent. There's no question about that. These are flawed people, but that's where drama comes from—from *the crooked timber of humanity*."[51] This reference, originally formulated by Kant in his essay on universal history, points to a need for universal laws and norms among individuals who are born morally autonomous.

If the space delineated by the family typically functions as a space of innocence within melodrama, the family in *Killer Joe* begins in a fragmented state and will be broken down even further and imploded from within. The film opens with a chaotic scene that takes place in a trailer park, late at night. Heavy rain falls while an unseen dog barks intimidatingly. Chris Smith climbs out of his car, runs through the mud, and pounds on the door of his family's trailer home while yelling at the dog to shut up. An exterior light comes on above the front door. As it opens, a woman's bare genitals appear eye-level with Chris. In stark contrast to the medium shot as it is typically utilized in narrative cinema, the woman who appears at the door is shown from the waist down, grotesquely depersonalizing her and reducing her identity to her sex. Sharla lets Chris inside and irritably explains she did not know it would be him as he enters the dimly-lit trailer home. Chris's father Ansel (Thomas Haden Church), in dirty long johns, enters the room, takes a beer from the refrigerator in the adjacent kitchen, and spits into the carpet, seemingly oblivious to the belligerence rising between his son and wife.

Following the chaos of the opening scene, Chris takes Ansel to a strip club to talk in private. While Ansel stares at the topless women, Chris explains that had he pushed his mother, Ansel's ex-wife Adele, against the refrigerator because she stole his stash of cocaine. He owes local gangster Digger Soames (played by Marc Macaulay) $6,000 and will be killed if he is not paid. Ansel does not have the money to help Chris, but they devise a plan. Adele has a $50,000 life insurance policy and his younger sister Dottie (Juno Temple) is the sole beneficiary of this money. Chris will hire Dallas detective "Killer Joe" Cooper to murder Adele. The funds from the payout will be divided three ways between Ansel, Dottie, and Chris. Ansel adds that he wants a four-way split, with his girlfriend Sharla also getting a cut. "I found her. She's my ex-wife," the father remarks, claiming her future corpse as his.

Throughout the film the Smiths violently abuse, cheat on, and steal from one another. For these reasons the Smiths remain largely unsympathetic. They are connected to each other, not in the emotional sense typically accorded to familial relations and the roles generally assigned to each member, but through relations of debt, guilt, and obligation. Among them they circulate pain, injury, and reconciliation according to the logic of tit-for-tat that has the character of binding contracts, always with conditions. Presupposing these ethical concepts is the quantification of life and thus the question of the value of Adele's unseen body, which is reduced to the amount of relief her death will bring to Chris's suffering. All the melodramatic and Oedipal meaning typically mobilized toward motherhood is evacuated here. Her being is reduced to pure exchange-value, an object that will be traded for cocaine money, to fund her own murder, and to pay off debts, both financial and moral, incurred by members of her immediate family. In *On the Genealogy of Morality*, Nietzsche explains this "primeval," transactional ethics that demands that the victim of injury respond to their victimizer with an equal and opposite quantity of pain.

> And where did this primeval, deeply-rooted and perhaps now ineradicable idea gain its power, this idea of an equivalence between injury and pain? I have already let it out: in the contractual relationship between *creditor* and *debtor*, which is as old as the very conception of a "legal subject" and itself refers back to the basic forms of buying, selling, bartering, trade and traffic.[52]

Chris's debt has a ripple effect that compels others in the trailer to escape their individual misery by claiming money and the right to extract pain from others. Ansel works at a mechanic shop and Sharla waits tables at a pizza restaurant. Both desperately want out of the situation in which they find themselves and to escape their life of meager subsistence by any means possible. They are characters who feel trapped and, as Friedkin has stated in interview, "who perceive they have few alternatives except to act in absurd and often self-destructive ways."[53] In this, perhaps a more accurate term may be that they do not act, but can only react to their immediate situations, becoming something like political animals as described by Aristotle.

The titular character is introduced through a montage of close-up shots: gloved hands, hat, gun, boots, and sunglasses. Wearing the police badge, Joe enters the dysfunctional Smith family with the hope perhaps that he will save them from their selfish and desperate ways. Instead, he will reiterate and intensify the transactional ethics that constitutes the relations between them. Joe meets the father and son in an abandoned pool hall during the day to discuss the terms of their deal. He explains that he has two conditions: one, if they are caught, they cannot implicate Joe, or they will be killed. And two, his payment is $25,000 cash in advance. They are to follow these rules and no exceptions will be made. Chris explains they do not have the money, but will obtain it once the job is finished. Yet Joe repeats, as if speaking in the voice of the sovereign, "No exceptions." He rises to leave but stops in the doorway, snapping his lighter while watching Dottie dancing outside the pool hall in the bright sun. Reiterating his power to decide when the law may be applied, to others as well as himself, Joe proposes that he take the virginal Dottie as his "retainer" until he can collect his money.

The irony that persists through *Killer Joe* is that Joe, a corrupt officer of the law, seems to be the only character to manifest a clear moral code. As both hitman and detective, Joe enforces and lives by a set of rigorous rules that guarantee moral culpability and violent punishment if one attempts to shirk their responsibilities—his clients obey his demands or he does not take them in as clients—which he impresses on the Smith family. He grants himself the right to dole out punishment and reward, and to hold others accountable, rights that are maintained by his being on the side of the law. For the first time in this scene, Joe mentions that he will carry out a criminal act by murdering Adele. Up to this point she has been quantified in terms of exchange-value, yet the exchange of contractual language serves to further entrap the Smiths into the dynamics of guilt and debt. Adele's murder is given a moral meaning, but Joe explains this only to assert power over them, not to enforce the law.

We already see here a paradoxical relationship to the law that Joe represents. He is an outlaw of a sort and exists in a moral universe beyond juridical law. When he enters the claustrophobic space of the Smith family trailer, the cop re-territorializes their moral universe so that they are individually beholden to him, financially and morally. The space of melodramatic innocence that seems never to have existed for the Smith family is taken over by Joe, who becomes their surrogate father figure. When he takes Dottie as his retainer and then seduces her in the living room, he also becomes their creditor. In that scene, he tells Dottie to recall her first love and they enact a fantasy where Dottie and Joe are thirteen years old and have sex for the first time. The actual age difference between them is disconcertingly stark. As she recalls her first boyfriend, Joe forces himself into her memory as he enters her from behind. The exchange of Dottie for money complete, Joe tethers himself to the Smiths by exploiting their plight further. Like McCann and Goldberg in *The Birthday Party*, he represents a force of menace that will violently upend moral norms and disrupt distinctions between victims and victimizers.

That Joe seems to embody a transgressive moral code is made more forceful in the violence depicted in the film's conclusion, for it quickly devolves into a spectacle of familial relations taken to their transgressive extreme. As with *Cruising* and *Jade*, the final scene of *Killer Joe* raises the moral stakes of what has come before it while exploding the ethical norms expected of the melodramatic mode. The family of four is about to have a dinner of Kentucky Fried Chicken together, including Joe as Dottie's boyfriend, in their trailer home. Sharla has been exposed for lying about the payout from Adele's life insurance policy, as she claims that the figure doubles in the case of accidental death. Growing impatient with her lies, Joe takes a small envelope of photographs from his jeans, removes one and accusingly asks Sharla, "Whose dick is that?" As we saw in *Jade*, Friedkin's male characters use explicit photographic evidence of a woman's infidelity to shame and blackmail her into what her lawmen/husbands hope will be a confession. Joe's incriminating question deems Sharla sexually and morally corrupt. Yet this evidence, used to trump Sharla's efforts to cheat her husband, reiterates how morality and money circulate between the members of the Smiths, now including Killer Joe. Sharla refuses to answer. Joe suddenly grabs her throat and slams her against a wall. She pleads for Ansel's help but her husband remains unresponsive while referring to Joe as "sir" and relinquishing his paternal authority. Sharla admits that it was Rex in the photos, Adele's former boyfriend and now Sharla's lover. The payout check, which Joe suddenly produces from his pocket, has been made out to Rex, complicating the relations between those inside and outside the family even further. Joe calmly takes off his watch and rolls his cuffs, then violently punches Sharla in the nose. He prepared similarly before taking Dottie's virginity in the same room, moments that connect his volatile body and its capacities for sex and violence to the space of the trailer home. A shot of Sharla's bloodied face heightens the shock of the assault, raising questions about whether her "punishment" can be seen as justified or excessively transgressive.

I discussed the assertion of sovereign power in terms of the logic of exception in Chapter 2, drawing from the work of Carl Schmitt. We saw how this assertion is manifest through many characters in Friedkin's films, particularly in the men who cross the fine line that divides ostensibly lawful policemen from lawless criminals. But the concept of sovereignty has another precedent in the work of Georges Bataille, who in Volume III of *The Accursed Share* thinks the problem of sovereignty in terms of transgression. He is quick to note that his theory of sovereignty "has little to do with the sovereignty of States, as international law defines it," thus making clear that his interest in sovereignty is as a kind of capacity or discourse that may be utilized by the state but is not identical to it.[54] Indeed, throughout Bataille's discussion of sovereignty in the *Accursed Share*, he speaks of it as grounded in the individual, the Nietzschean superman who gives birth to new values and to new notions of the human being. Sovereignty persists at the limit point of the profane, at the moment when the secular moral laws that govern the human world are rendered obsolete. "Alongside the man more or less constrained to serve, a sovereign man," he writes, underscoring with this juxtaposition the morality of the slave to that of the master.[55] Bataille extends this dichotomy, taken over from Nietzsche, by emphasizing that the sovereign man "refuses to accept the limits that the fear of death would have us respect in order to ensure, in a general way, the laboriously peaceful life of individuals."[56] While everyday man may be unwilling or unable to affirm death as intimately connected to life, remaining slavishly wedded to the anguish of its certain possibility, the sovereign man is somehow able to overcome this anguish, transgressing the sentiments and morals that the fear of death typically governs.

Indeed, transgression stands at the core of Bataille's theory of sovereignty in its profound defiance of the dictates of enlightenment modernity and the norms that underpin it. Yet this transgression is not an act of traversal whereby one passes from one self-enclosed stage of being to another. It emerges as a potentiality, as a capacity that is immanent to the actual and reappears in the virtual. The transgression of the sovereign does not simply settle in being, but is always unmade and made again in the capacity for perpetual potentiality which constitutes the very substance of sovereignty. We can think this more clearly in the context of melodrama and the rational ethics of reciprocity that forms its foundation. If sympathetic human victims are central to melodrama's production of virtue as a felt good, key to the production of the victim is a perceived moral imbalance between two parties. One commits an act of violence that affects another, constituting a relationship of moral credit and the production of a demand for reciprocal violence that is owed to the victim. This demand for reciprocity is typically called "justice," "righteous punishment," or "just revenge." Bataille's description of sovereignty transgresses this regime of ethical reciprocity, pushing its internal logic toward inoperability and ruination. This ethics transgresses the principles of justice and fairness, particularly within American democracy, that govern the give-and-take of punishment among individuals as well as the moral debts incurred by the memory of trauma. In so doing, it deigns to upend the very metaphysical foundations of melodrama itself and the concepts that typically underpin it, including that of the moral human being, the right to virtue, and the legitimate exercise of violence.

The depiction of violence in the final scene from Friedkin's *Killer Joe* escalates the melodramatic mode toward untenability, beyond that which may be justified through its ethical logic. Joe's violence transgresses the ethical metaphysics of melodrama from within it, yet precisely in doing so it provides the viewer with a glimpse of what Bataille calls sovereignty. Violence seems at all times ready to explode in these final moments. When it does so with Joe's sudden punch to Sharla's face, one is compelled to wonder if this shocking violence is just or necessary, while its lawfulness and ethics are thrown into question. Joe's upending presence destabilizes the underlying moral terms by which the viewer may judge the behavior of the characters in this film (Figure 3.4).

Figure 3.4 Smith family dinner

What happens next in *Killer Joe* takes the logic of transgressive violence even further. Joe dangles a KFC drumstick in front of his penis and demands that Sharla shamefully fellate it. He embodies the law in this scene, beating the truth out of Sharla, the one who has been deemed guilty by a figure who carries out violence with impunity, by any means necessary. She spits at Joe's feet. He grabs her by the throat and threatens her once more, "If you insult me again, I will cut your face off and wear it over my own." Friedkin frames this at a tight, low angle from the floor, forcing an uncomfortable intimacy between the viewer, Joe's animus, and Sharla's face smeared with blood, mascara, and tears. The morally compromised masks of *Jade* are exposed as such in *Killer Joe*, making visible the untenable violence exchanged between characters and the force of law without law that constitutes Schmitt's transgressive sovereignty. Finally broken, Sharla succumbs and sucks the drumstick between Joe's legs. Joe proclaims between heavy breaths that Ansel and Sharla must abide by their contract with him and not allow Chris to take Dottie. He did not receive his payment and the terms agreed upon dictate that Dottie now "belongs" to him fully. "I hold you all equally responsible," he accuses, between breaths. No exceptions. As Joe enforces his law, he also tests its discursive limits and capacity to transgress moral norms through his exercise of extreme violence. While he insists upon the ethics of reciprocity, which within melodrama justifies the use of violence by those who have suffered in the past, his enforcement of this very ethics is itself reiterated through cruelty, through sovereign power. The terror he invokes may be attributed to this transgression and the violent emergence of a moral order that renders the previous regime inoperable.

In enforcing his law, after proclaiming repeatedly that it had not been heeded, Joe lives up to his job as policeman and role as father and domesticates Sharla. The transgression that is depicted in this scene de-territorializes and re-territorializes the family structure, placing Joe, a violent force who arrives from outside the melodramatic space of the trailer, decisively at the head of the household. Through this, his presence allegorizes the violence that is at the foundation of the American family within capitalism and shatters the transactional ethics that typically constitutes its relations while taking the cruelty that is fundamental to this ethics to its self-destructive endpoint. Sharla's ostensible punishment, according to the film's moral logic, is not a result of her being unfaithful, but is rather because she does not acknowledge Joe's implicit and redemptive authority over her. Joe has Sharla prepare the table for supper and she obeys willingly. She will speak only once more, when Joe asks calmly about the iced tea she has prepared.

The trailer home becomes Killer Joe's domain. Within this enclosed space, the camera continues to stay in medium shot or closer. The quick editing matches the tension produced by McConaughey's volcanic performance, producing a sense of bewilderment with each cut while underscoring this actor's lean face and volatile body. This is Joe's show, after all, for he guides the movements, action, and the cinematography: when Sharla sets the table, Joe turns off one set of lights for another, changing the mood to a softer, more yellow ambience. This moment might even recall Grace Kelly's famous entrance in *Rear Window* when she switches on the lights for James Stewart's character. The violence that will explode after Joe changes the lighting remains unprecedented for both Hitchcock and Friedkin, however.

In a perverse moment, the family finally sits down to their chicken dinner. Joe asks Dottie if she wants white or dark meat, as well as any potato salad. Sharla, her face still bloodied and battered, serves tea. Dottie says grace. The Smiths sit around the table and, for a moment, portray the image of a kind of domestic innocence, becoming a reunited family about to eat at the same table. Joe taps his beer to make an announcement that he and Dottie are going to get married, inspiring protest and more vicious conflict. Chris challenges him and the men fight over the girl as if she were their property. (Significantly, Friedkin has written that, "Chris senses that there's a moral order to the world, but he can't quite grasp it."[57]) *Killer Joe* continues to swing between extreme moods, foregrounding the violence that threatens to break out at any moment from within the American family structure. Following some more scuffling with a steak knife and a can of pumpkin pie that results in more bloodshed, Dottie takes Joe's gun and shoots Chris and Ansel. With her gun pointed at Joe, she suddenly remarks, "I'm going to have a baby." Joe smiles, approaches Dottie with outstretched arms, and says, "A baby?" He apparently was not aware that she was pregnant. Friedkin cuts quickly to Ansel's and then to

Chris's decimated face. These close-ups identify the members of this newly constituted family, one where Joe steps in as the new father figure. The return to a space of innocence, typically delineated in relation to the nuclear family, is subverted fundamentally, inducing a dissonance in the bourgeois assumptions around who may be considered to be part of the family and who is deserving of sympathy. The absurdity of the final lines leaves the viewer profoundly unsettled with the prospect that this family will continue to exist in dysfunction. Friedkin cuts to a close-up of Dottie's finger sliding over the trigger. Clarence Carter's blatantly sexual song, *Strokin'*, from 1986, fades in on the soundtrack and the film abruptly ends.

The very last shot of the film is of Joe's smiling face, indicating that he looks forward to becoming the father of Dottie's baby and presumably her partner. Yet the sudden cut to the credits and the raucous song leaves viewers wondering what will happen next and compels them to reflect upon the violence that led up to this final shot. One may be left wondering whether Dottie pulled the trigger and killed Joe, or whether she gave in and acknowledged the new family to come. As the father of Dottie's baby, Joe is inducted as the new patriarch of the Smith household while the majority of the Smith family lies bloodied and dying. And with his induction, Joe also introduces the possibility of a new law, a new moral regime that will break away from the old secular law by inaugurating a new ethics, one that is to emerge following the death of the old gods. He becomes the sovereign father that explodes and recasts the nuclear family and is, as Foucault puts it, "made and unmade by that excess which transgresses it."[58] The reciprocal ethics that bound members of the Smith family, the violence exchanged between them, the guilt and debts that made them beholden to one another—this regime, one inextricably linked to the melodramatic mode, is transgressed and annulled, giving way to the possibility of new, yet unknown, forms of redemption, of justice, and of the moral human. As the Smith family is sacrificed while Joe emerges as their mad patriarch, one may be reminded of a question around transgression formulated by Nietzsche, to quote his *On the Genealogy of Morality* once more:

> "Is an ideal set up or destroyed here?" you might ask me . . . But have you even asked yourselves properly how costly the setting up of *every* ideal on earth has been? How much reality always had to be vilified and misunderstood in the process, how many lies had to be sanctified, how much conscious had to be troubled, how much "god" had to be sacrificed every time? If a shrine is to be set up, a *shrine has to be destroyed*: that is the law—show me an example where this does not apply![59]

Killer Joe makes clear that the creation of a new regime of morality is inextricably linked to violence, that which destroys, and to what may be perceived as profoundly unsettling. These stakes not only comprise Nietzsche's critique of morality but also the apocalyptic fantasy of Friedkin's film, the faith in a sovereign figure and the aspirational belief that only a "God" can save us.

NOTES

1. William Friedkin, *The Friedkin Connection* (New York: Harper, 2013), 369.
2. Arthur Bell, "Bell Tells," *The Village Voice*, July 16, 1979, 36.
3. Linda Ruth Williams, *The Erotic Thriller in Contemporary Cinema* (Bloomington: Indiana University Press, 2005), 135. See also William Friedkin, *The Friedkin Connection* (New York: Harper, 2013): "*Cruising* was going to be controversial and possibly offend everyone, but for me it was just an exotic background for a murder mystery" (365).
4. Quoted in Christopher Lane, ed., *William Friedkin: Interviews*, Conversations with Filmmakers Series (Jackson: University of Mississippi Press, 2020), 43.
5. Lane, *William Friedkin: Interviews*, 43.
6. Alexander Wilson, "Friedkin's *Cruising*, Ghetto Politics, and Gay Sexuality," *Social Text* 4 (Autumn 1981), 100.
7. Vito Russo, *The Celluloid Closet: Homosexuality in the Movies* (New York: Harper, 1987), 259.
8. Robin Wood, "The Incoherent Text: Narrative in the 70s," in *Hollywood from Vietnam to Reagan* (New York: Columbia University Press, 1986), 61.
9. Robin Wood, "The Incoherent Text," 59.
10. Guy Davidson, "'Contagious Relations': Simulation, Paranoia, and the Postmodern Condition in William Friedkin's *Cruising* and Felice Picano's *The Lure*," *GLQ: A Journal of Lesbian and Gay Studies* 11, no. 1 (2005), 25.
11. David Greven, *Psycho-Sexual: Male Desire in Hitchcock, De Palma, Scorsese, and Friedkin* (Austin: University of Texas Press, 2013), 186.
12. Eve Kosofsky Sedgwick, *Epistemology of the Closet* (Berkeley: University of California Press, 2008), 11.
13. Stephen Snyder, "*Cruising*: The Semiotics of S & M," *Canadian Journal of Political and Social Theory/Revue Canadienne de théorie politique et sociale* 13, no. 1-2 (1989), 103.
14. Friedkin, *The Friedkin Connection*, 369.
15. Williams, *The Erotic Thriller*, 136.
16. Thomas D. Clagett, *William Friedkin: Films of Aberration, Obsession and Reality* (Los Angeles: Silman-James Press, 2003), 250-1.
17. Erica Carter, ed., *Béla Balázs: Early Film Theory*, trans. Rodney Livingstone (New York: Berghahn Books, 2011), 194.
18. Davidson, "'Contagious Relations,'" 49.
19. D. A. Miller, "*Cruising*," *Film Quarterly* 61, no. 2 (January 2007), 71.
20. Gerald Walker, *Cruising* (New York: Stein and Day, 1970), 8.
21. Adrian Martin, "The Sound of Violence," *Undercurrent* 4 (October 2008), accessed February 14, 2021, <http://fipresci.hegenauer.co.uk/undercurrent/issue_0407/martin_cruising.htm>
22. Damon Young, *Making Sex Public and Other Cinematic Fantasies* (Durham, NC: Duke University Press, 2018), 153.
23. Young, *Making Sex Public*, 142.
24. Michel Chion, *The Voice in Cinema*, trans. Claudia Gorbman (New York: Columbia University Press, 1999), 126.

25. See "Norman; or, the Impossible Anacousmêtre" in Chion, *The Voice in Cinema*, 123–51.
26. Balázs, *Early Film Theory*, 205.
27. See James Lastra, "Sound Theory," in *Sound Technology and the American Cinema: Perception, Representation, Modernity* (New York: Columbia University Press, 2000).
28. Stephen Heath, "Narrative Space" in *Questions of Cinema* (Bloomington: Indiana University Press, 1981), 56.
29. Michel Foucault, *The History of Sexuality, Vol. 1*, trans. Robert Hurley (New York: Pantheon Books: 1978), 155.
30. Miller, "*Cruising*," 73.
31. Williams, *The Erotic Thriller*, 80.
32. See Edward Guthmann, "'Jaded' Is More Like It / It's got sex, murder and it's all in San Francisco," *SFGate*, October 13, 1995.
33. Barbara Schulgasser, "This 'Jade' Isn't Even Semiprecious," *San Francisco Examiner*, October 13, 1995.
34. Kenneth Turan, "Movie Review: Friedkin's 'Jade' Mines Familiar Territory," *Los Angeles Times*, October 13, 1995.
35. Irene Lacher, "William Friedkin takes a high-speech chase through his career," *Los Angeles Times*, May 12, 2013.
36. Friedkin, *The Friedkin Connection*, 408.
37. Clagett, *William Friedkin*, 349.
38. Terry Pristen, "Friedkin Signing Keeps *Jade* in Lansing Family," *Los Angeles Times*, 18 April 1994.
39. Williams, *The Erotic Thriller*, 139.
40. See Stephen Galloway, *Leading Lady: Sherry Lansing and the Making of a Hollywood Groundbreaker* (New York: Crown Archetype, 2017), 233–5.
41. Friedkin, *The Friedkin Connection*, 413–14.
42. Friedkin, *The Friedkin Connection*, 414.
43. Joe Eszterhas, *Hollywood Animal: A Memoir* (New York: Alfred A. Knopf, 2004), 597.
44. Eszterhas, *Hollywood Animal*, 597.
45. Sigmund Freud, "Fetishism," in *The Complete Psychological Works of Sigmund Freud, Vol. XXI*, trans. James Strachey (London: Hogarth and the Institute of Psychoanalysis, 1973), 154.
46. Linda Ruth Williams, "Erotic Thrillers and Rude Women," *Sight & Sound* 3, no. 7 (July 1993), 13.
47. Williams, *The Erotic Thriller*, 158.
48. "The Dick Cavett Show: Contemporary Directors: October 14, 1995 William Friedkin," Shout Factory TV, accessed February 14, 2021, www.shoutfactorytv.com/the-dick-cavett-show/contemporary-directors-october-14-1995-william-friedkin/57b6131db13fd60d1800abb7.
49. Christina Marie Newland, "Archetypes of the Southern Gothic: *The Night of the Hunter* and *Killer Joe*," *Film Matters* 5, no. 1 (Spring 2014), 33–8.
50. Friedkin, *The Friedkin Connection*, 470–1.
51. Lane, *William Friedkin: Interviews*, 127.
52. Friedrich Nietzsche, *On the Genealogy of Morality*, trans. Carol Diethe (Cambridge: Cambridge University Press, 2006), 43.
53. Naomi Pfefferman, "'Killer Joe's' William Friedkin: 'I could have been a very violent person,'" *Jewish Journal*, August 2, 2012.
54. Georges Bataille, *The Accursed Share Vols II & III*, trans. Robert Hurley (New York: Zone Books, 1989), 197.
55. Bataille, *Accursed Share*, 214.

56. Bataille, *Accursed Share*, 221.
57. Friedkin, *The Friedkin Connection*, 459.
58. Michel Foucault, "Preface to Transgression," in Donald F. Bouchard, ed., *Language, Counter-Memory, Practice: Selected Essays and Interviews by Michel Foucault* (Ithaca: Cornell University Press, 1977), 32.
59. Nietzsche, *On the Genealogy of Morality*, 70.

CHAPTER 4

Justice at the Limits of Popular Cinema

THE PEOPLE V. PAUL CRUMP (1962)

Friedkin was born and spent much of his childhood in Chicago's North Side, a working-class neighborhood populated by first-generation European immigrants—Jewish, German, Irish, and Polish—that arrived in the first half of the twentieth century. An only child, he lived in a small apartment on North Sheridan Road with his mother and father, and attended Hebrew School only a few blocks away. After he graduated high school in 1953, Friedkin began working in the mailroom of WGN studios and was promoted to floor manager for its television broadcast section. Here is where the budding director's education in film and media production began, not in film school, but on the television studio floor. He describes a typically hectic schedule in these early years:

> I was doing eight shows a day—kid shows, talk shows, variety programs; I became floor manager for the station's most important show, *They Stand Accused*, a live courtroom drama in which the lawyers were real, the judge was real, and the witnesses were all actors. All the participants were given a scenario earlier in the day, then we had an hour to rehearse before the show went out across the country, just before *The Jackie Gleason Show*.[1]

While attending a cocktail party in 1960—at this point he was working as a director at the local PBS channel WTTW—Friedkin met Father Robert Serfling, the chaplain at the Cook County Jail. The priest told the director about Paul Crump, a thirty-year-old, African-American death row inmate whom he thought might have been wrongfully convicted of murder. Friedkin was told of his forced confession and incarceration, and was later introduced to Crump. At the time, the inmate was in the middle of writing his semi-autobiographical novel *Burn, Killer, Burn!*, which would be published in 1962. Following his conversation with Crump, Friedkin decided to make a one-hour documentary about his case and asked cinematographer Bill Butler to film it. Butler would go on to work on a number of seminal films from the 1970s, including *The Conversation*, *Jaws*, and *One Flew Over the Cuckoo's Nest*. Both men began working in the WGN television studios and eventually entered the Hollywood industry at the same time, each having started out with minimal technical knowledge in cameras and film editing.

In *The Friedkin Connection*, published when the director was seventy-eight years old, he recounts a wealth of detail about the production of *The People vs. Paul Crump* (hereafter *Paul Crump*), including what Crump wore when they first met, what Warden Jack Johnson told him about the case, his dealings with gruff Chicago personalities such as Barry McKinley, the senior director at WGN, and Red Quinlan, the general manager of WBKB-TV, an ABC subsidiary in Chicago. Friedkin portrays himself as an ambitious young man with tremendous "street smarts" who, inspired by an innate desire for justice, breaks into documentary filmmaking to help a man he believes is innocent. Proposing the project to WGN-TV's Ed Warren, Friedkin implored at the time that, "There's a great documentary film in this. We could save an innocent man from the electric chair."[2] These and many other dialogues are recalled and presented to the reader verbatim in the autobiography, lending these recollections an in-the-moment drama. Friedkin apparently wrote the book largely from memory:

> The only thing I did was look up dates. I also went back and interviewed a number of people that I worked with. For example, I spent a week with Bill Blatty. It's all from memory. I wrote in longhand. It's the only way I can really think: from my brain, through my arm, to the pen and to the paper. It was a three-year process.[3]

In the short prologue to *The Friedkin Connection*, Friedkin explains his process of remembering and writing. Images and fragments of the past appeared to him "like fireflies" throughout the writing of the book.[4] Continuing to wax poetic, he describes how these fireflies flashed up at moments, illuminating, as if in a Proustian manner, "a dark corner of memory."[5] Nevertheless, as one works through the recollections narrated in his memoir, one cannot help wondering what is recalled with fidelity to historical reality and what details have been reconstructed and recast. Friedkin's fireflies illuminate the past, but the ontological status and veracity of what is illuminated remains in question. In my interview with him, Friedkin indicated that he is aware of the subjective nature of memory and during his process of reflecting on his life, he remarked:

> And you know what happens? Here's one of the things I learned. All of us are painting our own portraits. For ourselves and others. And we tend to, based on our own perspectives and styles, we tend to smudge out certain things. A self-portrait is often not in writing an autobiography, it's not a photograph, because you can even lie with a photograph, you can distort the lens, distort the light, you can distort the focus. And a lot of great artists have done all of that and more. The photographer I most admire is Cartier Bresson. Here it is, here's a snapshot of life. That's what I tried to do, but his camera is more honest than my prose.

These questions around memory and representation are posed in *Paul Crump* as they are presented through interviews, on-location footage, and re-enactments of Crump's memories. In Friedkin's first film production, the past is reconstructed in a manner that develops moral sentiment as a means to critically expose the violence of police brutality and the limits of criminal justice, a critique that we have already seen operating in many of Friedkin's films. It incorporates archival footage but rarely strays far from its mission to build sympathy for Crump's plight. If *Paul Crump* may be thought of as political documentary, it also veers toward the realm of docudrama, where historical events are dramatized and, recalling his early days working on *I Stand Accused*, the real Crump is cast alongside a number of individuals involved with his case played by actors. This penchant for bringing actors together with individuals who play actual roles in society is a practice that would find its paranoid culmination in *Cruising*, as we saw in Chapter 3.

Moreover, as a film that concerns itself with a man accused of murder and whose testimony remains in question, at least in the eyes of the law, *Paul Crump* asks the viewer to re-litigate Crump's guilt as if they were a sitting member of a jury at a trial. Evaluating the images and sounds of the film, linking cause to effect, the viewer is called upon to ascertain his culpability beyond a reasonable doubt and ultimately to judge whether he is deserving of the death penalty. The film's trial-like structure recalls Carol Clover's broad claim about the portrayal of suspected criminals in American cinema: "real-life trials become movies (by which I mean both film and television dramas) as easily as they do in the Anglo-American world both because trials are already movielike to begin with and movies are already trial-like to begin with."[6] In her essay, "Law and the Order of Popular Culture," Clover points to the adversarial nature of courtroom discourse and role of the jury as fundamental elements of the Anglo-American trial, elements that are readily translated into the popular mode of the cinema through the gathering of relevant data to induce competing narrative possibilities, the plot twist that manifests often adversarial possibilities, and the solicitation to the viewer to link guilt with villainy. For Clover, the interpellation of the viewer as a kind of jury member in the movies becomes relevant not only for the genre of the courtroom drama but also for a wide swath of Anglo-American film, television, and popular entertainment. Aside from the films by Friedkin that feature explicit courtroom sequences, such as *Rules of Engagement* and those featured in this chapter, we can also point to others such as *The French Connection*, *The Exorcist*, *Cruising*, and *Jade* as instances of films whose plots are already trial-like in the manner Clover describes, while critically engaging the practice of judgment in the cinema.

If *Paul Crump* introduces themes around judgment that the director will repeatedly return to throughout his oeuvre, it is seminal in another aspect, in a way that has more to do with the formal elements of this and many of his other films: montage. In 1975, the filmmaker remarked that, "To me, editing is more exciting, more interesting, more discovery prone, more important than any other facet of filmmaking."[7] He later remarks in the interview that he would be an editor full-time "if I could make as much money at it, if I could live the same life-style, as I do by directing."[8] Friedkin's films insist upon the juxtaposition of shots in linking action to characterization, and to this linkage the judgment of character. If memory is subject to the politics of melodrama in *Paul Crump*, both are constituted formally through this director's tendency to cut in a manner that heightens the tension between knowing and not knowing in relation to the moral orientation of a character on screen. After establishing some concepts between film form and the solicitation of spectatorial judgment, we shall continue to work with this problematic through three additional films that comprise three decades of the director's career: *Rampage*, *12 Angry Men*, and *Bug*.

Paul Crump quickly presents the alleged crimes that took place ten years earlier. Crump was incarcerated following his participation in a robbery at the Libby, McNeill & Libby meatpacking plant in March 1953. While a security guard was shot and killed during their escape, the five men involved managed to leave the scene with the stolen payroll money. A week later, they were picked up by police, arrested, and charged with robbery. Crump, twenty-two years old at the time, was charged with murder as well. Within two months he was convicted and sentenced to death. Throughout his time in prison, he maintained his innocence and was educated and rehabilitated under the tutelage of Warden Johnson, becoming a model prisoner and later an assistant in the medical ward. Between 1953 and 1962, Crump was given fifteen execution notices and was granted fourteen stays, experiences that subjected his life to the whims of the legal system.

The film opens with a shot of Crump and his two cell mates with someone playing the harmonica. A voice interrupts this forlorn music, quickly establishing a man's anguish: "Warden, Paul Crump has been up to the brink of doom and back down again, six, eight times, something like this?" Johnson's voice responds to the question, commenting on Crump's mental state:

> It's been eleven times, I think, for Paul on dates and about forty continuances in relation to his case over a period of eight years and this in itself is mental torture. These men live from day to day and of course with this pressure I'm inclined to think that they die daily with it.

The film's beginning solicits sympathy for Crump's beset condition and the emotional toil he has experienced as the state maintains power over whether he is to live or die. Subjected to the authority to decide that belongs to the power of the sovereign, the incarcerated man suffers as a result of its indecision and, with every juridical reversal, Crump is reminded of his own powerlessness with regard to his own destiny. The short exchange that opens *Paul Crump* also introduces the viewer to John Justin Smith, a critic and reporter for the *Chicago Daily News*, who asks questions of the warden and interviews key individuals related to the case. He also provides a running commentary on the visuals, offering at times a critical, moralizing perspective on the inhumanity of the justice system. When Crump tells his story, he is filmed being interviewed by Smith, who functions as a stand-in for Friedkin's role and may be aligned with his perspective as well.

Following the opening shots and credits, *Paul Crump* quickly settles into its fast-paced and elliptical style. The film does not simply present the events leading up to Crump's incarceration but re-presents them through re-enactment, showing the viewer short shots of a car heading to the stockyard, of cattle being let in to be fed and slaughtered, a guard manicuring his fingernails, women working in the meatpacking office, and five men getting out of the car and then entering the plant. A quick zoom onto an open bag of money, over $17,000 that will be paid out to plant employees, draws the viewer's attention to the stakes of the crime that will soon take place. Meanwhile, Smith's voice comments occasionally over the montage of images, telling the viewer that the payroll process proceeds like clockwork and that the factory guard is a family man. The solo guitar soundtrack rises in intensity as male and female employees are robbed, and as the family man is shockingly shot in the face. Throughout the sequence the voiceover remains unidentified, an acousmatic narrator without body, like the disembodied voice that signals the serial killer at the end of *Cruising*. It is only when the re-enactment of the robbery and subsequent murder take place that the narrator's voice identifies himself as Smith of the *Chicago Daily News*. Meanwhile, the man who shot and killed the guard is not the Crump we saw in the film's opening shot, but an actor (Brooks Johnson) playing a younger version of him. One may experience some bewilderment as the ontological status of these images and voices are never introduced and identified. *Paul Crump* disorients the viewer by reorienting elements that are constitutive of the reality of cinematic narrative: the relationship

Figure 4.1 Interview with Paul Crump

between sound and image (and by co-extension between voice and speaking body) and generic expectations that delineate documentary from re-enactment.

And while Smith begins narrating in the first person, thus identifying his voice as that of a newspaper reporter, Friedkin's film continues to develop this critical reorientation, provoking questions around the use of violence utilized by the Chicago police. Taking the viewer to the present moment, Smith interviews Johnson in standard shot-reverse shot format (Figure 4.1). These images embody the voices that were first heard at the start of the film. The warden explains that they employed Crump in convalescent care and that he has been taking care of prison inmates with physical and mental disabilities. While he speaks, the film cuts to documentary footage of Crump helping a man remove his shirt, shaving another inmate, and then interacting with a nurse. These are short shots that support and illustrate Johnson's belief that Crump has been rehabilitated and now attends to the "needs of his fellow man." While Johnson has clearly shown compassion by taking Crump under his wing, he also embodies a profound paradox for it will be his job to perform the execution if Crump is to be put to death.

This sequence recalls a similarly structured one where the voice leads the images in Fritz Lang's *M*, made in 1931. In this Weimar German film, which Friedkin knows well, the commissioner of police speaks to the minister about the procedures that have been deployed to pursue the child murderer, Hans Beckert, while images of the investigation accompany their conversations.

Sequences in *Paul Crump* are edited with a similar principle in mind, with the voice leading the images, allowing them to be organized not according to principles of linear space and time but according to the flow of what is narrated. And through this the voices of Smith and Johnson shift from being subjective to a kind of objective narration, becoming embodied, disembodied, and then, as their lips speak the words that the spectator hears, re-embodied again. The voices of Crump, his mother, and his lawyer will be introduced as well, entering into the film as if in a dream, later becoming embodied by the images of their speaking bodies. They will also acquire a narrational status as the film cuts to re-enactments from Crump's memory and play out his alibi of spending the night with a woman at the time of the shooting. We also see a re-enactment of the moment when Crump, played by the young actor, was apprehended at his mother's house. The mother is in turn played by his real-life mother, Lonie Crump.

Abrupt cuts continue to occur throughout the film. Most of these shots are not allowed to linger. They emphasize quick assessment, not contemplation, not the gaze but the glance, and provide only the information necessary to propel the narrative forward. This editing seems to attempt to depict what Slavko Vorkapich calls a "perception of the *shapes, of the motions* that things generate."[9] First published in 1959, Vorkapich's ideas on "true cinema" would come to influence Friedkin's ideas on montage after the director attended the lectures of the Serbian film theorist at USC in 1972.[10] Although he writes that hearing these lectures "increased my understanding of the possibilities of cinema," a number of key concepts introduced by Vorkapich could already be discerned in *Paul Crump*.[11] Specifically, the editing in Friedkin's film takes the viewer quickly toward possible actions and the capabilities of things, potentialities that connect them to other worldly things and bodies through the possibility of affecting and being affected by them. In contrast to the long take, which records the pro-filmic event as merely an "embellished" recording, montage reconstitutes the kinetic potentiality of objects through the visual impact that is specific to the cinema.[12] In the following passage, Vorkapich describes the process of teaching students how this visual impact may be discovered in everyday actions:

> The project following these exercises consists in a thorough observation of a complete simple activity or occupation where a limited variety of motions is involved. Again the emphasis is on the motions of objects, for example in the wrapping of a package, preparing food, loading of a truck, etc. The complete action is broken down into as many simple motions as possible and each shot from a great variety of angles. This kind of analysis, or overanalysis, is different from recording previously discussed. Here the motion-picture camera is in its natural element.

This process is really a filmic liberation of bits of dynamic visual energies, extracted from a simple event in reality. None is intended for an individual display as a "best shot" in the picture, not any more than a note is intended to be the best in a melody. In the recreation of the event in cutting, each filmic fact acquires value only by its place in the total filmic structure. And the student's sense for structure grows out of these exercises in analysis.[13]

In this and other passages, Vorkapich adopts the language utilized by Sergei Eisenstein, such as "energy" and the "melody," but deploys them in a manner that emphasizes how the vitality of events in reality may be recreated cinematically. Indeed, one may identify a distinctive Bergsonian streak in this thinking, one that is grounded in the capacity of bodies to affect and to be affected by others. The mission of the motion picture, for Vorkapich, is to express this vitality through editing, which for him consolidates the specific art of the cinema. Commenting on a sequence from Robert Flaherty's documentary, *Man of Aran*, where screen direction is confused, Friedkin mentions the theorist and writes that:

These shots are cut together rapidly and seem to draw our attention to the action more intently than if the proper screen direction had been maintained. It was a kind of cinematic cubism. Vorkapich said the most important function of a film director was to immerse the audience so deeply in a sequence that they would not be conscious of screen direction.[14]

Affective and emotional engagement in a film is paramount, in other words, more crucial than not violating the 180-degree rule and the prescriptions of linear time and space. For Vorkapich, continuity should not simply follow the principles of causality that ostensibly dictate external reality, but should, above all, reveal the "dynamic visual energies" that are constitutive of the movement of objects, the relations between them, and of the moving image as well.

This kinetic energy produced through fast montage sequences may be identified in key moments from Friedkin's cinema, including the chase sequences in *The French Connection* and *The Hunted*, the quick dialogues in *The Birthday Party* and *The Boys in the Band*, but also in the construction of spaces and actions that take place in *To Live and Die in L.A.* Interspersed with moments of standard "talking head" documentary, *Paul Crump* consists of passages that utilize a kind of "cubist" approach toward the recreation of subjective memory.[15] Sequences of images conform not to the rational organization of the external world but to the flow of discourse by characters in the film, bringing the spectator into the subjective interior of the remembered past. The movement depicted throughout

Friedkin's film thus does not simply express the movement of things in the world but also of memory and affect, their potentialities, of past perception recalled and made public as image and sound. The precise temporality of these images may seem confusing at times for they unfold through memory fragments in *Paul Crump*, expressing the sense of temporal dislocation that Crump must have experienced during his years in prison.

At the same time, as they are articulated and structured through sound design and editing, these images of matter and memory participate immediately in the moral sentiment and sovereign judgment that belong to the melodramatic mode. Melodrama structures and engages this sentiment through the elicitation of pathos before the image of Crump's suffering. In so doing, it draws attention to the historical criminalization of his body by white supremacist police officers and to the legacy of institutional racism that has historically dehumanized African-Americans. *Paul Crump* engages in what Linda Williams calls the "melodrama of black and white," bringing together in a chiasmus popular moving picture narrative, the redemptive aims of American justice, and the profoundly unequal relations produced by the problems of race.

This appeal to recognize Crump's victimization is made most forcefully in one particularly intense moment from the film, in the account depicting his interrogation by a group of white policemen. Tied up and shirtless, and starved of food for two days, Crump was fed information by the interrogators and induced to confess to the murder of the security guard at the meatpacking plant. Hung up by his arms, he is held up as a Christ-figure, questioned and taunted by the investigating officers like Jesus was by the Romans. "I started praying out loud," Crump recounts in voiceover, "I started saying the Hail Mary. I started saying Our Father." He had been a practicing Catholic his entire life and one may recall here the story that is signified by the Shroud of Turin. Close-up shots of the face of the actor playing Crump underscore his anguish. Breaking down emotionally on the dialogue track, the tormented man continues,

> One come up to me and he hit me in the stomach and told me to stop praying. He says, "You black son of a bitch, so what do you know about God?" He said, "What would the white mother of God want to do with a black son of bitch like you?"

Crump's voice breaks down once more while the image of his young re-enactor writhes in agony. The violent and cruel actions of the interrogators solicit the outrage of viewers who perceive the injustice of his persecution while sympathizing with Crump's despair. His body becomes a sign of his physical and emotional vulnerability, an image that expresses his subjective agony. For some, this image may compel the demand for action, to right the wrongs perpetrated by his victimizers. Meanwhile, the editing in this sequence is constructed according to the logic of affection that circulates between the bodies of the accusers and accused, those who judge and are judged, with close-ups of Crump's face, then of his tormentors, a clenched fist about to strike, and then a medium shot of the body of the accused twisting in pain. The violent intent issuing from the police interrogators and directed at Crump's body seems to inform the body of Friedkin's film and its expression of heterogeneity and dissonance. Like a fugue in two voices, the visual montage, in this and other sequences throughout *Paul Crump*, weaves into and coincides with his audio narration then returns to pursue its own logic, elucidating a dynamic visual energy circulating among things and bodies.

Friedkin had induced Crump's cries by shouting and even, at one moment, slapping him in the face. "The slap brought back the physical and psychological pain he had experienced at the repeated beatings," he writes, making clear that he knew that he had re-traumatized Crump in order to get an "authentic" performance for the film.[16] This technique, once again crossing the discursive boundaries between the real and the staged, remains ethically problematic, to say the least. In using this approach, Friedkin places himself in the position of sovereignty occupied by the Chicago police. Both utilize exceptional means to force Crump's body to produce a certain kind of truth, one that will attest to the delineation of its capacity to either carry out or be the recipient of violence. Friedkin's position, moreover, once more plays out the ethical questions raised when critically thinking the thin line between policeman and criminal, and which I have tried to elucidate throughout this book.

The final ten minutes of *Paul Crump* provide the opportunity for Crump to reflect upon his impending death. After Johnson states that he does not believe in capital punishment, Crump affirms that his fate in the electric chair will be decided by the will of God. In a single take longer than perhaps all the others in the film, he poetically describes the thought of his own imminent death and wonders what will be accomplished by it. These ideas compel him to assess how one might begin to appreciate human life while attesting to its quantification when one is made subject to the punitive logic of the criminal justice system. We cut to a shot of a dripping faucet, typically a signifier for the passing of time, that is made strange through the sound not of dripping water but of electronic blips. Close-up shots of the apparatus of death—showing how the head, arms, and legs of the condemned are to be restrained—highlight its grim purpose. Made of metal and wood, the electric chair seems positively medieval in its crude construction. As Crump questions the ethics of capital punishment and its ostensible aim of providing redemption for those who grieve for the murdered man, Friedkin's film critiques this premise and suggests that this exchange of one death for another remains a futile game of moral one-upmanship. This is followed by shots of Smith surveying a construction site where a small group of African-American kids play King of the Hill. Although one boy reaches the top of a mound of dirt, the film implies that he will likely be replaced by another.

Crump's execution that was scheduled for August 1962 was commuted once more, although it is not clear whether Friedkin's documentary, which was released at the same time, influenced the Illinois governor's decision. Crump remained in prison and in 1970 was denied any possibility of parole due to the interpretation of contested language in the proclamation of commuting. Following this legal development, somewhat inexplicably he admitted to killing the security guard in 1953. It was also during this time that Crump began to be transferred from prison to prison. He was deprived of his typewriter, disallowed opportunities to mentor young prisoners, and humiliated by the chaplain at the Pontiac Correctional Center. After 1970 he began to show signs of mental illness and was reported to see hallucinations while exhibiting increasingly bizarre behavior. Meanwhile lawyers and psychiatrists continued to advocate for his parole. These were repeatedly denied and Crump was moved back and forth between prison and the Menard Psychiatric Center in southwestern Illinois. When he was finally granted a release from prison in 1993, his emotional condition had deteriorated and his mental illness had already become acute. One of his sisters obtained a restraining order against him which he violated in 2000. He returned to Menard and died of lung cancer in 2002. While *Paul Crump* compelled sympathy for Crump's plight, it was after the film was released in 1962 that his disastrous decline became truly heart-rending.

RAMPAGE (1987, 1992)

Rampage also revolves around the problem of character construction in the cinema and its relationship to criminal culpability. As with *Paul Crump*, Friedkin's 1987 film features an accused murderer and centers on the ethics of putting him to death for his crimes. Unlike in the earlier film, however, there is no question in the plot that Charlie Reece (Alex McArthur) killed not just one individual but multiple men, women, and children. *Rampage* is based on a book by William P. Wood of the same title, which recounts the case of Richard Chase, the so-called "Vampire of Sacramento" who drank the blood of those he killed. Chase murdered six people between December 1977 and January 1978 in a series of gruesome deaths involving necrophilia and cannibalism. In his research notes, Friedkin writes that Chase's victims were arbitrarily chosen and that he expressed delusions of grandeur.[17] *Paul Crump* mixed documentary footage with re-enacted scenes, and while the narrative of *Rampage* was based on a real case, this story is reconstructed in the mode of docudrama that characterizes so many of Friedkin's films.

The Reece of Friedkin's film, good-looking like the historical Chase, has more than a passing resemblance to the killer(s) in *Cruising*, with his jacket (though it is red leather and not black), long hair, and dark aviator sunglasses. (Later in *Rampage* we will see the dismembered arm of a child washed up on a riverbank, rotted and discolored green, matching the severed arm that appears at the beginning of Friedkin's 1980 film.) Reece also drinks the blood of his victims in order, according to him, to restore its purity after it was poisoned somehow through an old Faustian bargain with the devil. Apparently it was Satan, whose voice he claims to hear on the radio, who instructed him to murder. "I had to do it," Reece calmly remarks, "it was all up to me." The fear of contagion, which I argued informs the construction of the male protagonists in both *To Live and Die in L.A.* and *Cruising*, returns through Reece's character, manifest in the delusional paranoia that his blood has been contaminated by a malevolent force outside himself.

Quickly presented in the first few minutes, the crimes committed by Reece are clear, but Friedkin is more interested in the ethical problems surrounding the judgment of these crimes. The last forty minutes of this roughly ninety-minute feature film is comprised of a courtroom drama that plays out the politics of the insanity defense. While the prosecuting district attorney, Anthony Fraser (Michael Biehn), argues that Reece was fully aware of the moral consequences of his actions, the public defender, Albert Morse (Nicholas Campbell), insists that he was legally insane and did not rationally understand these consequences beyond his own delusions. And if Reece is deemed unfit to stand trial, he would be exempt from consideration for the death penalty and therefore permitted exceptional status under the law. An affirmative insanity case would preclude criminal prosecution for the murders he committed and Reece would be granted not only legal leniency but also the chance to elicit sympathetic pity and even heroic martyrdom. The *mise-en-scène* of the courtroom itself is constituted as a lit theatrical space circumscribed by darkness, reiterating the claustrophobic space of melodrama and the closed film as defined by Leo Braudy. Asserting the ostensible separation between law and popular melodrama, the presiding judge advises the jury, before they enter into deliberation, to decide their unanimous judgment based on "evidence" and not "sympathy."

According to an interview with Friedkin by Thomas Clagett, the inspiration for *Rampage* comes from two well-known cases that were publicized in the media, in addition to the Chase case: that of John Hinckley Jr., who tried to assassinate Reagan in 1981, and that of John Wayne Gacy, who horrifically murdered dozens of boys and young men between 1972 and 1978.[18] In both, the defense counsel presented their clients as insane and argued that they were mentally unfit to stand trial. During Gacy's trial in early 1980, the defense argued for the insanity plea, but in the end, after less than two hours of deliberation, he was found guilty of all charges and sentenced to death. He was placed on death row and expressed no remorse for his crimes until he died by lethal injection in 1994. Hinckley claimed that he was inspired by Travis Bickle's character in *Taxi Driver* when he shot at Reagan as the president was leaving a hotel in Washington, D.C. in 1981. He also became obsessed with and stalked Jodie Foster, who played the child prostitute in Scorsese's film. At Hinckley's trial in 1982, he was found not guilty by reason of insanity, causing widespread outrage and dismay. For his part, Friedkin frustratingly commented that, "It seems to me a serious blip in the system . . . I think the insanity plea has gotten way out of hand."[19] In May of 1980, Richard Chase was found guilty of multiple counts of first-degree murder and sentenced to death. As in the film, the defense tried to claim that Chase was insane during his heinous murders, but their arguments were rejected by the jury.

In addition to the Hinckley and Gacy cases, which Friedkin researched, another infamous case emerges as relevant to *Rampage*. Toward the end of the film, during the jury deliberation scene, a woman juror references another murderer, whom she calls "insane," and whose story was still unfolding roughly contemporaneously when the film was shown, that of Dan White. White served on the Board of Supervisors in San Francisco from 1977 to 1978 and in November of 1978 he shot and killed mayor George Moscone and supervisor Harvey Milk in San Francisco City Hall. During the trial, a psychiatrist representing White's defense testified that their client was depressed and in a "diminished" mental state during the time of the murders. Lawyers then stated that he started eating junk food because he was so distraught. Journalists mockingly dubbed this the "twinkie defense." White was found guilty, not of first-degree murder, but of voluntary manslaughter, and sentenced to seven years in prison. In 1984, he was paroled after serving five years and the following year he committed suicide in his garage by carbon monoxide poisoning. While deliberating on how to judge Reece in the film, the unnamed woman in the jury reflects upon and highlights the problem of whether he was criminally responsible or of diminished capacity. "Anybody who did what he did is insane. Dan White was insane. Maybe the whole world is insane." The comparable case is evidently on her mind and, perhaps, was on the minds of viewers of Friedkin's 1987 film.

Fraser and his wife are politically liberal at the start of *Rampage* and both stand against capital punishment for morally principled reasons. However, as the film's narrative unfolds, the prosecuting attorney becomes ever more obsessed and agitated by his gradual unraveling of these principles as his pursuit of the death penalty for Reece becomes increasingly determined by his demand for moral certitude. Indeed, one is reminded of Friedkin's similarly obsessed men in *The French Connection* and *To Live and Die in L.A.*, vigilante police detectives who flout the law in order to pursue their own moral righteousness. Significantly perhaps, *Rampage* was produced immediately following the latter film. While these works marshaled the action and violence of their main detective characters in their pursuit of the bad guy, in *Rampage* Fraser marshals the law in vengeful pursuit of the punishment of Reece.

Moreover, while *Paul Crump* mobilizes melodramatic pathos in order to compel viewers to feel and judge the death penalty as appalling, immoral, and tantamount to state-sanctioned murder, *Rampage* acknowledges the necessity of capital punishment under certain, perhaps exceptional, conditions. When Friedkin was asked to comment on the difference in the representation of the death penalty between the two films in my interview with him, he responded:

> I still don't subscribe to capital punishment. Except, if somebody does something so evil that it's beyond the pale. Like, Hitler, like the Manson family. I don't find any way to excuse Jeffrey Dahmer. I don't find any way to excuse that behavior. That cuts you loose from the pack. And it can be argued that we can learn more from these people alive than just executed. If you read my book you know I saw a man die from the electric chair. And it was legal murder. It was murder, premeditated murder on the part of the state against this guy who allegedly burned his wife and kids in his own house, shot them and then burned the house. I liked him. His name was Vincent Ciucci and I liked him a lot.

On the one hand, one gleans from Friedkin's statements that figures like Hitler, the Manson family, and Jeffrey Dahmer remain moral exceptions, "beyond the pale," who make the case for when state-sanctioned execution is necessary. On the other, such figures may also be somehow "liked," even thought of as sympathetic, as in the example of Ciucci, who died in the electric chair in the year *Paul Crump* was produced. *Rampage* seems to address this ambivalence. Throughout the trial, the arguments of both the defense and prosecution remain unconvincing in their argumentation. Moreover, both sides are clearly morally compromised and driven by motives having little to do with reasonable judgment. Fraser works through the trauma of his young daughter's death as he sympathizes with the boy whose mother was murdered by Reece. The prosecutor challenges the discourse of psychiatry and critiques the shoring up of power, expressed in the language of moral righteousness, of men who deign to judge the killer's character. A number of scenes build sympathy for Fraser's frustration at the use of the insanity plea as a defense strategy.

In his review of the film, however, Roger Ebert writes that *Rampage* remains unequivocal: "Friedkin does not quite say so in as many words, but his message is clear: Those who commit heinous crimes should pay for them, sane or insane. You kill somebody, you fry—unless the verdict is murky or there were extenuating circumstances."[20] For Ebert, characters in the film who believe that

Reece undergoes some sort of victimization by the prosecution and are thus sympathetic to the serial murderer's "plight" are ultimately unsympathetic. Janet Maslin of the *New York Times* writes that while *Rampage* offers "discreet exposition about the murders and their aftermath," it also "becomes a tirade against a judicial system that would spare someone like Reece by deeming him criminally insane."[21] Such readings perhaps say more about these critics' own entitlement to judge than about the film's representation of the politics of capital punishment, or about Friedkin's own position for that matter.

If we consider the politics of melodrama in *Rampage*, we can perhaps begin to appreciate it not as a film that espouses a definite stance with regard to capital punishment but as one that highlights the difficulty of ascertaining the truth of Reece's moral and psychological nature. Indeed, beyond the problem of ascertaining the truth of Friedkin's own beliefs about the death penalty, his film provides an opportunity to think critically about the construction and narrativization of character in the cinema. *Rampage* does not offer a clear motive for Reece's multiple murders and while he is clearly disturbed, the film does not establish a definitive etiology that might explain his mental condition.

A comparison may be made with a case that was unfolding contemporaneously on national television at the time, which allows a parallel to emerge between the narratives of serial killing presented by the news media and Friedkin's film. One year before it was completed in 1987, Ted Bundy, then thirty-nine years old, was granted a stay of execution in Florida on account of his mental incompetency at his trial. His lawyer at the time was against capital punishment on principle and made efforts to plea for Bundy's inability to understand the charges he was facing. These charges are well known and stretched back years. Starting in 1973, Bundy kidnapped, raped, and sadistically murdered thirty young women in seven different states. He was incarcerated in Utah in 1975 when his Volkswagen was searched and items used for the killings, including a ski mask, handcuffs, and trash bags, were found in the back seat. Coincidentally perhaps, like Reece in *Rampage*, Bundy escaped incarceration due to police negligence. Bundy left for Florida, where he murdered four students at Florida State University and later a twelve-year-old girl. In 1978, he was incarcerated once more, again following a background check initiated by a traffic stop. Facing murder charges, Bundy bewilderingly took part in his own defense during the trial in 1979, making requests to the judge, grandstanding, and even cross-examining witnesses. It was the first to be televised nationally in its entirety, bringing popular scrutiny of his discourse and demeanor while becoming a real-life courtroom drama. Good-looking, educated, and well-spoken, his pathology remained unclear throughout his trials and professional psychiatrists diagnosed him at various moments as having bipolar disorder, schizophrenia, as being a sociopath, or afflicted with narcissistic personality disorder. His fitness to stand trial was only considered seriously after the Florida jury found him guilty and he was given the death sentence.

Beyond the heinousness of Reece's crimes, based in various ways on a number of real-life cases, *Rampage* above all shows us how popular narrative, which heavily informed reportage of Bundy's contemporaneous case in the news media, puts judgment and the question of justice at stake. Bringing these issues into relief, one begins to notice that throughout the film, individuals, experts and non-experts, are constantly postulating about Reece's nature. On the witness stand, a childhood friend remarks that Reece had many pets and went out of his way to avoid violence of any kind. His scoutmaster calls him a "good boy." A nurse at a hospital where Reece was a patient found his diary and saw dates, times, and places of animals he had killed. A high-school girlfriend testifies, in response to a question by one of the examining lawyers, that they had a "normal" sexual relationship. Finally, Dr. Ruden (Roy London), a psychiatrist for the state, remarks that he concluded Reece to be "schizophrenic, of the paranoid type," and that he harbored delusions that the Tippetts family, his last murder victims, were Nazis. When Fraser asks whether he believes Reece was aware that what he did to the Tippetts was a crime, the psychiatrist remarks that he "had a sense that he was killing but rationally didn't understand what he was doing." His response evidently prepares his characterization of Reece as lacking in mind and judgment, thus aligning him with the side of the defense and their appeal to the serial murderer being insane when the crimes were taking place. Providing a bit of fodder for melodramatic and psychoanalytic judgment, these testimonies reveal relatively mundane snippets of Reece's personal development, from childhood up to the present day, which may indicate the moral or psychic etiology of his violent impulses and paranoid delusions. However, the film's narrative ultimately does not bring any of these details together in any coherent way. There is very little circumstantial evidence presented in these courtroom sequences, as Reece has already been deemed guilty of the murders.

The fact that the film fails to allow this series of verbal testimonies to coalesce in a coherent manner only problematizes the relationship between the private self and malicious intent even further. As Fraser continues to examine Ruden, the profound problem of securing a causal link between Reece's will to murder and his culpability, beyond any impulse that may be deemed delusional or insane, becomes increasingly clear. As the state prosecutor puts it, somewhat reductively, "Delusions and abnormal states don't necessarily equal murder." It is possible, he continues, for a man to commit serial murders and still be found legally sane. He reminds the doctor that some time ago his staff had deemed Reece fit to leave the care of the hospital and that now, because of political expediency or for other reasons (which are admittedly not made clear in the film's narrative), Ruden finds him insane. Presupposed in all of these attempts to characterize Reece's mental condition is a private self that nevertheless possesses free will, who either willed premeditated murderous actions or was stymied and thus victimized by his own delusions. Fraser repeatedly attempts to causally link this abstract Cartesian self, one that exists outside of history and beyond mental illness, to crime. Indeed, the American adversarial trial needs precisely such a subject to scrutinize, a democratic subject who chooses to aggressively violate the social contract or fall victim to a set of uncontrollable circumstances. And it is this authentic, isolated self, apparently unsullied by mental illness, that is to be judged—by the lawyers, psychiatrists, the jury, and ultimately by the viewer as well.

In an effort to bring greater legitimacy to the claim of Reece's mental state during his murder spree, more experts are consulted and other empirical methods of reading the self are mobilized. Forensic evidence, including photographs and confiscated objects, indicate the possibility of premeditation. Other psychologists, Dr. Benjamin Keddie (John Harkins) and Dr. Leon Gables (Donald Hotton), lend their authority to the problem of Reece's characterization. The physiology of his brain through CAT scanning offers neuroimages that provide evidence of the health of the private self within. Reading these images, Dr. Gables observes that the brain of the murderer exhibits no structural lesions and that its size and shape are normal. On the witness stand, he testifies that Reece is in good health, knows right from wrong, and should be considered legally sane. Dr. Keddie contradicts Gables's evaluation and observes that Reece's actions were driven by psychotic delusions and so he cannot be held responsible for them. "The notion of free will in Mr. Reece's case is an illusion," the expert psychiatrist explains, his voice rising, "his behavior was conditioned by forces beyond his control." He goes on to argue that Reece should not be put to death but studied, so that other similar cases, other serial murderers, may be prevented. Later a PET scan of his brain unequivocally indicates abnormal patterns consistent with schizophrenia, a "picture of madness" that contradicts the earlier CAT scan. These digital images of Reece's brain function to connect a series of concepts around the self together, as Joseph Dumit elucidates in his comments on *Rampage*: "PET scan to brain, brain to schizophrenia, schizophrenia to insanity."[22] At the time of the film's release, the science of these connections remained unsettled in the medical and legal communities. Nevertheless, these connections are asserted implicitly and without question, linking signifier and signified in relations that are both natural and necessary (Figure 4.2).

The closing statements of the defense and prosecution remind us of the structural overlaps between the Anglo-American trial and popular American narrative. Each side aims to convince the jury of their story, one that stars Reece and whose stakes revolve around the problem of criminal intent. While Fraser at the end of the film is left uncertain about whether "execution is the answer," what we may glean from the multiple narratives that have been woven around Reece is the hermeneutic process by which external signs, his deeds

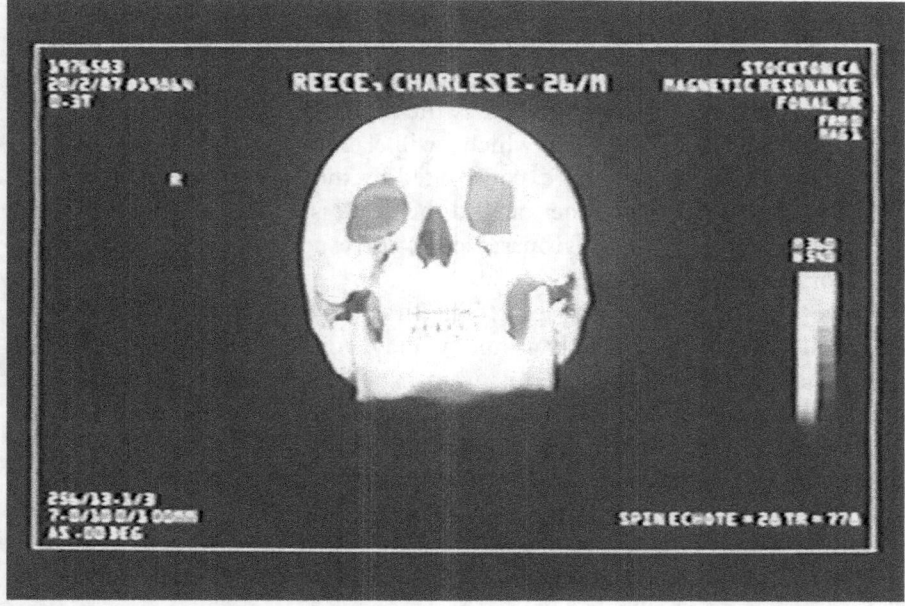

Figure 4.2 PET scan of insanity

that will tell us whether he harbored malice in his heart, are to be interpreted in order to reveal his essential moral nature. Indeed, the prosecutor's uncertainty, and by co-extension the spectator's, sheds light on a formulation from a text I quoted in Chapter 3, Nietzsche's *On the Genealogy of Morality*:

> And just as the common people separates lightning from its flash and takes the latter to be a *deed*, something performed by the subject, which is called lightning, popular morality separates strength from the manifestations of strength, as though there were an indifferent substratum behind the strong person which had the *freedom* to manifest strength or not. But there is no substratum; there is no "being" behind the deed, its effect and what becomes of it; "the doer" is invented as an afterthought,—the doing is everything.[23]

The moral nature of the doer is, the German philosopher would later elaborate, a narrative that is concocted after the deeds are done. Similarly for the narcissistic spectator of the cinema, the doer may be constituted only after there are deeds to judge. Signs of character reinforce the ideology that the nature of the self can be discovered and isolated. While *Rampage* underscores the arbitrariness of these narratives, it also proposes the disturbing thought that Reece's truth and the nature of his horrific crimes may ultimately be unknowable. For if he is deemed a legally sane criminal, we are still left with the troubling notion that these senseless murders were unmotivated by malicious intent. This critique may be extended to the various forms of narrativization and the institutions, such as the psychiatric and the legal, that are presented in the film and upon which I will elaborate further in *The Exorcist*. But what we are left with here, confronted by the failure of these narratives to discover a true self, the doer behind the deed, is a particularly Friedkinian explanation for how these discourses are to correspond with the hidden moral truth of the self: faith.

Two versions of *Rampage* exist. The first was produced in 1987 and was distributed in Europe for only a short while before the De Laurentiis Entertainment Group, who produced it, went bankrupt. Dino De Laurentiis, the famed producer of post-war Italian and later American cinema, had fruitfully worked with Friedkin previously on *The Brink's Job* but he had stopped answering the director's calls after *Rampage* was completed. In 1992, still in limbo, *Rampage* was acquired by Miramax and finally distributed in the U.S. after being recut. Upon its release, the film received decent critical reviews but did not do well at the box office. This was a particularly difficult period for the director and he remembers that:

> I was fifty-five years old and hit bottom. I thought about what else I might do with my life. There have been successful filmmakers of my generation, before and since, who didn't survive disasters like *Rampage*. They never directed another film. It was entirely possible the same fate awaited me.[24]

Friedkin goes on to describe that his personal life was a "shambles" as well. "I had been unhappily married and divorced three times," the director writes, "I had two young sons I dearly loved, but professionally, I was the instrument of my own downfall."[25] Between 1987 and 1992, in addition to *The Guardian*, he directed for television, including *C.A.T. Squad: Python Wolf* in 1988, the sequel to the *C.A.T. Squad* and which was co-written with Gerry Petievich, and an episode of the horror anthology series *Tales from the Crypt* called "On a Deadman's Chest" in 1992. This thirty-minute episode features a plot revolving around rage and jealousy between the singer and guitarist of a rock band, embodied in a tattoo that possesses unexpected supernatural properties.

The structure of the plots of both versions of *Rampage* are the same. Both relegate the third act to a courtroom drama, where the terms for delineating criminality from insanity are brought into dramatic conflict. The editing in the 1992 version of *Rampage* provides greater clarity for the motivation of the characters and includes shots not included in the previous version. The opening scene in 1987 quickly takes the viewer from a long shot of a farm field, in the midst of which Reece calmly walks, to an upper-middle-class residential area, and then into the home of his first victim. Through rapid cuts, the film depicts the murder, seemingly without premeditation, of a woman and her two elderly parents within three minutes of the film's credits. In the 1992 cut, there is no wide shot of the field as *Rampage* begins. Instead, we are immediately shown Reece walking through the residential neighborhood, then going to buy a gun, and then returning to the neighborhood to perform the murders—all of which take about two minutes longer than the corresponding scenes in the earlier version of the film.

The 1992 version also includes brief moments throughout that provide the viewer with more information about the characters, such as a short conversation between Fraser and the distraught Gene Tibbetts (Royce Applegate), who believes that God punished him by having Reece take his son away. Later in the 1987 film, a short, somewhat lurid dream sequence in the courtroom is not included in the later version of *Rampage*. In the earlier film, Reece is shown staring, with desire, at the female stenographer. Friedkin uneasily implicates the viewer in his gaze by moving the camera closer to her legs and then to her face as she smiles at him. Following a reverse shot of Reece sitting at the defense table, the stenographer surprisingly kisses the accused murderer on the cheek. By excluding this moment, which depicts Reece's subjective fantasy, from the 1992 cut, the viewer's attention is directed toward the problem of character judgment rather than toward his sexual and criminal etiology. Overall, the recut version of *Rampage* enables greater focus on this problem by including and excluding narrative details from the previous version of the film. Reece's premeditation is made more explicit in 1992, while this later version's overall dramatic trajectory is more focused and the continuity between scenes is more clearly delineated.

The most obvious difference between the two versions of *Rampage* is contained in their endings, however. In both versions, the jury renders a guilty judgment of Reece and in both he undergoes a PET scan. When the dye for the procedure is injected into his bloodstream, he voices anxieties about his blood being poisoned. In the early version of the film, Reece tearfully expresses remorse and a desire to make amends. When the scan finds that he is mentally ill, Morse goes to his cell to tell him that the results will relieve him of the death penalty. However, he is too late; Reece has ended his life in his cell, evidently from an overdose of pills his mother had given him. In the 1992 version of *Rampage*, following the trial verdict and PET scan, Reece is sentenced to undergo treatment at the state mental hospital. In the prison cell, he writes a letter to Gene Tibbetts explaining his need for his wife's blood to help him complete his "work." Reading it in voiceover, Reece sardonically invites Tibbetts to meet him in person, underscoring his schizophrenia and raising questions once more about his criminal intent. Perhaps for this reason Friedkin calls this ending "more ironic and unsettling" than the one for the 1987 version of *Rampage*.[26] Two intertitles conclude the film, one stating that Reece served four years and had a hearing to determine whether he would be eligible for release. The next indicates that he will have another hearing in six months, raising fears around the possibility of a sick man being freed who, as one juror put it, will be compelled to "live next door" to us and our neighbors.

12 ANGRY MEN (1997)

Friedkin's made-for-television movie is a remake of the well-known 1957 film of the same name. Reginald Rose wrote the screenplay for both films, both are based on his original 1954 teleplay, and both have their plots take place largely in the enclosed space of a jury deliberation room. As with the two versions of *Rampage*, comparison of the film versions of *12 Angry Men* draws attention to narrative details that differ between the two, reflecting their differing historical contexts. Friedkin's 1997 version of the classic courtroom drama responds to a pivotal drama of race and celebrity that took place in the news media and set the tone for discussion of these issues in this decade and after: the O. J. Simpson trial. Comparison with the short courtroom drama in *Rampage*, where the jury deliberates on Reece's fate, also helps us see how the filmmaker develops a series of issues related to judgment and visibility from this film to *12 Angry Men*. Earlier, I mentioned Clover's insight that real-life trials become movie-like in the Anglo-American trial world because of the ease by which the adversarial and deliberative protocols of the former are adapted to the popular mode of the latter. In the following, we will understand this connection further by placing greater focus on the characters that make up the jury. If the narrative drama in *Rampage* derives from the adversarial relationship that characterizes the arguments of the defending and prosecuting attorneys, in *12 Angry Men* it is the virtue of the individual members of the jury, who have gained personas and are thus anonymous no more, that is at stake.

The opening scene shows us the only woman who will appear in the entire film. Rose was asked whether he would like to include women in the twelve-person jury, but according to Friedkin the writer in the end decided against it because he did not want to change the title of the film. The defense and prosecution have just finished presenting their arguments and the female judge (Mary McDonnell) is instructing the jury to deliberate carefully and decide if the male defendant will be deemed guilty of first-degree murder. "It now becomes your duty to try to separate the facts from the fancy. One man is dead. The life of another is at stake . . . If there is a reasonable doubt, you must bring me a verdict of not guilty," she remarks, recalling dialogue from a corresponding scene in *Rampage*. The judge explains the terms and consequences of their judgment, not only to the jury, but also to the viewer. We are reminded that the decision must be unanimous, that if the jury returns a guilty verdict, no recommendation of mercy will be entertained by the court and that the teenager could ultimately face the death penalty. In contrast to the medium shots in the courtroom sequence in *Rampage*, which gave the viewer a sense of the courtroom space, Friedkin depicts this scene through cuts between close-ups of faces, between the judge and the young defendant, who is apparently Latinx. The judge looks into the camera as she speaks. After receiving their instructions, the twelve men are excused to gather in the deliberation room.

The plot is identical to the 1957 version in content and in the sequence of events. Both take place over the course of a single evening. The defendant has been accused of murdering his father in both films and the details of the case remain the same. With a view to deciding whether the boy is guilty or innocent of this crime, the twelve men of the jury reiterate facts presented during the trial by the defending and prosecuting lawyers. Viewers will recognize dialogue and moments that are in fact identical in both versions. The initial vote, tallied soon after they first sit at the long table, comes to eleven guilty and one not guilty, and compels the jury into intense deliberation until they all decide that a guilty judgment is impossible to determine beyond a reasonable doubt. Juror Eight (Henry Fonda in the earlier version and Jack Lemmon in the later one) is the leading protagonist in both films. He maintains skepticism about what claims may be assumed about the case by posing critical questions throughout the deliberation process. In the first dramatic moment of the film, he pulls out a knife from his pocket to illustrate that the murder weapon was not unique to the boy, but could have been purchased by, and thus belong to, anyone. The switchblade knives are stuck into the wooden table in both films, showing clearly that they are the same, allegorizing the irrelevance of distinguishing between the original and copy. Both versions of *12 Angry Men* contain a watershed moment when the credibility of a key female witness is questioned, triggered by a jury member who has marks left on the bridge of his nose from wearing glasses. Both films also feature a sudden thunderstorm in the second half, providing a moment of respite from the rising temperature of the room as well as the mounting tension between the twelve angry men. (In the 1957 version an electric fan is turned on and in 1997 an in-wall air conditioning unit.) One may also be reminded here of the sudden storm in *The Boys in the Band*, which caused the guests of a birthday to go indoors and begin their telephone game. In all of these films, the inclement weather outside marks the passing of time while also compelling the male characters toward greater intimacy, producing opportunities both to collaborate and further collide with each other.

Friedkin was apparently inspired to direct *12 Angry Men* when, as he explains in a 1997 interview, his son and friends "were around the house talking about 'What is a jury?' and 'What is reasonable doubt?' in the Simpson case."[27] He showed them the Lumet-directed film and while watching it was struck by the quality of the script and its seemingly enduring significance. "I started to think," the director continues, "that they just don't write them like this anymore and why aren't we making films like this and wouldn't it be great to do this with a superb cast today, and with every generation because it tells us a lot about ourselves as well as the American justice system."[28] He adds that in the previous year the 1964 stage version was revived by Harold Pinter in London. While the jury in the 1957 film consists only of white men, the 1997 television feature includes four African-Americans who take differing moral and legal positions on the accused and subsequently solicit differing levels of sympathy from the viewer. Juror One (Courtney B. Vance) serves as the foreman and maintains order through the deliberation process while also participating in it. He is a football coach who grieves for the broken heart of one of his star players. Juror Two (Ossie Davis) is an older gentleman who is reticent to speak, as his opinion perhaps is not yet fully formed, but nevertheless does not lose faith in the process. He raises decisive questions about how the boy stabbed a man who was at least six inches taller than him. Juror Five (Dorian Harewood) is about the same age as the foreman and has memories of growing up poor, enabling him to sympathize with the plight and impoverished upbringing of the defendant. Having grown up in a world where violence was a part of everyday life, like the accused young man, he provides important information about how switchblade knives are most effectively used to stab another person, underhanded and not downward apparently. Finally, Juror Ten (Mykelti Williamson) is a former member of the Nation of Islam and holds relatively uncompromising views about morality and criminality. He maintains a judgment of guilt throughout the entirety of the film, giving in to a vote of "not guilty" after cynically denouncing the entire process.

With the aim of thinking Friedkin's film in the context of the Simpson case, it may be interesting to draw correlations between these characters and a number of roles that African-Americans played in the trial itself. Aside from Simpson, these include Christopher Darden, one of the lead prosecutors, and Johnnie Cochran and Carl E. Douglas, who joined the defense team for Simpson. The high-profile lawyers who defended Simpson included Robert Shapiro, F. Lee Bailey, Robert Kardashian, and Alan Dershowitz and were dubbed the "Dream Team." The racial makeup of the potential jury was a point of concern. The court agreed that the trial would be held in downtown Los Angeles instead of Santa Monica where the crimes took place. The final jury was composed of nine African-Americans, one Latinx, and two white members. By insisting that the trial be held in L.A., the defense would avoid having to contend with a majority white jury. Polling data at the time indicated clearly that a plurality of white Americans felt that Simpson was guilty and a majority of African-Americans did not. With its fictional characters, Friedkin's film seems to attempt to reflect the demographic of the historical characters featured the trial, and in doing so, *12 Angry Men* enters into the discourse around race and the American justice system put into motion by the film's protagonists. Thus, the 1997 film imagines what the public could not directly see during the broadcast of the "Trial of the Century": the deliberations of African-American jurors and the melodrama surrounding these deliberations as they judge another American of crime.

In the last chapter of *Playing the Race Card*, Linda Williams extends her critical description of melodrama to the televised Simpson trial. She shows us how the emotional trajectory imputed through the melodramatic mode operates, not only in fictional moving image narrative, but also in televised non-fiction. Her argument turns on how black men have typically been narrativized within the history of American moving picture narrative and the act of judgment that responds to their images. This history is characterized as a "historically overdetermined repetition of the melodramatic racial trauma" that is "deeply bound up in the American justice system."[29] When this history of racial trauma is made into a spectacle, it solicits moral judgment and emotional response according to the melodramatic mode, thus gaining in supplementary meaning beyond the merely juridical. This solicitation becomes particularly acute when race and racism are not explicitly named as such, as was often the case in the Simpson trial. "In the visual field," Williams continues, "which evokes race without having to directly speak it, the black male body can be viewed as dangerous, threatening, and sexual, *or* as passive, victimized, and downtrodden."[30] Racism and moral judgment are inextricably bound up with each other, such that the accusation that the charge of "playing the race card," which was made at several key moments during the Simpson trial, already indicates a willful disavowal of the history of racial trauma that deeply informs the American justice system. In the visual field, shots of Simpson's face and body provide concrete evidence of his demeanor that lead the viewer to discover his virtue. Yet the (white) viewer operating within the melodramatic mode, by seeking the purity of Simpson's moral truth, nevertheless reads his racially marked body within a series of stereotyped signs: "was this a smiling villain under whose affable façade lurked a wild beast, or a genuinely friendly, falsely accused African American?"[31] Perpetrator of violence or victimized by the law: this binarized, racist characterization remains problematic as it distorts the long history of the relationship between race, moral judgment, the attribution of criminality, and the procedures of the American justice system.

In a later essay called "God Bless Juries!", Clover extends her insight that "trials are already movielike to begin with and movies are already trial-like to begin with" into a reading of the 1957 version of *12 Angry Men*.[32] There she argues, in counterpoint to critics at the time who thought otherwise, that Lumet's film should be thought of as a "consummate courtroom drama."[33] For while it does not technically take place in a courtroom, the plot of *12 Angry Men* still relies on the process of cross-examination, the production of supporting evidence, and adversarial dialogue to arrive at its conclusion. Far from standing as an exception to the genre of the courtroom drama, a claim based merely on the fact that it takes place in a jury deliberation room, the film in fact puts the juridical process itself under juridical scrutiny. "Most crucially," Clover adds, "despite its jury-room setting, it still plays to an off-screen jury. Perhaps it is because we sense our position as the film's object of address to be so secure that we can ignore or get beyond our diegetic competition."[34] Indeed, the film sheds light on a more generalized condition in the cinema. For when American films deal with questions of American law, they cannot avoid this juridical spectatorial address, even as the viewer's own discursive role is manifest and doubled on screen.

Friedkin's *12 Angry Men*, like the earlier film, does not employ proper names to identify individual jurors. But names seem unnecessary, for outward features and timbre of voice—elements unscored by the visual and auditory means of the cinema—allow spectators to distinguish one from another. And through this, these men of the jury are personified and personalized and, while they are tasked to ascertain judgment of the accused, they themselves are placed under moral scrutiny by the viewer as well, the viewer who is addressed as a kind of off-screen jury. We might be reminded here of the moments in *To Live and Die in L.A.* when the police are policed and specifically when their sovereign power to judge another of crime is critically foregrounded. Friedkin sets up these situations where those who are tasked with moral scrutinization are themselves scrutinized and the legitimacy underpinning their judgment is made into a potential object of critique. The jury watched witnesses cross-examined during the trial. Now it is their turn to be cross-examined, by the film audience.

By including black men in the jury, Friedkin dramatizes and personifies this key aspect of the Simpson trial, the claustrophobic, private space of the jury room that was not televised and thus not made available for visual and auditory scrutiny by the public. And in doing so, it provides audiences with the opportunity to assess the role of moral sentiment when African-American men are placed in a position of juridical and moral judgment. By depicting them as members of civic society who participate in the deliberative process—this depiction is admittedly politically weak, in any event—the viewer is reminded that African-American men are not only the victims of the system of American justice but can also be aligned with those who judge. Each of them embodies a different personality, perhaps in an attempt to represent the diversity of African-Americans more generally. And as in the televised Simpson trial, the problem of race and racism is not explicitly mentioned in the film's dialogue, except for a handful of moments. Somewhat late in the film, Mike Leigh's 1996 *Secret and Lies* is briefly discussed, which is described by Juror Four (Armin Mueller-Stahl), an older white man, as "a very touching story about a black woman." (Figure 4.3). He misremembers the title, however, and is corrected by Juror Two, who remembers it clearly. (In the 1957 version, two other films are recalled, *The Scarlet Circle* and *The Amazing Mrs. Bainbridge*, neither of which actually exist.) At another moment in *12 Angry Men*, after another vote is tallied, Juror Ten, the former member of the Nation of Islam, frustrated that Juror Two switched his vote to "not guilty," accuses the old man of getting "bulldozed by a bunch of these old white-washed intellectuals." He continues his angry criticism and faults him for being "just like some other folks your age, you're scared of the white man!" These charges enrage Juror Two and he responds by calling him a "loudmouth."

This interaction underscores the racist representation of Juror Ten as an unsympathetic villain who is cynical, stubborn, and impulsive—in short, the stereotypical angry black man. He refuses to accept any facts that contradict his narrative about what the accused did the night of the murder and, as the film unfolds, comes to reject the entitlement of due process that is fundamental to American justice. When another tally is counted and the results show nine to

Figure 4.3 Remembering past films

three in favor of not guilty, Juror Ten stands up in frustration and objects to the results of the vote: "These people are born to lie. Now that's the way they are and no intelligent man is gonna tell me otherwise. They don't know what the truth is!" As he continues, other jury members look down, becoming increasingly uncomfortable with where he is going with this line of thinking. "They think different, they act different and they don't need some big excuse to kill somebody either." Juror Five, who sympathizes with the accused young man, his struggles with poverty and being a person of color, rises from his seat in frustration and leaves to cool down in the restroom. "Smoking that crack . . . Nothing but crackheads! . . . Ok, look, nobody's blaming 'em for it. That's just the way they are by nature, you know what I mean? They're violent! And human life don't mean as much to them as it does to us." The angry man continues this discourse that separates "them," presumably those who share the race and class identity of the defendant, from "us," those present in the deliberation room. And soon he is deploying racist stereotypes. "They come over here illegally and they're multiplying five times faster than my people! That's five times, brothers," he remarks while looking at the other black jury members directly. Though he attempts to distinguish the world of the jury from that of the defendant, he instead alienates his fellow jury members with each dehumanizing and essentializing claim. Eventually he sits back down in a chair separated from the long table.

While eleven jurors become more or less sympathetic to the viewer throughout the course of the deliberations, each assumed to be operating in good faith within the norms of American democracy, Juror Ten is ostracized from this group. His performance is itself outrageous and extreme in its cynical lack of faith in the process. The process of deliberative judgment can take place only as a result of reasoned debate within the norms of the American democracy, the film seems to purport, and each individual is responsible for upholding these norms. On the other hand, Juror Ten's angry performances seem targeted to spread a sense of exasperation in their depiction of cartoonish intransigence, despite being met with general disapproval, especially from the other African-American men and Juror Four, who is an immigrant himself and speaks with a German accent. And with these nods to race and citizenship, Friedkin acknowledges the victims and perpetrators of violence in history, categories that turn on the sign of suffering and the production of virtue.

Within the space of a small room, Friedkin puts into motion a melodrama around race that offers viewers a glimpse into an allegorical space. Close-ups of faces and key objects tell the story of the film, providing viewers with the opportunity to assess the characters of the African-American jury members who were the subjects of public attention in the Simpson defense. In this, we might recall his *The Boys in the Band*, which shares the same parameters of space and takes place within the timeframe of a day. In both films, both derived from theatrical scripts, the drama unfolds within a hermetically sealed room that is separated from the world external to it. The sources of diegetic sound are located within the delimited space of the deliberation only and none are allowed to infiltrate from outside. In Friedkin's 1970 film it was the straight world, occupied by individuals desired by the film's characters in the past; in his 1997 production this outside is the Simpson trial and the melodrama surrounding its publicity. In both films he depicts a private space, making the invisible visible for popular scrutiny.

Two years later, another high-profile trial would replicate the conditions that constitute the melodrama of race in America. On February 4, 1999, four white New York City police officers shot and killed Amadou Diallo, a thirty-three-year-old immigrant from Guinea. The officers mistakenly identified the young black man as being or associated with a serial rapist who was at large for over a year. Diallo was standing in front of his Bronx apartment and when he was told to surrender, he removed his wallet from his pockets and the civilian-clothed police began shooting, putting nineteen bullets into his body. An internal investigation found that the officers were operating within policy. In late March, they were charged by the Bronx grand jury of second-degree murder, accusations that garnered a good deal of sensational national publicity. The cover of a *New Yorker* at the time showed a police officer aiming his gun at a family in a shooting gallery while newspaper editorials repeated the horrifying fact that the police shot at the unarmed Diallo forty-one times. While Mayor Rudy Giuliani called for due process for the officers, African-Americans were forced to consider the trauma of yet another black man who was the victim of excessive police violence, triggering memories of the Rodney King beating of 1993. Although race and the history of racial trauma were constantly disavowed in the juridical discourse, these issues were central in the vast realm circumscribed by the essentializing melodrama of race in the public sphere.

The defense attorneys for the four police officers were granted their request that the trial be held not in the Bronx where the crime took place but in Albany. At the time, about one in five people in the New York City borough was white compared to nine in ten in the upstate New York capital. The jury was made up of seven white men, four black women, and one white woman. The trial itself was televised on Court TV and covered extensively in the news. On February 25, 2000, after three days of deliberation, the jury came back with a judgment of acquittal for the officers for second-degree murder.

BUG (2006)

When *Bug* was released to theaters, critics heralded it as the seventy-one-year-old filmmaker's return to Hollywood auteurship, reminding audiences of the themes and tendencies that had characterized his more celebrated films. Roger Ebert, for instance, writes that:

> For Friedkin, the film is a return to form after some disappointments like "Jade." It feels like a young man's picture, filled with edge and energy. Some reviews have criticized "Bug" for revealing its origins as a play, since most of it takes place on one set. But of course it does. There is nothing here to "open up" and every reason to create a claustrophobic feel. Paranoia shuts down into a desperate focus. It doesn't spread its wings and fly.[35]

Rob Nelson in *The Village Voice* declares *Bug* to be Friedkin's best film since *The Exorcist* and that it is "more inventively unsettling than anything Friedkin has mustered in the quarter-century" since the latter film was released theatrically in 1973.[36] And Mick LaSalle, reviewer for the *San Francisco Chronicle* who praised *Cruising* in a 1995 review,[37] comments that:

> "Bug" is Friedkin's triumph, too, the film his fans have been waiting for him to make since "Cruising" (1980). This is not to dismiss two and a half decades of a respectable career, which includes "To Live and Die in L.A." among other titles. But "Bug" is the first time since "Cruising" in which it feels like Friedkin's personality is in every single shot. His Friedkin-ness, if you will, is not just a matter of stylistic embellishments or flashes of technique here. It's intrinsic. He suffuses the film in an atmosphere of unease from its first seconds.[38]

Deciding whether *Bug* is his "best" film since *The Exorcist* or *Cruising* will remain an open question but it does mark a shift in Friedkin's career, away from the big budget films that have generally underperformed at the box office (especially since *Sorcerer*) and toward smaller-scale projects that would afford the filmmaker opportunities to pursue aesthetic and thematic problems that continue to interest him. Produced with a budget of only $4 million, *Bug* did in fact reap modest profits.

Bug premiered theatrically on the London stage in 1996 and was Friedkin's first production whose script was written by Tracy Letts. *Killer Joe* was in fact Letts's first play, written in 1991 when the playwright was twenty-five years old. Friedkin attended a New York performance of *Bug* in 2004, about a year after completing *The Hunted*, and its effect seemed to have taken the film director by surprise. "The play was as powerful and compelling as anything by Harold Pinter," Friedkin writes, in a statement that also harks back to the kind of filmmaking that began his career.[39] In Chapter 3, I argued that the depiction of the Smith family in Friedkin's

2011 film of *Killer Joe* is undermined by a transgressive element, one that enters the trailer home of the dysfunctional Smith family. This element is embodied by the policeman Joe Cooper, who demoralizes the sentiments that typically underpin the structure of the family and who perverts the space of innocence associated with the home. In *Bug*, a similar perversion takes place, particularly around what can be known, what must be done, and what may be expected when there is a threat issuing from an external force. These questions revolve around the besieged subject and concern the kind of knowledge that may be accessed by this subject, manifest through the depiction of paranoia experienced by the two main protagonists. The film provides us with an opportunity to critically think these questions by taking them to their transgressive limits and through this *Bug* continues the mode of critique that was put into motion by *Killer Joe*. On the other hand, Friedkin's 2006 film is closely related to adaptations like *12 Angry Men* and *The Birthday Party* in that it takes place, for the most part, in a single room. Once more Friedkin exploits the narrative and formal elements of the stage drama to create a palpable sense of claustrophobia and, by co-extension, an awareness of a rigorous division between the inside and outside.

The plot of *Bug* begins auspiciously. It takes place, for the most part, in a "rustic" motel room outside of Oklahoma City. Agnes White (Ashley Judd) has taken residence in the rundown motel while working as a waitress at a lesbian bar. The opening scenes inside the hotel feature several brief phone calls from her ex-husband, with each ring of the phone piercing through the privacy of her room. (These phone calls may remind us of those in *The Boys in the Band* that connect past and present desire, as well as the enclosed space of Michael's apartment with the world outside.) Through a co-worker, Agnes meets Peter Evans (played by Michael Shannon, who was also in the London premiere of the play), a veteran of the Gulf War with a shy, awkward personality. After they get to know each other, Peter stays the night and sleeps on the floor of the hotel room. Cutting to the next morning, Agnes's ex-husband, Jerry Goss (Harry Connick, Jr.) unexpectedly emerges from the shower. He threatens her and hits her in the face, quickly demonstrating his violent and manipulative character. Peter returns to the hotel room and Jerry soon leaves, but not before taking Agnes's money. Very quickly, *Bug* establishes one man as sympathetic and the other as unlikeable. With the perceived threat gone, the new friends begin talking again. The sudden violence forcefully opens channels of trust and emotion between them, as well as between the cinema and the viewer. While these channels will make sympathy possible, they will also open paths for undesirable elements to circulate. Peter contends, somewhat inexplicably, that they are not safe because of the "technology, chemicals, and information" that have become a part of modern life. "Sometimes when you're lying in bed at night," he explains, "you can feel it—all the machines, people working their machines, the works, humming. . . ." Agnes opens up to Peter as well and recounts losing her six-year-old son in the grocery store ten years ago while becoming emotional. They have sex. Close-up shots of their intertwined bodies attest to the fluids that are exchanged between them.

Their traumas, insecurities, and paranoias also become intermingled and then exacerbated, rising in manic intensity until the explosive finale to the film. The next morning Peter suspects that their bed has been infested with aphids. His anxiety triggers memories of war, when he was given shots and pills to remedy symptoms of PTSD, invasive remedies that were themselves experienced as traumatic. In reaction to the invading bugs, the hotel room is adorned with long strips of sticky fly traps hanging from the ceiling, bug traps on the floor, and fly swatters on the tables. Peter inspects his blood under a microscope to check for miniscule bugs in this body and is convinced that the room is infested with "blood-sucking aphids." He lifts his shirt to reveal hideous sores and bites on his abdomen. While expressing views pointing to delusions of persecution, Peter gruesomely removes a molar from his mouth, believing that the government implanted bugs underneath his tooth. At some point in this trajectory of rising anxiety, Agnes also starts seeing the bugs Peter claims to see. She then expresses her love for him, becoming emotionally dependent, and begins to hallucinate unknown bugs infesting her body and the space of the hotel room.

The film continues to rise in intensity as Agnes and Peter become increasingly unhinged and disconnected from reality. By its ending scenes, they have become totally convinced of the rabid presence of these aphids. The bugs themselves remain invisible to the other characters in the film, to Jerry, Agnes's co-worker R.C. (Lynn Collins), as well as to Dr. Sweet (Brian F. O'Byrne), Peter's "consultant" who arrives later in the film. Significantly, Friedkin does not provide the viewer with any shots of the bugs that Agnes and Peter supposedly see, not only because they are so small, but also to highlight the question of their very existence. Indeed, the notion of a "blood-sucking aphid" is already preposterous in itself, but Agnes and Peter's insistence on their reality puts into relief the question of what else they might be perceiving. Despite apparent evidence that they have been bitten by bugs ostensibly hostile to their bodies, one begins to wonder if their bloody scratches and scars were self-inflicted and to speculate perhaps on whether the supposed infestation originates from internal delusions. Meanwhile, the chirp of a smoke alarm becomes that of a cricket, the sound of a helicopter flying overhead the sign of a military shakedown— from one to the next, the viewer is asked to definitively identify the nature of what is seen and heard, of signs symptomatic of Peter's mental state, and determine whether the threats he perceives are imagined or he is actually under siege from external forces.

These illusory bugs become full-blown delusions at the film's conclusion when Agnes convinces herself that she is the originating "super-mother bug" that gave birth to the infesting bug horde. This delusion of grandeur solicits spectators to ascertain her spiraling mental health as well and perhaps to analyze her psychotic fantasies as reflecting her desire to be a good mother and compensate for the loss of her young son. Dr. Sweet remarks that Peter may be "diagnosed as a delusional paranoid with schizophrenic tendencies, although personally, I'm not a big fan of labels." A contrast may be drawn between Friedkin's film and Kafka's *Metamorphosis*. While Gregor Samsa realizes that he must learn to cope with his status as a "monstrous vermin," Agnes and Peter cannot stand their own ontological status as non-human and are adamant about eliminating the bugs and thereby eliminating themselves as well. To see the bugs is to control them, to create the opportunity to destroy them, but Friedkin's camera, despite its capacity for close-ups and cut-ins, never gives the viewer this satisfaction.

The bugs, whatever they are, seem to be everywhere, disregarding boundaries between inside and outside, permeating the skin and found underneath a tooth. They are reviled pests invading the interior of Agnes's hotel room. In the final dialogue leading up to their mutual immolation, Agnes maniacally connects her ex-husband, R.C., and her lost son Lloyd to explain her own status as the super-mother. Peter's concerns about the malign "technology, chemicals, and information" that infects everyday life become a demonstration of psychotic conspiratorial thinking through her performance. The bugs invoke infectious disease ("typhoid, Legionnaires' disease, . . . AIDS," according to him), but also state surveillance ("some government screwup"), substance abuse, and disinformation, associations that bring together the science of entomology with postmodern knowledge and warfare. "We made them," Agnes declares, referring to the insects,

> We gave birth to them! And they will never leave us. They will never leave us because we made them. And those people . . . Those people are trying to come in here to kill us because the bugs won't go out into the world to do their work!

In her reading of Friedkin's film, Amy Rust suggests that this conspiratorial thinking responds to the relationship between humans and bugs and whose terms become increasingly interchangeable as the film unfolds.

> The bugs, it seems, no longer pose a threat from the outside alone; they also infest Peter's and Aggie's insides. Fighting back, the pair giddily maps the enemy's network of surveillance. But the further they reach, the more closely the bugs encroach. Soon, public pervades private and

private public, rendering proximity and distance, attack and defense, uncannily interchangeable. The many definitions of "bug" underscore this fungibility. Promising incursion ("a concealed microphone") as well as detection ("a burglar-alarm system"), "bug" comes to incorporate its opposite, denoting both "bugging" and "debugging" at once.[40]

Attack and defense become interchangeable, upending the hierarchy that typically organizes relations between infecting and infected, and between victim and victimizer. This reading sheds additional light on the intimidating presences of McCann and Goldberg in Meg's boarding house in *The Birthday Party*. Through this, the politics of blame that is so central to the narrative of contagion, the politics of identifying an origin of the outside that violates the private self, becomes upended as well. As Agnes illustrates, she has no one to blame but herself. Bug, buggy, to be bugged, to bug out, to bug another, to debug: like the chiasmatic reversibility that is integral to the meaning of the *Unheimlich*, the ways in which the word "bug" have been deployed in English as verb and noun, active and passive, attest to the fluidity of its definition.

These thoughts on the discursive effects of the bugs in Friedkin's film in fact steer us away from questions concerning their meaning, symbolic or otherwise. Instead of posing the question of what they straightforwardly represent, while anticipating an answer that often refers back to the human being as the exclusive creator of meaning, we might take the "fungibility" of the non-human bug further to see what happens to the concept of the human itself as it has been typically figured in popular cinema. Although her essay addresses Tracy Letts's theater play, Una Chaudhuri provides us with one way in which we might approach the problem of bugging, being bugged, and bugging out. Chaudhuri makes explicit that she intends to pursue an animal studies approach toward Letts's *Bug*, one that acknowledges

> the fact that the animal, which was for so long and so unquestioningly treated as a symbol or metaphor, a stand-in for human ideas and feelings, is now seen to be, and to always have been, also a representative of the real species to which it belongs.[41]

While implicitly acknowledging Rust's observation that the bugs embody a multitude of meanings, Chaudhuri attempts to isolate the "bugginess" of the bug by attempting to understand its lifeworld. Drawing from Giorgio Agamben's reading of Jakob von Uexküll's analysis of the *Umwelt* of the lowly tick, she describes the species life of the bug as distinct but also operating in conjunction with that of the human spectator.[42] Each lifeform, according to this analysis, is delimited by its own way of sensing and interacting with the world, limitations determined by its species-specific morphology and which exclude the *Umwelt*, or "surrounding world," of others. Bugs and humans may be thought to be triggered by their own *Umwelt*, each of which contains signs attuned to its particular being-in-the-world, or being-in-the-theater, as it were: the multitudinous, infectious, miniaturized, and seemingly technological world that embeds bugs and the signs of character that constitute the human being. These signs of bugginess disrupt the fantasy of humans being sovereign over a space that is in fact cohabitated by other non-human beings, reminding all the humans in the theater of their own particular form of species life. Chaudhuri describes this critique induced by Letts's play, as

> profound and potentially lethal uncertainty rooted in the vulnerability of the human body, the permeability of its surfaces, the extreme miniaturization of technology, and the pervasive reach of the state. Enlisting the spectators' bodies as much as the powers (and limits) of theatricality, *Bug* stages the contemporary *Umwelt* of extreme biopolitical vulnerability.[43]

This production of "lethal uncertainty" helps explain the play's disorientating experience, for one is reminded of the ubiquity of bugs, both organic and inorganic, in our everyday life. Unseen bugs, entomological and technological, are brought into consciousness through what is unfolding on the theater stage, provoking human audiences who typically share space inside the theater. Tiny bugs suddenly become objects of concern, registered as tiny insects, malignant disease, a contagious virus perhaps, but also as texts and tweets arriving on one's phone or outside entities mining the data produced by one's activity on it. In the performance of the play attended by Chaudhuri, she notes that the audience experienced a somatic sympathetic response to the actors as they itched, scratched, and swatted at unseen bugs. "These gestures are," she writes, "like yawns, affective and contagious—they are *catching*. Watching other people scratching themselves can cause people to start feeling an itch themselves."[44]

Indeed, these observations are particularly compelling within the space of the theater, but Friedkin's work allows us the opportunity to consider their meaning within the context of his cinema. Except in quick transitional shots, the camera seems purposefully to disavow the close-up shot on these tiny beings, never allowing the viewer a point-of-view shot on the bugs that Peter and Agnes insistently claim to perceive. The capacity of the cinema to attest to the truth of their reality is further challenged through montage, which André Bazin, describing the limitations of film, calls, "that abstract creator of meaning, which preserves the state of unreality demanded by the spectacle."[45] In contrast to filmic reality constituted through editing, Bazin prefers the long take for its "photographic respect" for the unity of dramatic space and the continuity of duration.[46] Above all, we must consider the reproducibility of the cinema image, which distinguishes the film medium most from the live theatrical performance. Within the heterotopic space of the film theater, the audience does not share the space of the bug-infested Oklahoma hotel represented on screen, perhaps thus lessening the somatic sympathetic response described by Chaudhuri above. The mediation of the camera, projector, and the aesthetics of narrative continuity place the film viewer outside the diegesis, one that interpellates the audience as an observer in relation to the world depicted in the film. Each showing of the film is a copy of the original performance, lacking, as Benjamin reminds us, "its presence in time and space, its unique existence at the place where it happens to be."[47] And so Friedkin's film, by the nature of its technical reproducibility, meets the viewer halfway, taking Letts's play beyond the theatrical stage, multiplying in and infecting the cinema theater so that it may be experienced by masses of individuals.

The extent to which the "aura" of *Bug* withers when it passes from stage to screen is perhaps of lesser importance here than the reminder that the film image itself circulates like an infestation. They escape the film theater and appear on home theaters, computer screens, tablets, and cell phones. Friedkin's film appears on the Amazon and iTunes platforms, allowing it to multiply across electronic devices. Moreover, captured still images on websites and copies of the entire film are distributed through bit torrents, part of a panoply of distribution modes for moving image media that make possible their influx into the everyday life of humans. On the other hand, as Jussi Parikka reminds us in *Insect Media*, bugs are not simply metaphors for infinitely reproducible and networked media, but constitute a technological ethos that gives rise to potentialities, affects, and intensities. "An animal has to find a common tune with its environment," Parikka writes, also working with von Uexküll's animal phenomenology, "and a technology has to work through rhythmic relations with other force fields such as politics and economics."[48] In this sense, insect media are always already ubiquitous, constitutive of the worlds that make life possible at all. A bug swarm is not simply like networked media, but both are fundamental to processes of individuation and of determining relations between a life and its surrounding world. The human being, or what is called the "human," is materialized through this swarm, in the relations between the human body and its *Umwelt* and the institutions that allow the human individual to appear as such.

In such an environment, it perhaps does not come as a surprise that Agnes and Peter remain maniacally fixated on conspiracy theories, so obsessed are they in maintaining the sovereignty of their humanity. Bugs violate the innocence of the true self in Friedkin's film. One is reminded of Frederic Jameson's well-known formulation that the conspiracy theory "is the poor person's cognitive mapping in the postmodern age."⁴⁹ When he wrote this in 1990, Jameson was speaking about the status of knowledge in the age of late capitalism, and the inability of the Enlightenment subject to cognize and totalize its systematicity. Making paranoid efforts to cut themselves off from the bugs they fear so intensely, Peter and Agnes become the experts of their own self-diagnosed condition. They demonstrate this intense solipsism and paranoid fantasy in Letts's 1996 play, but Friedkin's 2006 film reminds us of the constitutive role that technological media plays in the couple's obsessive production of conspiracy theories. Peter, as we saw from one of the film's very first scenes, is particularly observant. "There's stuff in it," he remarks, looking at a cheap reproduction of a painting on Agnes's motel room wall, "Hidden stuff. People and things, if you really look at it." Moments later he deduces that Agnes has a child, though she lied to him about it. This capacity of insight, the ability to uncover the truth beneath the surface of things, an ability that is fundamental to the melodramatic mode, is amplified and taken to its paranoid, utterly distrusting limits by the end of *Bug* (Figure 4.4). The belief in hidden truths puts the faculty of insight into increasing crisis, turning understanding almost imperceptibly into conspiracy. Anything can be connected to everything, and indeed these connections are desperately followed by the protagonists of Friedkin's film, if only to shore up the sovereignty of the human being in the world.

In an era when empiricism is the primary means by which knowledge may be verified and legitimated, unseen bugs pose a fundamental problem to this means of knowing, bugs that are themselves constituted through modern, empirical science. As the difference between truth and lies is called into crisis,

Figure 4.4 Peter threatens his consultant Dr. Sweet

confidence in the legitimacy of modern institutions quickly wanes in an age when the act of perception itself may be characterized as simultaneously empirical and delusional. The means for deducing the existence of the bugs go haywire, while panic around contagion is exacerbated in turn through the very failure of these means and as the very act of deduction starts to be understood like a contagion. Correspondingly, the possibility of sympathizing with others also opens up the possibility of contamination, of the spread of paranoid knowledge and disinformation. The infested body, then, becomes the sign of a horrific transgression when the outside has broken into the ostensible innocence of the soul. Early in the film Peter explains to Agnes that, "You have a center, right? I mean, a place, inside, that's just you, that hasn't been spoiled. I think it's important to try to keep that place sacred, in some sense, on some level, but sex, or relationships, they cloud that space." With this, the film illustrates how the self is bugged by that which has been deemed other to it through the very manifestation of discursive boundaries that are paranoically transgressed. We have seen this image of the bugged self in films such as *To Live and Die in L.A.* and *Cruising*. In the next chapter we will attempt to develop it further with *The Exorcist*.

The year *Bug* was released in film theaters, Twitter was founded and Facebook opened its membership to anyone with an e-mail address, drastically increasing its numbers. In March of 2006, the Patriot Act came into effect, allowing the National Security Division access to business and medical records with a court order and the wiretapping of phone calls. These are forces that put the human being, as understood within the melodramatic mode, constantly on the defensive against fake news, hacking, phishing, trolling, and disinformation campaigns. Melodrama engages viewers sympathetically while also enabling their contaminations by these "alternative" discourses. Yet *Bug* reminds us that these bugs that infiltrate our world also constitute the technical means for critically thinking them. In their demand for individual liberty and the frenzied purge of the non-human, Agnes and Peter act out a profound ambivalence that persists between two states: the coherence of the individual and its occupation by outside forces that threaten its sovereignty.

NOTES

1. William Friedkin, *The Friedkin Connection* (New York: Harper, 2013), 27.
2. Friedkin, *The Friedkin Connection*, 36.
3. Casey Burchby, "Fifty Years of Filmmaking: An Interview with William Friedkin," *Los Angeles Review of Books*, May 1, 2013.
4. Friedkin, *The Friedkin Connection*, 4.
5. Friedkin, *The Friedkin Connection*, 4.

6. Carol Clover, "Law and the Order of Popular Culture," in Austin Sarat and Thomas R. Kearns, eds., *Law in the Domains of Culture* (Ann Arbor: University of Michigan Press, 1998), 99.
7. Christopher Lane, ed., *William Friedkin: Interviews*, Conversations with Filmmakers Series (Jackson: University of Mississippi Press, 2020), 10.
8. Lane, *William Friedkin: Interviews*, 19.
9. Slavko Vorkapich, "Toward a True Cinema," in *A Montage of Theories*, ed. Richard Dyer MacCann (New York: E. P Dutton, 1966), 177. One of the few essays written about him is Sheri Chinen Biesen, "'Kinesthesis' and Cinematic Montage: An Historical Examination of the Film Theories and Avant-Garde Mediation of Slavko Vorkapich in Hollywood," *Studies in Visual Arts and Communication: An International Journal* 2, no. 1 (2015).
10. See Friedkin, *The Friedkin Connection*, 218–19.
11. Friedkin, *The Friedkin Connection*, 218.
12. Vorkapich, "Toward a True Cinema," 174.
13. Vorkapich, "Toward a True Cinema," 178.
14. Friedkin, *The Friedkin Connection*, 219.
15. In transcripts for the Harold Lloyd Master Seminars from 1992 and 1994, he speaks directly toward this. From September 2, 1992:

"What I thought would be good is . . . there was a show in New York at that time of cubist painting. You know the cubist paintings, where they would take an object and fragment it and show . . . on one flat canvas they'd show you front, back, side, rear of a face or a violin or whatever . . . a vase of flowers. So I would see this and I thought, 'Why couldn't you do that with a film?' Which is also, you know, basically a two-dimensional medium like canvas; the film is just height and width, the canvas is just height and width. So now, to get an illusion of reality, I thought it would be wonderful to let the camera go from here around to here and over to here and over there and back whenever possible in a kind of, what I called a sort of cinematic cubism. You have a scene where Gene Hackman is running down the steps of an elevated platform, he comes down, the camera follows him over here where he tries to stop a car, the car blows by him, he then comes running by and I show what's over here and then take him over there and we went 360-degrees as often as we could. Now one reason, as you all know, why you don't normally go 360-degrees is 'cause usually back here is the camera crew, lights, guys standing around eating sandwiches, drinking pop, doing their thing. You can't pan over here, on the average movie set, 'cause there ain't nothing to see except the crew. And I thought, 'Get the crew the hell outta here. The camera is going to go anywhere.'"

And from March 16, 1994:

"Deep immersion . . . And he would show other things where he would break the left/right continuum and he said, 'People don't even notice that if they're involved in a scene. If they're not involved in the scene, they see everything. They see all the flaws if they're not involved. But if they are involved, the technical rules of filmmaking mean very little.' And in *The Exorcist* I set out to prove Vorkapich right. I have a scene where this priest is in the little girl's bedroom and he's got a tape recorder on, and he's taping her voice. And when I shot the scene I made a wide shot of this guy reaching down to turn on the tape recorder with, I believe, it was his left hand. Then I made a close-up of him turning on the tape recorder with his right hand and no one has ever noticed it. When I was mixing the picture, we'd run the scene over and over and I asked the mixers, 'Do you see anything wrong?' 'No, nothing.' Nobody ever noticed it. They were involved in the scene. And so you can shoot what is the best angle for you within a scene, even if it breaks the left/right continuum, if you've got the audience involved in the characters and the story. Technique is of less interest than character and story."

16. Friedkin, *The Friedkin Connection*, 48.
17. A poem that was kept in Friedkin's papers was apparently written by Chase: "when you think you see us / when you think were (*sic*) not there / we are around the corner / I will end the world by/ flooding if I get killed/—Gott."
18. See Thomas D. Clagett, *William Friedkin: Films of Aberration, Obsession and Reality* (Los Angeles: Silman-James Press, 2003), 308.
19. William Friedkin, *Rampage Symposium*, University of Southern California, November 19, 1987. Quoted in Clagett, *William Friedkin*, 309.
20. Roger Ebert, "*Rampage*," *Chicago Sun-Times*, October 30, 1992.
21. Janet Maslin, "Review/Film: Random Murder Spree in a Friedkin Thriller," *New York Times*, October 30, 1992.
22. Joseph Dumit, "A Digital Image of the Category of the Person: PET Scanning and Objective Self-Fashioning," in *Cyborgs and Citadels: Anthropological Interventions in Emerging Sciences and Technologies*, eds. Gary Lee Downey and Joseph Dumit (Seattle: University of Washington Press, 1997), 92.
23. Friedrich Nietzsche, *On the Genealogy of Morality*, trans. Carol Diethe (Cambridge: Cambridge University Press, 2006), 28.
24. Friedkin, *The Friedkin Connection*, 401-2.
25. Friedkin, *The Friedkin Connection*, 402.
26. Friedkin, *The Friedkin Connection*, 401.
27. Lane, *William Friedkin: Interviews*, 77.
28. Lane, *William Friedkin: Interviews*, 77.
29. Linda Williams, *Playing the Race Card: Melodramas of Black and White from Uncle Tom to O. J. Simpson* (Princeton: Princeton University Press, 2002) 265.
30. Williams, *Playing the Race Card*, 266.
31. Williams, *Playing the Race Card*, 269.
32. Clover, "Law and the Order of Popular Culture," 99.
33. Carol Clover, "God Bless Juries!" in *Refiguring American Film Genres*, ed. Nick Browne (Berkeley: University of California Press, 1998), 270.
34. Clover, "God Bless Juries!", 270.
35. Roger Ebert, "Without a Net," *Chicago Sun-Times*, May 24, 2007, accessed February 14, 2021, <https://www.rogerebert.com/reviews/bug-2007>
36. Rob Nelson, "JitterBug," *The Village Voice*, May 15, 2007, accessed February 14, 2021, <https://www.villagevoice.com/2007/05/15/jitterbug>
37. Mick LaSalle, "'Cruising' Back From the '80s," *SFGate*, May 12, 1995, accessed February 14, 2021, <https://www.sfgate.com/movies/article/Cruising-Back-From-the-80s-3033280.php>
38. Mick LaSalle, "This thriller will have your skin crawling," *SFGate*, May 25, 2007, accessed February 14, 2021, <https://www.sfgate.com/movies/article/This-thriller-will-have-your-skin-crawling-2591949.php>
39. Friedkin, *The Friedkin Connection*, 449.
40. Amy Rust, "Plugging In and Bugging Out: The Torturous Logic of Contemporary American Horror," *Quarterly Review of Film and Video* 31, no. 6 (2014), 515.
41. Una Chaudhuri, *The Stage Lives of Animals: Zooesis and Performance* (Abingdon: Routledge, 2017), 133.
42. See Giorgio Agamben, *The Open: Man and Animal*, trans. Kevin Atell (Stanford: Stanford University Press, 2004).
43. Chaudhuri, *The Stage Lives of Animals*, 147.
44. Chaudhuri, *The Stage Lives of Animals*, 147.
45. André Bazin, "The Virtues and Limitations of Montage," in *What is Cinema? Vol. 1*, trans. Hugh Gray (Berkeley: University of California Press, 1967), 45.

46. Bazin, "The Virtues and Limitations of Montage," 46.
47. Walter Benjamin, "The Work of Art in the Age of Mechanical Reproduction," in *Illuminations*, ed. Hannah Arendt, trans. Harry Zohn (New York: Schocken, 1968), 220.
48. Jussi Parikka, *Insect Media: An Archaeology of Animals and Technology* (Minneapolis: University of Minnesota Press, 2010), xiv.
49. Frederic Jameson, "Cognitive Mapping," in *Poetics/Politics: Radical Aesthetics for the Classroom* (London: Palgrave, 1999), 167.

CHAPTER 5

"The Power of Cinema Compels You"

THE EXORCIST (1973)

In a hand-written letter addressed to Friedkin, dated January 22, 1976, a budding young filmmaker extols the extraordinary effect that *The Exorcist* had on him:

> Seeing the risks of being labeled a supreme egotist, among other things, I can only say that the effects of this film on my entire being, after 9 viewings, are that of metamorphosis and rebirth brought about by the power of the real Exorcist, William Friedkin, to exorcise from me all the distorted blocks of misunderstanding about sex and religion which society has created. He has done this by showing those distortions taken to their ultimate power, and the effects of those distorted powers on everyone involved, including the audience, in arriving at a new awareness. These distortions exist in our own society, in every walk of life, but we refuse to look, or pretend they do not exist; all the while maintaining a façade of Purity and Righteousness. We have Chris McNeil and her rich, chic, very near sterile house and Regan behind closed doors foaming at the mouth, the White House and Watergate with the FBI and the CIA to follow; Father Karras' rich priestly robes with his guilt, repression, and his mother alone and sick in a New York ghetto, the Church's supremacist politics and its repressed followers, and the government's politics and the psychologically oppressed masses. These are all distortions of power that exist. It is the recognition of this distortion of the power of the unconscious which is symbolized for me as the demonic stone image, seen at the beginning in Iraq and reappearing in Regan's bedroom in the end, as knowledge through experience.[1]

The author of this letter was then thirty-year-old David Lynch, who composed it one year before he released his first feature film, *Eraserhead*, in 1977. Lynch expresses a sentiment that was perhaps shared by others at the time, namely an increasing dissatisfaction with old ways of thinking and a disillusionment with American institutions throughout the decade. *The Exorcist* served as a lightning rod for increasingly cynical audiences in the late '60s and into the '70s who were critical of the constrictive norms of American morality and sought to rethink the role of America in the world. Early in 1973, the Paris Peace Accords were signed, ending U.S. involvement in the Vietnam War. This signaled capitulation in the war and squandered tens of thousands of American lives. The oil embargo of 1973 was a calculated strategic move by members of OPEC to retaliate against nations that were supportive of Israel, including the U.S., during the Yom Kippur War of October. The sense of moral righteousness that served to justify American involvement in world affairs seemed to lose legitimacy at this time.

The most significant news of the second half of 1973, however, was the ongoing Watergate scandal. On November 17, during a press conference given in response to the impeachment proceedings that were already underway, Richard Nixon remarked that, "people have got to know whether or not their president is a crook. Well, I'm not a crook." While he repeatedly denied the veracity of the charges against him, specifically around his alleged abuse of power and obstruction of justice, Nixon's acknowledgment of them nevertheless inflamed the judgment of the public. *The Exorcist* premiered in U.S. theaters on December 26, 1973, offsetting the spirit of the holiday season with its dark and somber tone. It opened to only thirty theaters but quickly became a bona fide blockbuster within weeks, first by word of mouth and then through the media attention given to the incredible success of the film. In an interview in 1974, where he comments on the loss of control experienced by the young female protagonist in *The Exorcist*, Friedkin remarks that, "I think a large part of our entertainment today is a result of the national nervous breakdown since the three assassinations and the Vietnam War. I think we are coming out of another kind of seizure with the Nixon administration."[2] Earlier in the summer of 1973, the Senate Watergate Committee began holding hearings on the events that took place in the Watergate building the previous year. These hearings were televised on PBS for two weeks, playing to a moralizing jury made up of millions of Americans watching from their living rooms. On October 20 of that year, a day that we now refer to as the "Saturday Night Massacre," the country was gripped by the shocking news that the president fired Special Prosecutor Archibald Cox. Cox had subpoenaed hundreds of hours of phone conversations Nixon personally recorded from the Oval Office between himself and administration officials, family, and friends. These tapes revealed a particularly unpresidential side of Nixon, showing him speaking like a gang leader replete with profanity and tough guy talk. They would all but confirm testimony provided by the White House Council that an extensive cover-up of illegal activities had taken place. Nixon would go on to try and discredit his investigators by sowing confusion and undermining faith in the process. His efforts themselves became integrated into the continuing scandal. The declining trust among the populace in American judicial and political institutions, the transformation of the counterculture, the continuing sexual revolution, and the rise of alternative, spiritual, and even conspiratorial worldviews seem to have been reflected and amplified by *The Exorcist*.

For Lynch personally, *The Exorcist* drove out "distorted blocks of misunderstanding about sex and religion which society has created" by "showing those distortions taken to their ultimate power."[3] The film's steady pacing raises the emotional intensity of its transgressive imagery, like a gradual crescendo, through the violent transfiguration of its main characters to its climatic, yet ambiguous, ending. Meanwhile Nixon's presidency pushed up against the limits of executive authority and constitutional law, inducing fundamental questions about what can be believed about politics during those exceptional times while compelling Americans to reconsider what they wanted their president to do. Toward the end of his essay, Lynch continues writing:

> William Friedkin made violent love to his audience and I for one had a desperately needed orgasm. I accepted my nature in all its glorious ugliness, and now I can love it, mold it, create with it, and make love with it if I chose. I am Free. I no longer need to work on a self-destructive level, because I know it had just become a bad habit that had to be broken and can be broken.[4]

Throughout this book, I have tried to show how Friedkin's films critique moral and ethical "distorted blocks of misunderstanding" that are reproduced through popular cinema, misunderstandings that are repeated like bad habits and "that had to be broken." The films do this through their narrational trajectory, pushing their moral logic to their limits, thus laying bare the contradictions and violence that are typically papered over to serve the experience of moral certainty by the viewer. Films like *The French Connection*, *To Live and Die in L.A.*, and *Killer Joe* problematize legal and moral distinctions that separate policemen, who are generically supposed to abide by the law, from criminals. In *The People v. Paul Crump*, *Rampage*, *12 Angry Men*, and *Rules of Engagement*, I have argued that at stake is the right to critically judge another of criminal transgression itself. And in films like *The Birthday Party*, *The Boys in the Band*, and *Bug*, all based on original theater plays, I tried to highlight how enclosed spaces delineate spaces of melodrama where questions of virtue are raised, virtue consolidated through distinctions between an innocent, often nostalgic, interiority set over-against a threat that is thought to be exterior to it. In all of Friedkin's films analyzed so far, I tried to show how they reveal relations of violence and lay bare their ethics in order to provide spectators with the opportunity to break bad habits. For the director of *Eraserhead*, *Twin Peaks*, *Mulholland Drive*, and many other film and television productions, breaking bad habits means to cease working "on a self-destructive level" and to refuse the cycle of violence associated with the act of moral judgment.

I would like to continue these lines of critique into *The Exorcist*, a seminal work for Friedkin, not only because of its massive financial success but also because it engages with ideas around morality and faith that would occupy the filmmaker throughout his career. Adjusted for inflation, *The Exorcist* still counts as one of the top ten highest grossing films of all time. Its foundational status in film history has legitimized the horror film among art house audiences and forever altered the scope of the genre. While Friedkin acknowledges its incredible success in interview, he also mentions that he never set out to make a horror film but instead intended to work through what he has described as the "mystery of faith." In this chapter, we will examine how this mystery is articulated over the course of his 1973 film and see that it emerges through a series of epistemological failures. These failures, the result of a series of attempts to conclusively identify the source of Regan MacNeil's (Linda Blair) horrifying condition, delineates a line of critical thinking that isolates how belief, particularly belief in that which is rationally impossible, might be possible at all. In turn the power of this film inheres in its capacity to induce the possibility of this belief for the modern film spectator. If the melodramatic mode attests to the persistence of virtue in a post-sacred world, *The Exorcist* operates within this popular mode of moving picture narrative in order to herald the uncanny return of the sacred, manifest through a religious battle between Father Lankester Merrin (Max von Sydow) and the demon Pazuzu. And if melodrama helps explain how characters in a narrative are humanized and deemed worthy of sympathy, Friedkin's film takes this affective mode to its limits through the tension that arises between the pathetic victimization and progressive demonization of Regan's character.

The Exorcist opens with Father Merrin on an archaeological expedition in Nineveh, located in northern Iraq. A number of ominous images are shown in this opening sequence that will reappear later in the film: a demonic figurine found at the excavation site, a small amulet with the words "Sancte Joseph, ora pro nobis" ("Saint Joseph, pray for us") engraved on it and which is apparently "not of the same period" as the figurine, Merrin shakily consuming a nitroglycerine tablet to calm his nerves, a woman in a carriage who will resemble the elderly mother of Father Damien Karras (Jason Miller), a shot of snarling dogs fighting each other, and of course the large statue of Pazuzu. The film cuts to a large house at nighttime in Georgetown. While

Chris MacNeil (Ellen Burstyn) annotates a script in bed, she hears strange sounds in the attic. She goes to check on both the noises and her daughter Regan. Regan is asleep but the window to her room is wide open, allowing the cold winter air to rush in.

Within the first ten minutes of the film, Friedkin shows that something from northern Iraq has come to invade this home in Georgetown through the juxtaposition of these locations, through a cut. We may be reminded of the cuts in *The French Connection* that juxtaposed Marseille and New York, Charnier and the two detectives Popeye and Cloudy. Mark Kermode comments that in the film's introduction, "which seems on the surface to have little narrative import, Friedkin has conjured an ancient, exotic battleground between good and evil, and injected it directly into the home of a modern, wealthy, single, white mother with no apparent religious connections."[5] Additionally significant for us is the logic of contagion that explains the source of narrative tension for Friedkin. Like the bugs in *Bug*, the spirit of Pazuzu remains unseen and infiltrates the interiors of both the home and the body of an innocent girl. At the outset of *The Exorcist*, the viewer is made privy to the distinctions between the domestic and foreign as well as between the secular and sacred, while the characters in the diegesis are subject to a growing sense of terror through their pursuit of a supernatural power that remains unknown to them. Like detectives, Chris and Karras set out to name this pagan entity that originates from outside the ostensibly modern and secularized U.S.

Nevertheless, one is left unsure about how to read other ominous signs in the film's prologue. What are we to make of the clouded eye of a blacksmith, of whether a clock stops for mechanical or intangible reasons, or of the sounds of rattling in the attic that may be caused by rats or something else? One quickly gleans that rational but also superstitious modes of discernment will be necessary for reading these signs, a tension that will increase as the film continues. In the face of this uncertainty, the viewer perhaps desires nothing more than to see the face of Pazuzu himself, if only to confirm who or what is the source of the acousmatic noises coming from various rooms in the house. Later Chris goes to the attic holding a lit candelabrum, putting herself into potential danger, in a moment that almost dares the demon to appear. The sounds of scratching are heard again. When she turns to look they confirm not the presence of rats but of their Swiss housekeeper Karl (Rudolf Schündler), who has come to check on her. The scene leaves the viewer unsettled, since the visual form of whatever was lurking in the attic remains unconfirmed, eluding the empirical look that demands knowledge, even of that which remains invisible.

Chris is an actor on a film called *Crash Course* and is only taking temporary residence in in this colonial-style house (which apparently was modeled to look like the house of Texas democrat Senator Lloyd Bentsen). Her old house in Los Angeles has been sold and she is waiting for a new one to be built.

While Chris is preparing a scene on the Georgetown University campus, we also see Father Karras for the first time, observing Chris from a location in front of Healy Hall. The scene emphasizes the fact that some of *The Exorcist* was itself filmed on location in Georgetown while also reflecting the student activism and anti-war sentiments of the counterculture at the time. According to a *Washington Post* article from 1972, the Catholic church reportedly thought that the student extras that showed up for this scene looked like "freaks."[6] Later in the scene, reversing the relationship between observer and observed, Chris sees Karras expressing doubt about his own faith to another priest in the Saint Michael parish. "There's not a day in my life that I don't feel like a fraud," the priest and psychiatric counselor remarks, quickly establishing that his character is undergoing a crisis of faith. We also find out that he has an ailing mother in Brooklyn and is burdened by guilt for having left her alone in his dimly-lit childhood apartment. Karras tells an older colleague that he wants to be reassigned to be closer to his mother. "I want out of this job. It's wrong, it's no good," he remarks.

One soon begins to sense something out of the ordinary in a scene where Chris and Regan play with an Ouija board. Though they do not touch it, the small planchette suddenly moves of its own accord (one of the many images in *The Exorcist* that will be repeated in subsequent horror films). Regan reports that it is the doing of "Captain Howdy," her imaginary friend. In the 2003 recut of the film, signs of the unexplainable first appear when the twelve-year-old girl is taken to a medical center to undergo a physical exam. During an EKG test, while the camera holds on a medium shot of Regan lying in bed, Friedkin inserts a brief shot of a demonic face, indicating the invasion of Pazuzu into her character. Dr. Harold Klein (Barton Heyman) diagnoses her with "a disorder of the nerves" and remarks that she shows the symptoms typical of such a disorder, including hyperactivity, "her temper," and weak "performance in math." He then proclaims that "nobody knows the cause of hyperkinetic behavior in a child" and prescribes Regan ten milligrams of Ritalin a day. (At this point in the film, one may wonder if in our time she would simply have been diagnosed as having ADHD.) In the original theatrical version, Regan is shown receiving a medical exam for the first time after she interrupts Chris's party and chillingly tells a group of singing revelers that, "You're gonna die up there," while urinating on the floor through her nightgown. This is also the first time her bed is violently shaken. In his office, Dr. Klein diagnoses Regan with a "type of disturbance in the chemical-electrical activity of the brain" located in in the "temporal lobe." He somehow connects the shaking bed with "a kind of seizure disorder" that can cause personality changes, even "criminal behavior." At this point, one may also begin to wonder whether Regan's malady may be diagnosed as a medical condition at all: is she simply acting out or is she really sick? Does her conduct reflect the antisocial behavior perceived of the "freakish" counterculture, dismissively depicted with the young protestors in *Crash Course*?

In any event, the portrayal of Dr. Klein's medical assessments (which remind one of a similar conceit around insanity at the end of *Rampage*) attests to the ways in which medical knowledge produces a discursive object, the patient, that is to become subject to scientific interrogation and diagnosis. Friedkin consulted radiologists and physicians to make certain that his depictions of Regan's examinations were authentic and as up-to-date as possible. "These doctors had all witnessed similar behavior," the director recalls, "and it seemed to resemble hallucinations derived from paranoid schizophrenia."[7] The body of the patient is bestowed a geography within this discursive mode as its surfaces are divided into a series of regions connected to specific functions, allowing for further categorization and classification. Regan's corpus will thus be expected to betray signs of disease, ailment, and various "conditions." The medical institution will also determine what counts as legitimate and illegitimate knowledge, and dictate what may be known and unknown about the body, as well as delineate divisions between correct and incorrect diagnoses of it. The clinical gaze, according to Foucault in *The Birth of the Clinic*, constitutes its object of observation, "the tangible space of the body, which at the same time is that opaque mass in which secrets, invisible lesions, and the very mystery of origins lie hidden."[8] In doing so, this gaze reiterates the relationship between the examining look and the examined patient, between expert insight and medical ignorance. One participates in this mode of assessing the body when struggling to decide whether Regan is acting out antisocially, whether she is just a "rotten kid," or truly sick.

This clinical gaze, as I have described in an earlier chapter, operates in parallel with that associated with the melodramatic mode in its quest to find virtue at the heart of every human character depicted on screen. In this way, Dr. Klein shifts his analysis almost imperceptibly from a medical discourse to a moralizing one as he offers his analysis. His expert opinion, on the other hand, is considered to be ostensibly ideologically unbiased and unclouded by untruths, politics, and superstition. The medical and juridical discourses in which he operates have been empowered by modern institutions to produce a secular truth about the self and its invisible interiority.

The scene in which the apparent scar on Regan's brain is scanned through cerebral angiography manifests this discourse and reveals its macabre, violating curiosity. After a catheter is inserted into her neck, which immediately spurts blood, three large X-ray devices are moved close to Regan's head. They thud loudly and repetitively, like a jackhammer, as they scan her brain (Figure 5.1). The depiction of these machines recalls that of the electric chair at the end of *The People vs. Paul Crump* in their necessary violence, the chair as a technology of death that

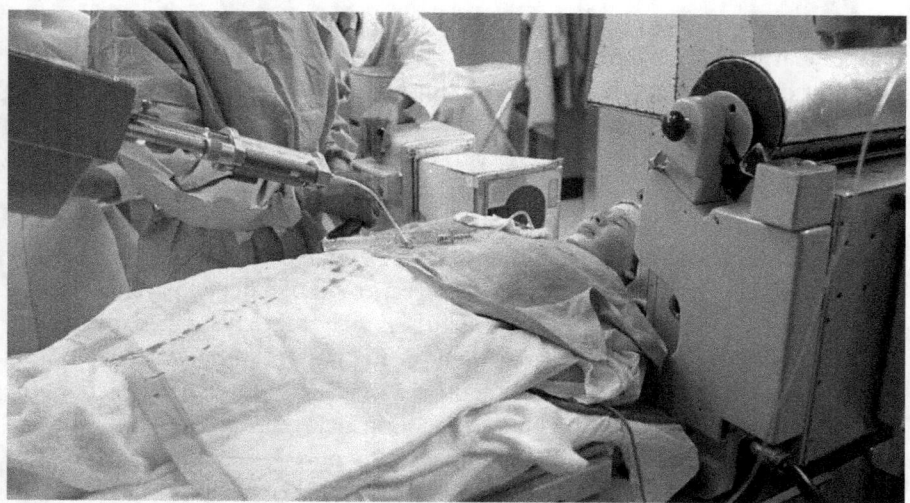

Figure 5.1 Scanning for Regan's malady

seems both medieval and modern and which instantiates Foucault's genealogical historiography. The images that are produced by the angiography realize the fantasy of making the medical sensible, of making visible and even tactile a condition that she embodies, a frozen image of her condition, so that it may be made objective and thus available for judgment. Assessing the results, the medical professionals, Dr. Klein and Dr. Taney (Robert Symonds), are surprised to learn that there is in fact no lesion, "no vascular displacement at all." Meanwhile at home, the demon seems to have finally taken possession of Regan as she exhibits increasingly unexplainable and blasphemous behavior. On her bed, she obscenely tells both doctors to "fuck me" repeatedly. Having failed to locate the brain lesion, they hand the patient over to a psychiatrist, but not before advising that they perform a pneumoencephalogram on her first, another invasive X-ray process that involves a spinal tap.

The psychiatrist (Arthur Storch) begins by hypnotizing Regan, asking if she is comfortable, asking her age, and whether there is "someone inside you?" He addresses the "person inside of Regan" directly and asks if it is Captain Howdy. When she is asked about the identity of this interiorized person, Regan violently seizes the psychiatrist's genitals with her hand. It is at this moment that the film suddenly cuts and Karras, who is shown jogging, is introduced to detective William Kinderman (Lee J. Cobb). Kinderman is investigating the death of the director of *Crash Course*, Burke Dennings (Jack MacGowran). The presence of the detective introduces additional discursive modes into the film, that of the legal and investigative, reprising the policemen and detectives that appear in Friedkin's other films. Kinderman tries but fails, to coax Karras's opinion as to any priests that may have reason to harm Burke. Curiously, the detective invites the priest to the movies to see *Othello* (without clarifying whether he is referring to the 1965 film starring Lawrence Olivier or Orson Welles's 1955 version).

The Exorcist then cuts to Dr. Barringer (Peter Masterson), the director of a large psychiatric clinic. He diagnoses Regan's condition as a "somnambular-form possession," a rare disorder whose etiology originates in a psychic conflict and eventually leads to delusional fantasies that the patient's body has been invaded by an "alien intelligence." He is speaking before a group of a dozen psychiatrists, all seated around a conference table, with Chris at its head. Sensing her frustration, Barringer asks if she or Regan are religious in any way and proposes that an exorcism may be effective in this case. As soon as he suggests this course of action, the psychiatrist condescendingly rebuffs the notion that there may be any spiritual validity to the procedure and remarks that, "It's pure force of suggestion. The victim's belief in suggestion is what caused it, so in that same way the belief in the power of exorcism can make it disappear." The analytical aim of the psychiatrists, as we saw with the medical doctors and the detective, is to insistently confirm that all claims about the truth of Regan's mental and physical hygiene will fall within the discursive realm of the secular, a realm circumscribed by Enlightenment reason and empirically discernable virtue. This realm will operate in juxtaposition to superstition, deviancy, delusion, and madness.

Meeting for the first time, Chris later asks Karras how one might go about getting an exorcism if a person is "possessed by a demon or something." The priest responds despondently that, "I'd have to get them into a time machine and get them back to the sixteenth century." The ostensible man of faith has also apparently renounced some of the more superstitious practices of Catholicism. All are at their wits' end, however, and so the priests and psychiatrists place Regan back in her bedroom where the exorcism will take place.

Notably, the type of psychiatry represented in *The Exorcist* is not psychotherapy, but hypnosis. Widely practiced in the 1970s in medical and forensic contexts, hypnosis reproduces the hierarchy of doctor and patient through the roles of the controller and the controlled, while lending the entire dynamic between the two a telepathic, paranormal tinge. If the former demands that a symptom of disease show itself empirically in order that it may be legitimated, the doctor-as-hypnotist makes this demand especially focused by locating it in the psyche of the individual. The truth will reveal itself through the words and behavior of the patient herself. The aim of the hypnotist, then, is to remove the emotional and psychic blockages that prevent this access. At roughly the same moment that *The Exorcist* was selling out theaters worldwide, Foucault lectured on the workings of psychiatric power in Paris and specifically about the technique of hypnosis and suggestion:

putting the subject in a situation such that, on a precise order, one will be able to get a perfectly isolated hysterical symptom: paralysis of a muscle, inability to speak, trembling, etcetera. In short, hypnosis is used for precisely this purpose, placing the patient in a situation such that he will have exactly the symptom one wants, when one wants it, and nothing else.[9]

His observations here should be read in relation to his genealogy of the concept of insanity in modernity and the institution of psychiatry in *Madness and Civilization*. Like the medical institution that thrives on constituting discursive distinctions between the sick and healthy, psychiatry operates by reiterating and concentrating long-standing distinctions between the insane and the sane. The medical clinic, hospital, the psychiatric clinic, the bedroom: these are spaces where panoptic surveillance will take place, where Regan's pre-teen self is to be compulsively inspected, coercively categorized, and where her behaviors will be measured and controlled. When the psychiatrist commands the person inside Regan to "come forward" and asks, "who are you," he receives a painful response that is both highly sexual and explicitly aggressive, belying both the theory of latent drives as well as any bad faith about the practice of psychiatry.

As medical and psychiatric means are deployed to diagnose what is happening to Regan, the game of soul-searching, of finding malady in the other, results in the repeated failure of these means. Through Regan's inability to explain her intractable condition, the narrative to *The Exorcist* unfolds through the unraveling of scientific certainty. What we are left with, then, is an understanding of her supposed truth that can only be arrived at through a leap of faith, an uncanny belief in that which has been deemed impossible by modern science. The existence of evil spirits may be "possible" and "necessary," to quote another film by Friedkin based on a Harold Pinter play. A review of the film that appeared in a 1974 issue of *Cinefantastique* expresses some sense of how *The Exorcist* arrives at this conclusion:

> Science fails; the law—a detective (Cobb) who keeps smelling religious maniac—fails. Even that most spiritual of all institutions, motherhood, falls short. By the end of the movie, the only institution left to keep that demon up in its room is God: or whatever force in man passes for God.[10]

The possibility of alternative beliefs and metaphysical explanations, particularly those associated with the new spiritual discourses of the counterculture, come into the picture. In this, *The Exorcist* seems to resonate with the sensibilities expressed by *Chariots of the Gods*, a bestseller throughout the 1970s and after, and which posits that ancient artifacts, perhaps like the pagan figurine featured at the beginning of the film (or the embedded monolith in Kubrick's *2001:*

A Space Odyssey [1968]), were produced by intelligent aliens that arrived on earth long ago. Regan's condition is presented through a similarly impossible narrative of the return of the repressed. The filmic adaptation of this book of pseudoscience was nominated for best documentary feature at the Academy Awards in 1971, so popular were its wild conceits. In Friedkin's 1973 film, a demonic spirit, thought to have been banished to the realms of superstition, deviancy, delusion, and madness, has returned and infested Regan's body.

The Exorcist thus proceeds through critique, by applying secular, institutionalized means of knowing the self, what Carol Clover calls "white science" in her analysis of the horror film, and then showing how they fail to capture what is at the heart of Regan's rationally improbable malady.[11] At stake is not merely the condition of her body, the origin of her intentions, or her psyche, but her moral soul. We are reminded here of the references to the story of Abraham in Friedkin's *The Hunted* that delineate how faith appears through the suspension of the universal, faith as exceptional to modern ways of knowing that insist upon empirical and scientific correctness. In Chapter 2, I tried to show how Abraham's trial of faith is framed through a critical ethics of filicide in Johnny Cash's recitation of the lines to Bob Dylan's song, "Highway 61 Revisited," which recounts and recasts the original parable, and a postcard reproduction of Rembrandt's painting, *Sacrifice of Isaac*. Faith, absurd and irrational, comes to the fore when rational, critical explanations about the morality of Abraham's intent to murder his son Isaac fail to help us understand the nature of his murderous and profoundly unethical motives. Yet it is precisely in its maddening absurdity that one may begin to perceive the uncompromising nature and impossibility of faith. As with the fundamental absurdity of Abraham's passion, the "person inside" Regan remains unseen throughout *The Exorcist*. Pazuzu's presence is constantly mediated through symptoms that appear on her face and body, or other signs of the supernatural that appear in the film, like a drawer that opens on its own, a shaking bed, or an inhuman voice. After medicine and psychiatry fail to link these signs to an originating cause, the signs of melodrama lead the viewer to an uncanny realization—the return of the pagan gods and the arrival of harbingers of evil in the world.

Scholarship around Friedkin's best-known film is multitudinous and encompasses an astonishingly wide variety of fields. These accounts, like the medical and psychiatric discourses depicted in the film, may themselves be thought to constitute a "white science" in their attempts to explain the meaning of *The Exorcist*. Such accounts typically perform symptomatic readings to assess the interiority of the filmic text, holding it up to illustrate broad concepts about culture and the self. And like the discourses associated with the doctor and the psychiatrist, they attempt to make sensible hidden truths that lie beyond the surface of the film. There are accounts that claim the film reiterates primal narratives that concerned our "Paleolithic and Neolithic forebears" long ago, including the fear of the other, which developed and later became manifest in the Christian tradition through the figure of Satan.[12] Friedkin's film taps into fundamental, genetically determined fears and anxieties that have enabled humans to survive in a world of threat. It represents a response to a sense of meaninglessness in contemporary culture by confronting its "deep horror."[13] These scholarly accounts bear some troubling resemblance, perhaps, to the narrative of repression in *Chariots of the Gods*. On a less essentializing track, *The Exorcist* has also been seen as reflecting Jesuit tenets, including the tradition of self-questioning through education and scholarly rigor.[14] When Karras undergoes his crisis of faith he is posing the question, tantamount to Jesuit belief, of whether his will corresponds with that of God. On the other hand, this theodical concern is at the heart of many critical accounts of the film that see it within other theological contexts. Horror films like *The Exorcist* reflect uncertainties about the very existence of the Christian God and ambivalences about the question of whether these uncertainties matter at all in our secular age.[15] Such broad issues certainly were relevant at the time the film was released, following the election of John F. Kennedy in 1960, who won by overcoming an overwhelming anti-Catholic bias, and less than ten years after the close of the Second Vatican Council. In this regard, Friedkin's film has been understood to mark a turning point in the representation of Catholicism in Hollywood. Following the collapse of the Production Code, *The Exorcist* resurrects the gothic and occult aspects of this tradition that had remained, for the most part, suppressed until the late 1960s.[16]

The film depicts the institution of psychiatry, but in terms of the available academic writing on *The Exorcist* that delves into the psyche of the characters or narrative, the majority of them take up psychoanalytic approaches that enable critical discussion of childhood, motherhood, sexuality, and issues revolving around gender. The relationship between Chris and Regan, according to many of these accounts, can be understood in terms of the Oedipal drama and specifically of the journey the little girl must undertake to replace her mother with her father as her favored figure of attachment. Instead of acquiescing to becoming a proper "daddy's girl," Regan embodies a monstrous-feminine rejection of this patriarchal order as the film unfolds, both in appearance and behavior.[17] Her appearance is also the result of self-inflicted wounds that reflect a masochistic impulse through the coercion of forces that threaten the delineation of proper femininity.[18] In effect, the story of her possession is an allegory about the rejection of the Oedipal complex in order to return to an originary dyadic relation between the mother and daughter. On the other hand, if one turns to Blatty's text, we can observe that this process of ego formation is not only left troubled and incomplete in the story of *The Exorcist*, but also reiterates taboo relations between fathers and daughters as well as between patients and doctors. Regan's transgressive and repeated invitations for sex with the men in the novel may be interpreted as expressing an incestuous desire for her father, who, as in Friedkin's film, remains largely absent from the narrative.[19] From these accounts of the family romance one may read the figure of the possessed child as linked to cultural perceptions of "failed" parenting. As tropes of contagion, narratives of possession allegorize the consequences of negative societal influences, including the media, on children.[20] From this perspective, the film seems to anticipate themes that would appear in Alice Miller's international bestselling book, *The Drama of the Gifted Child*.

In any event, these psychoanalytic accounts may be supplemented with audience studies that consider the phenomenon of "cinematic neurosis" and trauma that viewers experienced while watching *The Exorcist*. These viewers show symptoms similar to individuals in crisis or experiencing borderline personality disorder. The anxiety, dissociation, and paranoid ideation that are represented in the film are reported to have been experienced by individuals after seeing it, raising once again issues of suggestion and hypnosis and the adverse impact of Friedkin's film on sensitive viewers.[21] The traumatic experience of *The Exorcist* becomes itself an object of scientific scrutiny as viewers are subjected to the effects produced through the apparatus of the cinema.

* * *

While continuing to consider these critical perspectives, I would like to return to the critical logic around the "mystery of faith" I have been trying to elucidate here and throughout the book. We are left with the conclusion that Regan's condition can be accounted for only by supernatural explanations and thus we are take seriously the presence of evil in the world, embodied by the demon Pazuzu. Friedkin's film attests to the return of sixteenth-century occult practice into everyday social life. Once the exorcism begins, the viewer is invited to consider the image as documenting a series of spectacular events that are typically considered impossible in reality. It tests the limits of Octave Mannoni's formulation, appropriated by Christian Metz, that summarizes the logic of disavowal integral to the cinematic apparatus: "I know very well, but all the same . . ."[22] And by allowing for the possibility of that which repeatedly escapes explanation, in the authentic representation of the highly improbable, *The Exorcist* re-evaluates the meaning of exorcism in terms of the institution of cinema and raises the issue of whether its images can be believed as true. The problem of faith, whose logic so interests Friedkin, parallels the problem of the spectator's own faith in what is depicted on screen. These are concerns that inform Friedkin's recent documentary of a "real" exorcism, *The Devil and Father Amorth*. The initial two-thirds of *The Exorcist* set out to make visible the invisible condition Regan embodies. The spectacle of the exorcism, comprising the last third, will showcase clear signs of her demonic possession, inscribed on her body as well through the *mise-en-scène* of her bedroom. The critical logic delineated through the film's narrative structure, first the depiction of a series of attempts to explain Regan's condition scientifically followed by the conclusion that it can only be explained by recourse to the supernatural, is crucial for building evidence in the cinematic legitimacy of the film's conclusion.

When Karras first sees Regan, restrained so she does not harm herself, she famously projectile vomits (pea soup) in the priest's face. He throws holy water on her and while she writhes in pain from the burning sensation caused by it, he records her screams and speaking in tongues. Karras consults the bishop of his parish in his large office—the Church, like the modern institutions depicted earlier, has its hierarchy of institutionalized power as well—and they decide to send Merrin to perform the exorcism. The solemn arrival of the old man at the MacNeil house seems to quickly dissipate any doubts as to the fact of Regan's possession. "The demon is a liar," Merrin tells his younger colleague, "He will lie to confuse us. But he will also mix lies with the truth to attack us." Like soldiers marching into battle, they slowly climb the stairs and enter her room. In the battle between the forces of good and evil, the discourse of Catholic theology, as elaborated in the *Rituale Romanum*, will function as a weapon. Prayer and the throwing of holy water is met with profanity and the animation of inanimate objects aimed at attacking the priests. When they chant, "the power of Christ compels you," Regan's face suddenly relaxes, her eyes become fully white, and her body levitates off the bed.

The exorcism showcases the spectacle of what inhabits Regan's interiority and so the special effects during these well-known scenes must maintain the belief in the reality of spiritual warfare. Vomit tubes, piano wire, a life-size Linda Blair dummy with a fully rotatable head, a foam rubber tongue, flying objects, the refrigerated set, latex molds, crew members aggressively shaking Regan's bed: the mechanical means to portray the supernatural in the cinema must maintain faith in the authenticity of what is seen and what cannot be diagnosed by medical, psychiatric, and forensic science. Pauline Kael, who otherwise has never been a fan of Friedkin, seems to sense the director's aims here when she writes in her review of the film that "the movie—religiously literal-minded—shows you a heaping amount of blood and horror. This explicitness must be what William Friedkin has in mind when he talks publicly about the picture's 'documentary quality.'"[23] Music from George Crumb's *Black Angels*, Anton Webern's *Five Pieces for Orchestra, Op. 10*, but also sound effects created from guinea pigs running on sandpaper and buzzing insects keep audiences guessing as to their diegetic source. Meanwhile, the well-known overdubbing of Mercedes McCambridge's emphysemic voice, made hoarse after years of chain-smoking and alcohol, makes, as Michel Chion remarks, "multiple voices—old woman, monster—come out of the 'possessed' girl."[24]

This mismatch between body and speech is heightened through the fact that McCambridge's voice was recorded on the soundtrack and not the dialogue track. This discrepancy led to a number of legal disputes around how she should be credited in the film and about who had legal possession of the sound for *The Exorcist*, two issues that highlight the "proprietary" nature of sound effects in the cinema more broadly.[25] Karras records Regan's voice and plays it in a language learning room later, revealing that English is spoken, but backward. As in Led Zeppelin's fourth album from 1971, backmasking hides secret satanic messages in the recording. At stake is the very hermeneutics of audio recording and what it reveals. In this connection one might consider the nature of the Nixon tapes, which were never released during his presidency, and their meaning for the truth of his actions while in office. (Merrin's warning, that "he will lie to confuse us. But he will also mix lies with the truth to attack us," seems to gain additional relevance in this context.)

Friedkin's film culminates in Regan's bedroom, again a closed space of melodrama, where characters are implicated in an explicit Manichean conflict between good and evil, where the space of innocence that is Regan's childhood is at stake, and where, above all, what takes place aims toward the legibility of virtue. In his psychoanalytic reading of *The Exorcist*, Andrew Hock Soon Ng notes that Regan's bedroom functions as a site of intimacy and transgression, where private, forbidden incestuous desires are expressed. "Here, both spaces, body and bedroom," he writes, "are collapsed into a single desire, whose agitation necessarily affects them together."[26] The melodramatic mode informs the entire unfolding of *The Exorcist* but, in its pursuit of moral legibility through the dialectics of pathos and action, is gradually shorn of its associations with science and medicine. Holy water, the reciting of sacraments, a floating bed, cracking walls, the sign of the cross: these signifiers have meaning within Regan's bedroom, pointing back to the legitimizing of the sacred in an ostensibly post-sacred age. By the final exorcism sequence, the modern and post-sacred mode of moral feeling that is radicalized in many of Friedkin's films becomes, in effect, re-sacralized and ironically turns out to be constitutive for the appearance of unearthly evil. On the other hand, while the film's fantastic visual and auditory elements seem to lift it above the mundane melodrama of American politics, they nevertheless contribute to the reiteration of melodrama as a kind of political theology. The spectacular scenes depicting Regan's exorcism, the excessive display of the vulgar and profane that operates in the lineage of the "cinema of attractions," are not simply the other to cinematic narrative but are fundamental for externalizing internal moral values and thus for realizing the aims of melodrama. The manipulations of voice, soundtrack, image, and mechanical effects attest to the power of cinema to compel viewers to emotionally invest in this impossible spectacle.

The space of melodrama delineated by Regan's bedroom takes us back to a film that was discussed in Chapter 1. In an interview from 1974, the director makes a connection to *The Birthday Party* in order to explain why the reasons for Regan's possession must remain inexplicable:

> My feeling is that the demon just arrives at that point in the story when we want it to arrive, just as any character walks in the door. As in *The Birthday Party*, Goldberg and McCann just walk in. What is it about this little girl that made her possessed? Who the hell knows? It's not the author's province to speculate.[27]

In *The Birthday Party*, the concert pianist Stanley is asked whether he recognizes "an external force, responsible for you, suffering for you," and about the relationship between necessity and possibility. Earlier, I argued that the claustrophobic room in Friedkin's cinema is treated like a theatrical stage, reflecting the relationship of the two forms in the adaptation from one to the other. Similarly, in *The Exorcist* the walls of Regan's bedroom delineate the space where the forces of good and evil, between the human and non-human, are forced to confront each other face-to-face, confined within a small space. During their momentary respite, Merrin responds to the question of why Regan was chosen to be possessed: "I think the point is to make us despair. To see ourselves as animal and ugly. To reject the possibility that God could love us." This dialogue, apparently written by Blatty and reluctantly included by Friedkin for the 2000 version of the film, articulates the horror of the possibility that God has been alienated from man. But it is the confined space that brings this confrontation between man and his opposite, "animal and ugly," to fruition. As we have seen in many of his other films, Friedkin creates claustrophobic spaces, functioning like laboratories of moral sentiment, where ethical dramas are taken to their breaking point, as we saw in key moments from the director's other films, such as the bars depicted in *Cruising*, the jury deliberation room in *12 Angry Men*, a motel room in *Bug*, and the trailer home in *Killer Joe*.

But like the morally compromised characters depicted in these moments, ambivalence pervades these conclusions and encourages moral uncertainty within the melodramatic mode. As in films like *The French Connection* and *To Live and Die in L.A.*, one is encouraged to experience sympathies, divided and conflicted, as Regan becomes increasingly monstrous. This experience revolves around the problem of her identity—one may be confused as to whether she is an innocent girl victimized by an external force or a victimizer, her possessed body an evil agent of violence. While Karras gently wipes her forehead with a hand towel during a respite from the exorcism, Regan takes on the voice of his dead mother. "Dimmy, please, I'm afraid," she remarks, speaking in Greek while reminding the priest of the guilt he feels for letting her pass away alone in a mental clinic. "You're not my mother," he angrily responds. This moment prepares the viewer emotionally for Merrin's later death at Regan's hands. When Karras sees her giggling, the priest calls her a "son of a bitch," throws her on the floor, and punches her repeatedly in the face. As Todd Berliner puts it in his account of the "conceptual incongruity" of Friedkin's film, "Regan is both evil and its innocent victim, both revolting and sympathetic"[28] (Figure 5.2). She embodies a contradiction that arises from within the popular melodramatic mode, one that remains unresolvable between virtue and villainy, innocence and utter defilement. In order that she may be saved, Regan becomes at the same time an object of Karras's violence. And in the end, he sacrifices himself, as we know, by letting the demon possess and contaminate his body.

The representation of this claustrophobic space in *The Exorcist* helps us see how these restricted rooms that appear throughout Friedkin's oeuvre may additionally be characterized as heterotopias. These spaces self-reflexively appeal to the ontological heterotopia of the cinema theater itself, an indoor space that provides an opportunity for individuals to judge images that refer to things and worlds outside the cinema. The boundary between the sacred, enclosed space of the room and that of the world of outside is permeable, vulnerable to contagion. For Foucault, a heterotopia is a counter-site, "a kind of effectively enacted utopia in which the real sites, all the other real sites that can be found within the culture, are simultaneously represented, contested, and inverted."[29] Films like *The Exorcist* and *The French Connection* may be understood as melodramas that draw from historical events, while each delineates a non-site where these events

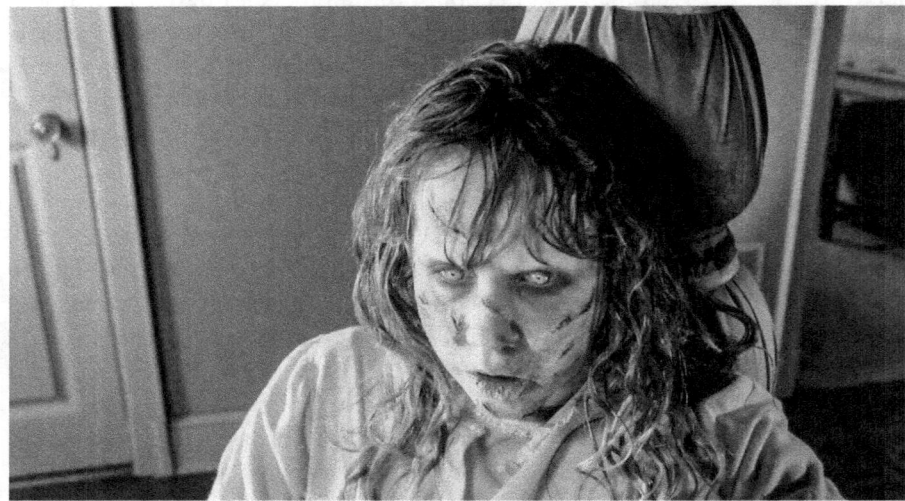

Figure 5.2 Innocence and defilement

are represented and inverted. Inside and outside the film's diegesis, inside and outside the theater, one term, and then one binary, crosses over into the other, fiction and history, secular and sacred. "Thus it is that the cinema is a very odd rectangular room," Foucault writes, "at the end of which, on a two-dimensional screen, one sees the projection of a three-dimensional space."[30] To identify these spaces and settle into them is to engage with the melodramatic mode in order to inhabit a place from which one may morally judge the other.

Let me end this section with some commentary on Friedkin's own views on claustrophobic space. As Karras struggles with the loss of his mother, and as Regan taunts him for leaving her on her own, a haunting image of her sitting on Regan's bed appears during the exorcism. It is a quick shot from Karras's point of view and appears as a subjective hallucination. The demon already knows the deep guilt the priest still feels. In my interview with Friedkin, the director spoke wistfully of the loss of his own mother, before he experienced his meteoric success in the 1970s with *The French Connection* and the *Exorcist*:

> One of the things that really crashed my world was the death of my mother. I loved and respected her so much and then she was gone, just gone. I was away doing *The Boys in the Band* in New York and I had leased a house out there. It was my first house. And she was walking down the street and dropped dead. And I got a call at four in the morning from my business manager. I was in New York and it just shattered my world. I was editing *The Boys in the Band*. I've never really gotten over it.

This was in 1969, as Friedkin was finishing his 1970 film. Continuing, he spoke to me of the feeling of safety present "in this little room and with my parents," recalling Marcel Proust's biography. Although Friedkin acknowledges that he and the French writer were raised differently, he explains that Proust "captures the child's sense of loss and love for a parent, that I could identify with." The son of immigrants, like Karras, like the scriptwriter Blatty, Friedkin seems to express some of his regret in being unable to share his success in Hollywood with his mother who according to the director had "sacrificed her life" for him.[31] Adding significance to the claustrophobic rooms that I have tried to identify and analyze throughout this book, Friedkin told me:

> I think we all live in a claustrophobic way, and occasionally venture out, you have a girlfriend, a wife, close friends that take you out occasionally. But see, I'm almost never out of that world even though I love my wife, I have two sons that I love, I'm never outside that world. Never. When a light goes off, you are there alone with whoever the fuck you are. No matter who's next to you, or in the room with you. And I'm very

conscious of that. That's somehow in all of my films, and in the things that interest me. And they're all basically solo statements. Miles Davis appeals to me, but he's a voice in the wilderness. Bill Evans, the jazz pianist, and Kleiber's interpretations of classic Beethoven.

It is art that has helped him cope with a life lived with limitations, with reminders, not only of incredible success, but also of failure and disappointment. Again, the claustrophobic space is where these all-too-human anxieties and concerns are negotiated.

You think we live in a perfect, peaceful world? You're safe in your own perimeters. We're all safe in the little worlds we build around ourselves. Try to think beyond that, this is what great art and literature can do. It can take away that invisible shield we all live by. The sense that we're going to live forever. Life, liberty, and the pursuit of happiness? And then, some horrible thing happens to you, or your friend or relative, and it just shatters these illusions.

And yet, the prospect of venturing out beyond one's own perimeters, one's fears, is addressed in all of his films as well. To continue living and working, despite the confrontation with impossibilities that prevent their success and the unsettling uncertainties that lie outside one's own "little world"—this impulse seems to constitute the encounter with the mystery of faith for Friedkin. And to commit oneself to this encounter, to reach out toward that which transgresses the self, is to comport oneself toward what the director calls "fate." We turn to its mystery in the section that follows.

SORCERER (1977)

Nixon addressed the nation in a televised address on August 8, 1974 to announce his resignation from public office. He did not admit to any criminal activities relating to the Watergate scandal but claimed he was resigning because he knew that he had lost the support of Congress and thus would not be able to "carry out the duties of this office in the way the interests of the Nation would require." Nixon then went on to tout his own accomplishments in the area of foreign policy and declared to have ended the Vietnam War and opened the door to relations with China. He took responsibility for making friends of "one hundred million" people in Arab countries and took credit for the denuclearization in the Soviet Union. He tendered his resignation the next day and just one month later, President Gerald Ford, in a highly controversial move, pardoned Nixon in order to achieve the "greatest good of all the people of the United States." Ford's own televised speech attempted to elicit sympathy for his shamed predecessor, calling it an "American tragedy in which we all have played a part."

Nixon the private citizen avoided the limelight until he sat down with British journalist David Frost for a series of taped interviews in 1977. They were broadcast on television and radio in four ninety-minute parts in May, drawing tens of millions of viewers and listeners. In the interviews Nixon defends his decision to deploy illegal means, such as burglary and electronic surveillance, during his presidency to contain anti-war and countercultural activities. In effect, he granted himself the sovereign power to decide legality under purported conditions of political emergency. "When the president does it," Nixon infamously stated, with the camera close up on his face, "that means that it is not illegal." It is this logic of the exception that impugned and damaged the reputation of the presidency, following the burglaries in the Watergate building and the subsequent cover-up operation. Throughout the interviews, Nixon would continue to deny that his actions while in office were in any way immoral or illegal. Watching the careful shot-reverse shots between the men, the viewer is invited to scrutinize the images of his facial expressions, reactions, and physical demeanor in order to consider his stated motives and thus assess the virtue of the former president.

Throughout this book I have tried to elucidate a series of key themes and problematics that characterize Friedkin's thinking through the discursive mode of popular cinema. These include the problem of sovereignty, its relationship to law, the question of the legitimate exercise of violence, and of legal and moral transgression, problems that are played out in what the director calls the "thin line between policeman and criminal." Another concerns the problem of faith in the modern era which, as I tried to show above, is realized through critique. These issues are staged in claustrophobic spaces of melodrama which provide the conditions for both the elaboration of the ethical underpinnings of this popular mode of moving image narrative as well as their overturning. The narrative of the Nixon scandal in fact resonates with many of these Friedkinian themes in their content and scope. His presidency tested the limits of both executive authority and constitutional law. At the same time, investigative journalism and narratives of grand conspiracy in the news media, of corruption going "all the way to the top," fostered a growing cynicism about American democracy and a waning of faith in the legitimacy of its institutions. The morally ambivalent characters that appear in Friedkin's cinema, particularly in the films of the 1970s, knowingly transgress moral norms, as if to reflect the chaos that was perceived to be unfolding in the American news at the time. On the other hand, I have been trying to show through this book that his films do so in order to provide viewers with the opportunity to critically think these norms and their relationship to the law. Indeed, it is precisely the depiction of transgression that defines his work and, in pursuing it, Friedkin's films test the limits of how moral human beings are to be depicted in popular cinema. This problematic not only centers on whether what viewers see and hear in the cinema counts as true, but also on whether it can still provide spectators with the experience of redemption (as it reportedly did for David Lynch while watching *The Exorcist*).

One month after the Nixon/Frost interviews were broadcast on television, *Sorcerer* premiered in U.S. cinemas on June 24, 1977. The opening shots betray little of the story that will unfold. The title of the film appears while in the background the face of a totem or fetishistic object fades in over a soundtrack composed of discordant, organ-like noises, inspiring the question of whether this film will continue the supernatural and pagan themes featured in *The Exorcist*. But the film quickly cuts to a long shot of the Zócalo plaza in Veracruz, Mexico City, indicated by a caption in the bottom corner of the screen. A man overlooks the bustling area from the balcony of his apartment. While putting out his cigarette, another man wearing dark sunglasses steps in the door and calmly shoots him with a pistol. (Perhaps *Sorcerer* will resemble *The French Connection*, with this opening depicting an assassination that echoes that of the earlier film?) Friedkin next cuts to a shot of the Damascus Gate in Jerusalem and slowly zooms in on a young man wearing a yarmulke. He meets up with two others, they sit and rest a bit, and then board a bus together. A bomb suddenly explodes and these three men, undercover Palestinian terrorists, are chased by the Israeli police.

We then cut to Paris. Starting with a shot of the Arc de Triomphe, we are taken to the bedroom of a wealthy couple who are discussing research that is about to be published. She is editing a book about a "soldier-poet" named Étienne DeBray of the French Foreign Legion. He receives an anniversary present from her, a watch with the words "For the tenth-year of our eternity" engraved on the back. But the businessman has been accused of criminal fraud and bribery, charges that will bankrupt him and his firm. Desperate demands for help from his father-in-law are not successful and his financial advisor commits suicide. Finally, we have another cut to a scene that takes place in Elizabeth, New Jersey. Four Irish gang members, including one played by Roy Scheider, get out of a car and enter a Catholic church, rob its ample tithes, and kill one of its priests. Driving away, they are involved in an accident and only Scheider's character makes it out alive. The killed priest is the brother of the leader of a rival gang, who vows to pursue the injured but surviving gangster, remarking that, "I don't care where he is or what it costs." Scheider leaves New Jersey to let things blow over and is helped to do so by his friend Vinnie. Vinnie is played by Randy Jurgensen, the New York police officer who advised

Friedkin on *The French Connection* and who will also play Detective Lefransky in *Cruising*. The troubled gangster knows nothing about where he is being sent, except that he will need a passport to get there.

At this point, almost one-quarter of the way into *Sorcerer*, the viewer is provided with four seemingly unrelated plotlines. Each location is indicated by a caption and given only a brief depiction, each episode becoming progressively longer. As in *The French Connection* and *The Exorcist*, which begin with prologues set in Marseille and Northern Iraq, Friedkin's film from 1977 begins by delineating the film's international scope, then cross-cutting between the distant locations. English is not spoken until the Elizabeth sequence, already more than fifteen minutes into the film. Meanwhile, victims and perpetrators of violence in each episode are quickly identified, mostly through generic means. As in the prologue to *The Boys in the Band*, each character is introduced as having individual lives before coming together to move the main plot forward. The assassin, terrorist, corrupt businessman, and the gangster—each of these characterizations implies film genres yet are not elaborated upon. Little information is given that allows these episodes to be grounded in real contexts and historical events. A slaying in Mexico, terrorism in Israel and the Middle East, corruption in France, mob activity in New Jersey: each remains historically vague, like the facile depiction of the Kosovo War in *The Hunted*. As we have seen, popular melodrama reduces the political complexities of history in order to serve its morally binarized aims. These melodramas generally take place in tourist spots, marking images of cultural specificity that also have the status of commodified images. What is more, no credits are provided at the opening of *Sorcerer*, breaking with expectations, as if to emphasize that any and all proper names will be unnecessary to the film. These episodes seem to suggest that Friedkin's film will not center on a single individual-hero, but will concern a group of four morally compromised delinquents as each flees the scenes of crime they were responsible for creating. And like Nixon, these four men will refuse to take responsibility for their illegal actions.

In lieu of opening credits and more conventional character development, these episodes function as an extended introduction to *Sorcerer*. It turns out that Scheider's character has been taken to an unnamed rural location in Latin America. A cut abruptly takes the viewer there, as with the sudden transition to Vietnam in Michael Cimino's *The Deer Hunter*, and without a caption as in the previous four episodes. Brief shots show a dilapidated village with animals lingering around, a close-up of a rooster's head, a naked child walking through the mud, a man sleeping on the ground, piles of trash crawling with crabs, then a silkscreened poster of a state official in military uniform with the words "Unidos hacia el futuro" ("United to the future") underneath it. We find out that the name of this village is Porvenir, coincidentally another translation for "future" in Spanish. Soon we will see that the four men from the introduction have all come to settle here. Apparently, some time has passed, as their scruffy appearance indicates that they have already acclimatized to the hotter, more humid, and less privileged climate of Porvenir. Indeed, the contrast with their lives in their home countries is stark. And as expatriates, their livelihoods have already been integrated into the local economy for they have taken up low-paying, physically demanding jobs for an oil production company, apparently owned by Americans. They partake in the local black market for forged passports while paying off corrupt government officials and policemen. The four men have taken up aliases to hide their identities: the assassin in Veracruz (played by Francisco Rabal) is Nilo, the terrorist in Jerusalem (Amidou) is Martinez, the French businessman (Bruno Cremer) is Serrano, and Scheider's gangster is Juan Dominguez. Criminals and moral offenders in their home countries, in Porvenir their criminal histories seem to matter very little. Nevertheless, this new Latin American context is like a prison for these characters as the poor village functions as one of the many spaces of melodrama featured in Friedkin's films, such as Regan's bedroom, where laws, and one's responsibility to uphold their norms, have been suspended.

Viewers who know Henri-Georges Clouzot's film from 1953, *The Wages of Fear*, and know that this film and *Sorcerer* are both based on a story by Georges Arnaud, will likely recognize the images of the village. These establishing shots from *Sorcerer* are analogous to those of Las Piedras, Puerto Rico that opens the earlier film. As its story unfolds, many key plot developments and narrative details will be quickly recognizable as well. Friedkin has repeatedly disavowed, in interviews and in his memoirs, charges that his film is simply a remake of Clouzot's work. Instead, he has claimed that *Sorcerer* is another version of the original novel from 1952. Yet while the American director was in France promoting *The Exorcist*, the night his film opened in Paris he met Claude Chabrol, François Truffaut, and Clouzot for dinner. Friedkin requested permission to make *The Wages of Fear* that night and was apparently granted the rights to engage in the project by the French director. Friedkin later found that Clouzot in fact did not own the rights. According to a gossipy account provided by Peter Biskind, the American director apparently assured Clouzot that, "I promise you I will not do it as well as you did."[32] Nevertheless, the older director remained puzzled as to why Friedkin would want to make another version of the story.

If we take seriously Friedkin's claim that *Sorcerer* is not a remake, but rather another version of the original story, we should reconsider the notion that this film is merely an imitation of Clouzot's work. In my discussion of *12 Angry Men*, I tried to argue that we should see Friedkin's film not simply as a remake of the 1957 work directed by Sidney Lumet but as another version, another manifestation of the problematics raised by the 1954 television play by Reginald Rose as well as the adaptation for the theater stage of 1964. Each of these productions might be thought of as differing performances of a jazz composition, each one an improvised variation of a basic melody and a progression of chords, each taking their cues from an originating concept. They all put the problem of American juridical judgment into motion and all draw from a text written by Rose, but the differences account for the differing historical time of their productions. Nevertheless, critics seemed to have been stubbornly unconvinced by the director's stated motivations for making the film. A 1977 review of *Sorcerer* in *The Washington Post* calls it a "sinful copy" of *The Wages of Fear* and unequivocally considers the earlier film the "original," the text against which the later film is to be judged.[33] It criticizes Friedkin's version for "copying the situations from 'The Wages of Fear' up to a point and then backing off at the climaxes, an indecisive style of imitation that plunges them abruptly into anticlimax time after time."[34] Reviews raise the question of why Friedkin made *Sorcerer* at all while stating that the remake is implicitly flawed and debased. For the purposes of this chapter, instead of deeming *Sorcerer* an imitative remake of an original work, I intend to see it as a text that enriches Arnaud's book while also bringing it into the scope of Friedkin's larger aesthetic and ethical concerns. In doing so, I would like to withhold critiques based on morally overdetermined binaries such as original vs. remake, authentic vs. counterfeit, so that we can consider the discursive effects, particularly those I have repeatedly identified in this director's work, produced by the film.

Nilo, Martinez, Serrano, and Dominguez are forced to toil together in order to pursue a shared goal. An oil well has exploded hundreds of miles away in Poza Rica, causing it to go up in endless flames. The only way to extinguish it is to explode the area again using dynamite. Small crates of highly combustible nitroglycerine are recovered in Porvenir, now in powder form. However, because the material is easily ignitable, it cannot be transported by air. The oil company announces that they will hire four drivers, to be paid lucratively, to transport six crates of the nitroglycerine through dense jungle and across hundreds of miles of treacherous road. (The distance between the actual Porvenir in Chile and Poza Rica in Mexico is thousands of miles.) A short scene demonstrates just how explosive this material is—a few globules of water containing the nitroglycerine explode like firecrackers when dropped on the ground. Only a few years before *Sorcerer* was released, members of OPEC declared an embargo on oil that would be targeted at nations supporting Israel during the Yom Kippur War in October 1973. Oil prices in the U.S. quadrupled while shortages became rampant for gas stations across the country. Although the embargo ended on March 1974, the economy entered into recession until 1975 and revealed the importance of oil and the bargaining power wielded by the twelve members of OPEC. On the other hand, the questions of U.S. involvement and the exploitation of resources in Porvenir never come up explicitly in *Sorcerer* (in contrast to Clouzot's film), nor does the fact that the four men were hired by an American oil company to shore up their losses.

Martinez and Serrano take one large army truck, named "Sorcerer," while Nilo and Dominguez will drive another called "Lazarus." The title of the film is directly referenced for the first time. A montage sequence shows the men working together to prepare their trucks for the trip, paralleling a montage in *The Hunted* that depicts two men preparing their weapons for the imminent melee between them. Although only one crate of explosives is required, the oil company makes clear that it wants an additional truck as backup, revealing that it expects one of them to not make it to the end. Indeed, the tension rises as soon as the large trucks set off on their journey, lest any sudden movement explode the nitroglycerine. Sympathetic viewers may be compelled to remain anxiously still in their seats as the precariousness of the trip is maintained throughout the film. According to Friedkin, he chose to name this film *Sorcerer* because he was listening to Miles Davis's album from 1967 of the same name. "Sorcerer" was also "an intentional but ill-advised reference to *The Exorcist*."[35] Friedkin had originally wanted the title *Ballbreaker*, but Lew Wasserman of Universal rejected it, perhaps not surprisingly. In my interview with Friedkin, he revealed another suggested title:

> I was gonna call it *No Man's Land*. And then Harold Pinter wrote a play called *No Man's Land* before I finished shooting. And that was his new play. I could have used the title, but I wouldn't. You can't copyright a title. But that was a much more accurate title, as was *Ballbreaker*.

Like a jazz quartet, the four men are forced to work together, to quickly react to what they see and hear, and improvise solutions to unforeseen problems that arise on the way. While navigating narrow dirt roads, their first major obstacle is a feeble rope bridge that spans a rapid river, in a thrilling scene that for some viewers may recall David Lean's *The Bridge on the River Kwai*. Heightening the tension, the film shows both trucks managing to cross the bridge in the midst of low-light at dusk while hindered by strong winds and heavy rain. Later, they encounter an enormous tree that has fallen, blocking the road ahead. The four men concoct a detonation device using tree branches, a stone some string, and a box of nitroglycerine. When the box explodes, the path is cleared for the trucks to move again. Nilo, Martinez, Serrano, and Dominguez stand silently in the same shot together, appreciating what they have done, and allow themselves a brief moment of respite before continuing toward their goal (Figure 5.3).

In addition to *The Wages of Fear*, Friedkin has stated numerous times in interview that his interest in *Sorcerer* was indebted greatly to John Huston's

Figure 5.3 Male collaboration

Treasure of the Sierra Madre from 1948. Both films feature financially desperate characters who fundamentally distrust each other but nevertheless must cooperate if they are to secure their lucrative prizes. Before crossing the treacherous bridge, an exasperated Dominguez says to Nilo: "We're going across that bridge, and you're going to guide me, because I can't do it alone." Scheider's look in Friedkin's film parallels Bogart's rugged, unshaven, persistently sweaty appearance in Huston's film. Compared to Clouzot's version of the story, much less time is devoted to male bonding in Porvenir as they remain strangers to each other for most of the course of *Sorcerer*. But animosity gradually gives way to something like goodwill, emerging precisely after this scene of male collaboration. In a forward included in the Blu-ray release of the film, Friedkin writes that he sees *The Wages of Fear* as "a metaphor for the warring nations of the world, who had to find a way to cooperate or blow up in a nuclear disaster."

This sense of the necessity of cooperation seems to be brought into greater relief in some later scenes from *Sorcerer*. After the four men continue on their way, for the first time they ask each other about their respective pasts, as if to remind viewers of the spaces of innocence they had left after arriving in Porvenir. The wife that Serrano had abruptly left in France is recalled when he shows Nilo the engraved watch she gifted to him the last time they were together, seemingly long ago. For the first time in the film, they seem more human through their mutual appreciation that they have come this far while looking forward to completing the hazardous mission and their imminent return home. And for a brief moment, they are perhaps seen as sympathetic characters who recognize themselves as having personal histories and a future destiny.

If the narration in the first two-thirds of *The Exorcist* operates within discourses of modern medicine and psychiatry, institutions that are deeply invested in producing the patient and locating malady in Regan's body, *Sorcerer* is implicated in the discourse of illegality, put into motion by the prison institution and specifically through the status of delinquency. The prison, for Foucault, reproduces distinctions between the legal and illegal through the organization of space and the disciplining of criminal bodies. Yet this delineation of criminality has the effect of diffusing techniques of disciplinary power into many secular cultural norms, establishing a kind of open illegality that also encompasses the very definition of delinquency. Delinquency is thus "an illegality that the 'carceral system', with all its ramifications, has invested, segmented, isolated, penetrated, organized, enclosed in a definite milieu," a kind of controlled illegality that is allowed to persist outside the prison but within civil society.[36] By emphasizing the criminal backgrounds of the four protagonists in the first thirty minutes, *Sorcerer* highlights their delinquent status in Porvenir, as criminals but not incarcerated, and thus subject to the broader carceral system that characterizes civil life in modernity. This status perhaps accounts for the seeming unlikeability of the characters throughout most of the film; according to the director, he "purposely set out to make these characters hard to 'root for.'"[37] When they arrive at the poor village, they are shorn of national identity, of ethnic community, and cut off from family ties. This is also a location where the American petrol company can treat the local workforce as expendable and less than human by obviating labor laws typically enforced for companies on U.S. soil. When a large tree trunk falls on a Latin American worker, seriously injuring him, his bloody body is brought back to Porvenir in a truck with armed soldiers. The sight of the injured man and of others who died working sends the people of the village into chaos as they scream "Asesinos" ("Killers!") and "Hay que matar a esos gringos!" ("The gringos must be killed"). With growing unrest and an uprising imminent, the people throw rocks at the posters that proclaim "Unidos hacia el futuro."

Sorcerer constitutes this exceptional space, and the delinquency produced through it, as the discursive starting point for the 218-mile trek to the fictional Poza Rica. In the men's perilous journey toward their goal, the film resembles a chase film whereby the traversal of space is construed through the overcoming of a series of physical obstacles. And through the depictions of their surmounting, the film also builds cinematic narrative, connecting events in a linear fashion through time. In my discussion of *The Hunted*, I looked at how this construal is fundamental to narrative cinema more generally as Friedkin was especially interested in exploring the chase in this film. *Sorcerer* may be understood similarly with its gripping sequences that depict the overcoming of a precarious bridge and the explosion of a giant tree. The film and the trucks press forward, toward a goal they must reach yet without knowing what obstacles still stand in the way. As they continue on, the film allows for only brief moments of reflection, after they have overcome obstacles and seem to have reasserted themselves as drivers of their own destinies. But just as Serrano is telling Nilo about the time he met his wife, momentarily directing their thoughts away from the here and now ("It's five minutes before 9:00 in Paris"), the truck hits an obstruction in the rocky road that blows the tire and causes the truck to veer off and immediately explode into flames. At the moment the film relaxes the tension and the narrative solicits the sympathy of the viewer, the human characters are suddenly eliminated. Ironically, the obstacle remains invisible, a sharp stone in the road that could not have been foreseen or avoided by the drivers.

In my interview with him from 2017, Friedkin states that, "*The Exorcist* is about the mystery of faith, *Sorcerer* is about the mystery of fate. And those are the extremes that interest me." If we take this as a cue, we might consider trying to understand his 1977 film as a chase film that seems to pursue what he calls "fate" and compel a confrontation with the unknown that inspires irrational fear. He explains himself, waxing philosophical while quoting words written by one of his favorite artists:

> Are you looking forward to dying? Are you looking forward to dying slowly and painfully? Is it possible that you will? Do you have any control of that? No. There's a great line from Bob Dylan, "Those not busy being born are busy dying." And that's not a comforting thought. None of Bob Dylan's lyrics are comforting, but they're profound. "While preachers preach of evil fates, teachers teach them knowledge waits, can lead to hundred-dollar plates, but goodness stands outside the gates. And sometimes even the president of the United States must have to stand naked. And if my thought-dreams could be seen, they'd probably put my head in a guillotine. But it's alright, Ma, I'm only dying." I mean that's profundity, but that's the way it is. I've never heard it put better. That's irrational fear.

I remember my astonishment when Friedkin cited these lines by Dylan from memory and explained their meaning to me in the terms presented in *Sorcerer*. The film flirts with fate through the structure of the chase film and Friedkin here indicates that he sees this structure as allegorical of the lifespan. Indeed, the tension sustained throughout the film is comprised of its continual unfolding that may be interrupted at any moment with the threat of absolute ruinousness if the nitroglycerine were to explode, with any slight, unanticipated movement. In this, the very experience of the film's unwinding is paralleled to the experience of life itself as it lives toward death, toward an event that is certain but cannot be foreseen in terms of when and how it will come to pass.

In its being-toward-death, human existence for Friedkin seems to find its most appropriate medium for thinking life, not in abstract theorizations, but in the existential phenomenology that is constituted by the unspooling of the film in the projector. From law, citizenship, security, and the time and space of innocence, the film unfolds toward disintegration, inevitably, irreversibly, toward the unforeseen that is also certain. To continually confront the unknown challenges of life, according to *Sorcerer*, is to confront the possibility of death at every moment. This confrontation, for Friedkin, is tinged with irrational fear. Despite this, the vitality of film lingers.

If we consider that it is fate that the four men in *Sorcerer* pursue, this thought can only be considered from the perspective that what transgresses the self is also destructive to the self. I am reminded of what the director said to me in the interview I conducted with him, quoted above: "Life, liberty, and the pursuit of happiness? And then, some horrible thing happens to you, or your friend or relative, and it just shatters these illusions." This trajectory is borne out by the film as the truck driven by Serrano and Nilo, "Sorcerer," explodes and the one driven by Dominguez and Martinez continues on. They are stopped by a group of four guerrilla fighters, all of them armed, and engage in a scuffle. Martinez shoots three of them and Dominguez beats another one dead with a shovel. Another obstacle is surmounted but Martinez has been shot and bleeds out on the floor of the truck. He dies and the truck runs out of gas with less than two miles left. Desperate and alone, yet still obsessed with completing the mission, Scheider's character carries a crate of the nitroglycerine by hand and delivers it to the workers at the flaming oil well. He is the last survivor of a grueling journey, bringing an end to the sustained tension that began when the precarious explosives were loaded onto the trucks.

Sorcerer concludes with a final appearance of fate. Dominguez is taken back to Porvenir, still tense and a bit shell-shocked from the journey, where he receives his check for $40,000 at the bar where he met Serrano for the first time. He will travel to Bonao in the Dominican Republic and from there perhaps return to the U.S. His future plans remain unclear. A plane is waiting for him, but he requests a few minutes so he can dance with the barmaid. They do so, while a ballad played by Charlie Parker swells on the soundtrack. The camera pans away from them, taking the viewer outside the bar while a taxi pulls up and two men step out. The first is a hitman associated with a figure from his former life in New Jersey, Carlos Ricci, whose brother was shot by Dominguez's gang. He has come for payback. The other is Dominguez's friend, Vinnie, who helped him leave the U.S. for Porvenir. Played by a cop-turned-actor, Vinnie has apparently betrayed Dominguez's location to the rival gang. With the camera capturing the location from a high angle, the two men enter the bar and the menacing soundtrack by Tangerine Dream returns. A gunshot is heard. As with the conclusive shot at the end of *The French Connection*, it remains unclear who shot whom. But the larger message is clear—despite Dominguez's efforts to stay out of trouble and successfully leave the jurisdiction of the U.S. and its laws, his past returns like fate to punish him for his sins. As with the moral currency that circulates in *Killer Joe*, money and debt constrain human action in *Sorcerer*, despite all attempts up to this point to depict human agency and to master one's own destiny through a series of individual decisions. Ultimately, it is death that awaits Dominguez at the end. Redemption exists, but not for the film's human heroes. Death comes when it is least expected, when one's defenses are down, as was the case for Serrano, like a figure coming in from outside who embodies threat and "irrational fear." Explaining this threat, Friedkin remarks in a 2015 interview:

> There is a force of evil in the world that causes all these problems. Life is actually a beautiful gift, but people regard it not as something that is vulnerable, but as something that they take for granted. The major powers in the world just keep threatening each other, attacking each other, and there's going to come a point where there's enough nuclear proliferation to destroy the world. So yes, that is the metaphor behind *Sorcerer*.[38]

Once again, the dichotomy between interiority and exteriority is overturned in *Sorcerer*. What was thought to have infiltrated and endangered the self was part of it all along.

This overturning is played out through the uncanny depiction of nature in *Sorcerer*. Throughout the film, rural Porvenir and the South American jungle are figured as more primitive, presumably less civilized, than the four locations depicted in the opening of the film. When the four men arrive, they quickly acclimatize to their new surroundings as their characterization as criminals are seemingly diffused from their bodies. The abilities that were important in their previous lives become less so and they become like human animals, acquiring skill sets that are necessary only for survival in the harsh environment of the jungle. Nature is hostile, but the machines, most importantly the trucks, seem to take on a threatening existence as well. The front of "Sorcerer" seems to acquire a monstrously toothed face. At a peculiar moment in the film, while Serrano and Nilo cross the tenuous bridge, a bundle of branches floating in the water seemingly attack the Frenchman. The discordant soundtrack at this moment underscores the apparent hostility of the aggressive brushwood and this hindrance compels them to cross the falling bridge extremely slowly, as if by crawling. Another moment at the end of *Sorcerer* emphasizes the dehumanized, de-individualized place of the protagonists, specifically when Dominguez drives through a seemingly alien landscape before his truck breaks down. The image here is desaturated and tinted dark blue, while Scheider's face is superimposed on the bizarre surroundings through reflections on the windshield of the truck (Figure 5.4). On both the image-track and soundtracks, earlier moments from the film are recalled while confusion emerges with the

Figure 5.4 An alien landscape

hallucinatory vision of Martinez laughing. All this recalls earlier moments for the viewers as well and summarizes the film's journey, through the progressive development of male obsession that veers into delusion. On the other hand, these moments also subvert the hierarchy of humans controlling nature and machines, while lending the non-human signifiers throughout *Sorcerer* an impenetrable quality. The film's *mise-en-scène* gains a kind of agency that exceeds what is typically construed as human and the cinema seems to grant it a power of life that exposes the futility of thinking the inherent supremacy of human life in the world.

Along this line of environmental thinking, we might recall the ethos depicted in *Bug*, where the two main protagonists gradually become paranoid about their contamination. I tried to show that their conspiratorial paranoia is driven by the very thing they wish to expel—Enlightenment truth. To bug and be bugged, this is the circular hermeneutics that infests the two main human characters, but their anxiety ultimately stems from their insistence upon a strict division between a threatening exteriority over-against a consecrated interiority. A similar encounter between humans and their environments seems to be put on display in these peculiar moments that depict the phenomenology of nature in *Sorcerer*. Friedkin's film presents a gradual stripping away of individual virtue and individuality as it is typically construed in the melodramatic mode. Their possibilities of being are defined primarily by the morphologies of their bodies and the capabilities of their trucks—all are technologies that are equipped to pursue the chase. Throughout the trajectory of the film, the four men gradually shed the pretense of their humanity within the bourgeois melodrama, becoming human animals, or possibly human-trucks, that are meant only to survive until their demise.

* * *

It is perhaps significant that the truck that carries the film's name is the one that explodes. When *Sorcerer* was released to theaters in the summer of 1977, it bombed at the box office and was generally panned by the critics. After a series of delays that forced the production to go over budget, *Sorcerer* eventually cost $22 million but reaped only $9 million worldwide. Audiences found the characters to be unrelatable and, with expectations inspired by its elusive title and prior experience of *The Exorcist*, expressed disappointment that it was not a film involving magic and fantasy. Others were put off by the lack of English dialogue in the opening scenes. At some screenings, a disclaimer was posted, indicating that "two of the opening sequences were filmed in the appropriate foreign languages—with sub-titles in English," while assuring audiences that, "Other than these opening scenes, 'Sorcerer' is an English language film." A week after it premiered, showings of the film were cancelled at the Chinese Theatre on Hollywood Boulevard and replaced by *Star Wars*. The latter had a limited release one month before Friedkin's film, but its popularity expanded rapidly due to word-of-mouth among viewers and soon dominated screens in the U.S. Meanwhile, in his scathing review for *The Village Voice*, Andrew Sarris writes that *Sorcerer* embodies,

> everything that is wrong with current movies: no narrative flow, no psychological development of characters, no interaction of performers, no true unity of locale amid all the exotic locations, no feelings, no build-ups, no pay-offs, no structure, not a single line of resonant dialogue, not a single scene with dramatic tension.[39]

Looking back, this series of assessments strikes one as unduly denigrating and largely unwarranted. The Francophile critic states at the beginning of his review that he has never been the kind "who froths at the mouth at the mere mention of remakes" and then goes on to judge *Sorcerer* as merely a remake of *The Wages of Fear* while also damning it as exemplary of what he disapproves of in contemporary American film.[40] What "current movies" he is thinking about is never made clear in the review. And while Sarris is clearly enamored by Clouzot's film, such that he grants the French director the status of auteur, he does not extend the same to Friedkin and suggests that *The Exorcist* and *The French Connection* cannot join the ranks of art cinema.

To his credit, the director has never denied that a number of mistakes and perhaps some bad decisions were made during the production of *Sorcerer*, including his choice of title and its downbeat ending, which likely confused and frustrated general audiences. The enormous success of his previous work made him prone to targeting by film critics, particularly those who perceived Friedkin to be making movies that were mere empty sensationalizing or, as Pauline Kael puts it, "jolts for jocks."[41]

During the production process Friedkin was unwavering in his mission to realize his artistic vision. According to his own recollections, while urgent questions came from executives at Paramount and Universal about when the film would be finished, he ignored these requests and let his co-workers receive the brunt of their ire. "I was becoming detached from reality," the director remembers.[42] After the film was finished, he believed that it would gross $90 million, so convinced was he in his accomplishment; it was a film that he believed to be his magnum opus. Within the context of this heightened self-importance, the subsequent critical and financial failure of *Sorcerer* dealt Friedkin an especially great blow both professionally and personally. The director became morose, partly from the malaria he was diagnosed with after the film's production, but also from the harm that *Sorcerer* would strike to his reputation. Like Dominguez, Friedkin left his home country to escape his troubles and went to Paris to recuperate. Reflecting back on how this first significant career failure affected him and the work he would do afterward, he writes that, "My films became more obsessive, less audience-friendly, and would turn even darker in the future. They would continue to portray the American character as psychotic, fearful, and dangerous."[43] This portrayal would indeed be developed in the characters, especially the men, of Friedkin's oeuvre, as my analyses have tried to illustrate.

In retrospect, we can see how critics of *Sorcerer* in 1977 repeatedly deployed the discourse of art and the myth of originality to ground their judgments, discourses that deemed the film a flawed derivation of a unique film. While Sarris remarks that it is "sacrilegious" to "remake" Charles Vanel's character in *The Wages of Fear*, when he criticizes "Friedkin's noncharacters," we can sense another ideological formation that the critic imposes on the film, namely the bourgeois individual who attests to the power of psychological realism in the cinema and which remains central to melodrama.[44] Other than Roy Scheider, the men who play Nilo, Martinez, and Serrano would have been unfamiliar to American audiences and likely less sympathetic. Friedkin has repeatedly expressed regret in failing to accommodate Steve McQueen's conditions for his participation in the film, noting that his star power would have brought greater visibility to the production. *Sorcerer* generally gives more screen time to Scheider's character and Bruno Cremer's Serrano, but its plot utilizes and treats the four main protagonists equally. "I said," the director remembered thinking, "'I don't need stars, I'll just make it with four good actors.' And I did."[45] In the end the film does not reiterate the cult of personality or work within clear distinctions that separate virtue and villainy, as is the case with

Star Wars, on which this ideological formation depends. Viewers steeped in the habits of the melodramatic mode, like Sarris, who writes that the protagonists "barely give each other the right time, and so there are never any emotional connections," will likely be disappointed in the ambitions of Friedkin's film. While the construction of fully fleshed out, believable characters was important for Friedkin, it was apparently less an end in itself and more a means to realize his conceptual obsessions. Whether one deems it successful or not, *Sorcerer* nevertheless seeks to elaborate cinematic ideas while staging ethical problems within the epistemological constraints of popular cinema.

Still, *Sorcerer* has typically been understood not only as a failure within Friedkin's oeuvre but also as a signal film that marked the end of New Hollywood, sounding a death knell to this generation's conceit of commercial auteurism. Along with films such as Michael Cimino's *Heaven's Gate*, Martin Scorsese's *New York, New York*, and Francis Ford Coppola's *One From the Heart*, Friedkin's film has been seen as an exemplar of the outsized dreams of the generation born after the war, who chased projects driven by obsession veering into self-indulgence. The aesthetic concerns of this group of filmmakers, who often had connections with French, Italian, Japanese, and other new wave cinemas, were overcome by the demands of the culture industry and the steady rise of the hit-driven blockbuster film. The increasing prevalence of cable television and the proliferation of video compelled viewers to consume content at home while the success of films like *Jaws*, *Star Wars*, and *Saturday Night Fever* confirmed broader economic and industry trends already taking place throughout the 1970s. *The Exorcist*, of course, should be considered one of these blockbusters but despite its pretensions around the mystery of faith it remains an outlier in Friedkin's oeuvre in its wild financial success. New marketing strategies, advertisements, and product tie-ins, as well as the increasing importance of the youth market drove the industry toward films directed not by auteurs but by producers and studio executives. As David A. Cook notes,

> the extent to which film production had become an investment-specific strategy by the latter part of the decade was quite unprecedented, and it warped the shape of the industry for years to come, driving production and marketing costs to hitherto unimagined levels.[46]

Films are commodities, first and foremost, and box-office performance is the clearest marker of their success, particularly in the opening weeks of release. Confidence quickly waned among the New Hollywood auteurs and they were forced to reassess and adapt.

While accepting the fate of *Sorcerer* within the changing landscape of Hollywood, Friedkin began working on a new film that would allow him to return to the orbit of issues around *The French Connection*. *The Brink's Job* tells the story of the 1958 robbery of the Brink's security company in Boston. Featuring Peter

Falk, Gena Rowlands, and Paul Sorvino, it was filmed at the location where the crime took place twenty year earlier. Although its plot seems to follow that typical of the heist film, where a group of thieves hatch a plan for breaking into a secured building, *The Brink's Job* quickly shows that this is not the case. The film depicts the need for collaboration among competing men, ambivalent about each other personally, toward the accomplishment of a shared goal, as in *Sorcerer*. But their incompetence is coupled with the depiction of the surprisingly lax security standards of the security company, conveying the sense that the incredible success of their crime depends not on the masterminding of a genius plan but on chance and on conditions beyond their control. More cynical than *The French Connection*, *The Brink's Job* finds incredulity and humor in the circumstances that enabled a group of relatively unsophisticated working-class men to steal millions of dollars and become popular heroes by the film's end. In the last scene, Falk's character is celebrated by adoring crowds after he is released from prison, recalling the ironic endings of Scorsese's *Taxi Driver* and *The King of Comedy*, and that feature criminals celebrated as heroes through the publicity produced by the news media. Nevertheless, *The Brink's Job* ultimately was another box-office loser. While most of the auteurs of this period had fallen victim to industry-wide changes, Friedkin's fall was perhaps the most dramatic since he had experienced the heights of success only a few years earlier. His career would continue in ways that seemed to illustrate his growing pessimism and resentment about how he believed fate informed the morality of the times.

Throughout this book, I have shown how the popular melodramatic mode serves as a backdrop to the operation of Friedkin's films. We have seen that they radicalize and upend many of its most salient expectations and induce experiences of moral unease while inspiring questioning into the ethics that typically ground the melodramatic mode. In its production of moral sentiment, the melodramatic mode is particularly reliant on the timing of "too late" that moves viewers to feel heartbreak and loss. Yet in contrast to the backward-looking orientation of this aspect of melodrama, fate for Friedkin looks forward to a future that is as yet unknown. It is an orientation that seeks an experience of redemption more transformative than that which can be offered by popular melodrama, toward that which transgresses its limits and its interiorized claustrophobia. In my conversation with the director we had spoken about our shared appreciation for Carlos Kleiber's recording of Beethoven's Fifth Symphony in C-minor. This particular piece is famous for its four-note theme, "fate knocking at the door," that is developed through its four movements and ends in triumph. "I watch basically the same films over and over again," Friedkin remarks in a 2015 interview, "like reading a novel again, or listening to a piece of music again. I never tire of listening to the Fifth Symphony of Beethoven conducted by Carlos Kleiber."[47] Individual works by Beethoven, Cartier Bresson, Proust, Rembrandt, and Vermeer serve as touchstones for the director, in addition to films such as Raoul Walsh's

White Heat, Carl Dreyer's *The Passion of Joan of Arc*, and others I have not discussed in this book. Above all of these, for Friedkin, stands Orson Welles's *Citizen Kane*. These are "great works of art" that he had experienced through recordings, reproductions, and Blu-ray discs, experiences that he enjoyed repeating in his Bel-Air home. In moments of disarming modesty, he told me that he had not achieved this sense of greatness in his own films. The works by these masters are "universal and timeless. I don't have anything like that in my quiver. If I were you, I would take everything you've written about me and throw it into a shit can and write a book about Sidney Lumet." (He is particularly fond of this director's 1982 film, *The Verdict*, starring Paul Newman.) But what remains so compelling about Friedkin the human being is this gaze that continues to seek "greatness" to come, a greatness that has yet to be realized. His gaze remains uncompromising and critical but constantly open to the possibility of that which remains unanticipated and the seemingly impossible. But precisely because Friedkin continues to seek out this impossible greatness, and precisely because it remains outside his reach, so do his films strive to realize experiences that transgress the constraints of popular cinema.

NOTES

1. From the Friedkin papers at the Margaret Herrick Library archives.
2. David Bartholomew and Dale Winogura, "The Exorcist: The Book, the Movie, the Phenomenon," *Cinefantastique* 3, no. 4 (1974), 17.
3. From the Friedkin papers at the Margaret Herrick Library archives.
4. From the Friedkin papers at the Margaret Herrick Library archives.
5. Mark Kermode, *The Exorcist, 2nd Edition* (London: BFI, 1998), 25. Kermode is particularly obsessed with *The Exorcist* and this short book is where any serious study of the film should begin.
6. Sally Quinn, "Exorcism: Beating the Devil," *Washington Post*, November 6, 1972.
7. William Friedkin, *The Friedkin Connection* (New York: Harper, 2013), 253.
8. Michel Foucault, *The Birth of the Clinic: An Archaeology of Medical Perception*, trans. A. M. Sheridan Smith (New York: Vintage Books, 1994), 122.
9. Michel Foucault, *Psychiatric Power: Lectures at the Collège de France*, trans. Graham Burchell (New York: Palgrave, 2006), 312.
10. Harry Ringel, "The Exorcist," *Cinefantastique* 3, no. 2 (1974), 40.
11. Carol Clover, *Men, Woman, and Chainsaws: Gender in the Modern Horror Film* (London: BFI Publishing, 1992), 66.
12. See Carrol L. Fry, "'We Are Legion': Primal Dreams and Screams in the Satanic Screen," *Journal of Religion & Film* 19, no. 2 (2015).
13. Robert F. Geary, "The Exorcist: Deep Horror?", *Journal of the Fantastic in the Arts* 5, no. 4 (1993).
14. See Colleen McDannell, "Catholic Horror," in *Catholics in the Movies*, ed. Colleen McDannell (Oxford: Oxford University Press, 2008).
15. See Douglas E. Cowan, "Religion and Cinema Horror," in *Understanding Religion and Popular Culture: Theories, Themes, Products and Practices*, eds. Terry Ray Clark and Dan W. Clayton (Abingdon: Routledge, 2012).

16. See Thomas Doherty, "The Rise and Fall of Catholic Hollywood, or from the Production Code to *The Da Vinci Code*," in *Moralizing Cinema: Film, Catholicism, and Power*, eds. Daniel Biltereyst and Daniela Trevari Gennari (Abingdon: Routledge, 2018).
17. See Barbara Creed, *The Monstrous-Feminine: Film, Feminism, Psychoanalysis* (London: Routledge, 1993), which is still the most insightful in this respect. Many others have followed up on Creed's work, including Allison M. Kelly, "A Girl's Best Friend is Her Mother: *The Exorcist* as a Post-Modern Oedipal Tale," *Journal of Evolutionary Psychology* 25, no. 1-2 (2004) and Daniel Humphrey, "Gender and Sexuality Haunts the Horror Film," in *A Companion to the Horror Film*, ed. Harry M. Benshoff (Malden: Wiley-Blackwell, 2017).
18. See Aviva Briefel, "Monster Pains: Masochism, Menstruation, and Identification in the Horror Film," *Film Quarterly* 58, no. 3 (2005).
19. See Sara Williams, "'The Power of Christ Compels You': Holy Water, Hysteria, and the Oedipal Psychodrama in *The Exorcist*," *Literature Interpretation Theory* 22, no. 3 (2011).
20. See Karen J. Renner, *Evil Children in the Popular Imagination* (New York: Palgrave, 2016).
21. See Bruce Ballon and Molyn Leszcz, "Horror Films: Tales to Master Terror or Shapers of Trauma?", *American Journal of Psychotherapy* 61, no. 2 (2007).
22. See "Disavowal, Fetishism," in Christian Metz, *The Imaginary Signifier*, trans. Ben Brewster (Bloomington: Columbia University Press, 1982).
23. Pauline Kael, "The Exorcist," *The New Yorker*, January 7, 1974.
24. Michel Chion, *The Voice in Cinema*, trans. Claudia Gorbman (New York: Columbia University Press, 1999), 171.
25. Jay Beck, *Designing Sound: Audiovisual Aesthetics in 1970s American Cinema* (New Brunswick, NJ: Rutgers University Press, 2016), 188.
26. Andrew Hock Soon Ng, "Intimate Spaces, Extimate Subjects: The Bedroom in Horror Films," in *Spaces of the Cinematic Home: Behind Screen Doors*, eds. Eleanor Andrews, Stella Hockenhull, and Fran Pheasant-Kelly (London: Routledge, 2015), 155.
27. Bartholomew and Winogura, "The Exorcist," 17.
28. Todd Berliner, *Hollywood Incoherent: Narration in Seventies Cinema* (Austin: University of Texas Press, 2010), 135.
29. Michel Foucault, "Of Other Spaces," *Diacritics* 16, no. 1 (Spring 1986), 24. For more on the cinema as heterotopia, see Hye Jean Chung, *Media Heterotopias: Digital Effects and Material Labor in Global Film Production* (Durham, NC: Duke University Press, 2018).
30. Foucault, "Of Other Spaces," 25.
31. Friedkin, *The Friedkin Connection*, 150.
32. Peter Biskind, *Easy Riders, Raging Bulls: How the Sex-Drugs-and-Rock 'n' Roll Generation Saved Hollywood* (New York: Touchstone, 1999), 224.
33. Gary Arnold, "A Sinful Copy of 'The Wages of Fear,'" *The Washington Post*, June 27, 1977.
34. Arnold, "A Sinful Copy."
35. Friedkin, *The Friedkin Connection*, 329.
36. Michel Foucault, *Discipline and Punish: The Birth of the Prison*, trans. Alan Sheridan (Vintage: New York, 1995), 277.
37. Friedkin, *The Friedkin Connection*, 322.
38. Christopher Lane, ed., *William Friedkin: Interviews*, Conversations with Filmmakers Series (Jackson: University of Mississippi Press, 2020), 130.
39. Andrew Sarris, "A Devil of a Bad Movie, But Not Diabolical," *The Village Voice*, July 18, 1977.
40. Sarris, "A Devil of a Bad Movie."
41. Pauline Kael, *Deeper Into Movies* (New York: Little, Brown, 1973), 317.
42. Friedkin, *The Friedkin Connection*, 335.

43. Friedkin, *The Friedkin Connection*, 347.
44. Sarris, "A Devil of a Bad Movie."
45. Lane, *William Friedkin: Interviews*, 76.
46. David A. Cook, *Lost Illusions: American Cinema in the Shadow of Watergate and Vietnam* (Berkeley: University of California Press, 2000), 156.
47. Lane, *William Friedkin: Interviews*, 133.

Bibliography

Adler, Renata. "Screen: 'Night They Raided Minsky's':1920's Film Directed by William Friedkin Starts Run at 86th St. East and at Victoria." *New York Times*, December 23, 1968.
Agamben, Giorgio. *The Open: Man and Animal*. Translated by Kevin Atell. Stanford: Stanford University Press, 2004.
Agamben, Giorgio. *State of Exception*. Translated by Kevin Atell. Chicago: University of Chicago Press, 2005.
Arnett, Robert. "Eighties Noir: The Dissenting Voice in Reagan's America," *Journal of Popular Film and Television* 34:3 (2006).
Arnold, Gary. "A Sinful Copy of 'The Wages of Fear.'" *The Washington Post*, June 27, 1977.
Atkinson, Michael. "Man's Pest Friend." *The Village Voice*, March 18, 2003.
B., Scott. "An Interview with William Friedkin." *IGN*, last updated May 20, 2012. <https://www.ign.com/articles/2003/03/11/an-interview-with-william-friedkin>
Ballon, Bruce, and Molyn Leszcz. "Horror Films: Tales to Master Terror or Shapers of Trauma?" *American Journal of Psychotherapy* 61, no. 2 (2007).
Bartholomew, David, and Dale Winogura. "The Exorcist: The Book, the Movie, the Phenomenon." *Cinefantastique* 3, no. 4 (1974).
Bataille, Georges. *The Accursed Share Vol. II & III*. Translated by Robert Hurley. New York: Zone Books, 1989.
Bazin, André. *What is Cinema? Vol. 1*. Translated by Hugh Gray. Berkeley: University of California Press, 1967.
Beck, Jay. *Designing Sound: Audiovisual Aesthetics in 1970s American Cinema*. New Brunswick, NJ: Rutgers University Press, 2016.
Bell, Arthur. "Bell Tells." *The Village Voice*, July 16, 1979.
Bell, Matt, ed. *The Boys in the Band: Flashpoints of Cinema, History, and Queer Politics*. Detroit: Wayne State University Press, 2016.
Benjamin, Walter. "The Work of Art in the Age of Mechanical Reproduction." In *Illuminations*, edited by Hannah Arendt. Translated by Harry Zohn. New York: Schocken, 1968.
Berlant, Lauren. *The Female Complaint: The Unfinished Business of Sentimentality in American Culture*. Durham, NC: Duke University Press, 2008.
Berliner, Todd. *Hollywood Incoherent: Narration in Seventies Cinema*. Austin: University of Texas Press, 2010.

Biesen, Sheri Chinen. "'Kinesthesis' and Cinematic Montage: An Historical Examination of the Film Theories and Avant-Garde Mediation of Slavko Vorkapich in Hollywood." *Studies in Visual Arts and Communication: An International Journal* 2, no. 1 (2015).

Biskind, Peter. *Easy Riders, Raging Bulls: How the Sex-Drugs-and-Rock 'n' Roll Generation Saved Hollywood*. New York: Touchstone, 1999.

Bordwell, David. "Intensified Continuity: Visual Style in Contemporary American Film." *Film Quarterly* 55, no. 3 (2002).

Braudy, Leo. *The World in a Frame: What We See in Films*. Chicago: University of Chicago Press, 2002.

Briefel, Aviva. "Monster Pains: Masochism, Menstruation, and Identification in the Horror Film." *Film Quarterly* 58, no. 3 (2005).

Brooks, Peter. *The Melodramatic Imagination: Balzac, Henry James, Melodrama, and the Mode of Excess*. New Haven: Yale University Press, 1995.

Burchby, Casey. "Fifty Years of Filmmaking: An Interview with William Friedkin." *Los Angeles Review of Books*, May 1, 2013.

Burnham, David. "$10-Million Heroin Stolen from a Police Office Vault." *New York Times*, December 15, 1972.

Canby, Vincent. "Screen: Unsettling World of 'The Birthday Party': Pinter's Adaptation of His Play Arrives Film Playing at Coronet Directed by Friedkin." *New York Times*, December 10, 1968. Available at: <http://www.nytimes.com/movie/review?res=9A00EEDA1230EF34BC4852DFB4678383679EDE>

Carter, Erica, ed. *Béla Balázs: Early Film Theory*. Translated by Rodney Livingstone. New York: Berghahn Books, 2011.

Chaudhuri, Una. *The Stage Lives of Animals: Zooesis and Performance*. Abingdon: Routledge, 2017.

Chion, Michel. *The Voice in Cinema*. Translated by Claudia Gorbman. New York: Columbia University Press, 1999.

Chung, Hye Jean. *Media Heterotopias: Digital Effects and Material Labor in Global Film Production*. Durham, NC: Duke University Press, 2018.

Clagett, Thomas D. *William Friedkin: Films of Aberration, Obsession and Reality*. Los Angeles: Silman-James Press, 2003.

Clover, Carol. "God Bless Juries!" In *Refiguring American Film Genres*, edited by Nick Browne. Berkeley: University of California Press, 1998.

Clover, Carol. "Law and the Order of Popular Culture." In *Law in the Domains of Culture*, edited by Austin Sarat and Thomas R. Kearns. Ann Arbor: University of Michigan Press, 1998.

Clover, Carol. *Men, Woman, and Chainsaws: Gender in the Modern Horror Film*. London: BFI Publishing, 1992.

Cook, David A. *Lost Illusions: American Cinema in the Shadow of Watergate and Vietnam*. Berkeley: University of California Press, 2000.

Cowan, Douglas E. "Religion and Cinema Horror." In *Understanding Religion and Popular Culture: Theories, Themes, Products and Practices*, edited by Terry Ray Clark and Dan W. Clayton. Abingdon: Routledge, 2012.

Creed, Barbara. *The Monstrous-Feminine: Film, Feminism, Psychoanalysis*. London: Routledge, 1993.

Davidson, Guy. "'Contagious Relations': Simulation, Paranoia, and the Postmodern Condition in William Friedkin's *Cruising* and Felice Picano's *The Lure*." *GLQ: A Journal of Lesbian and Gay Studies* 11, no. 1 (2005).

Derrida, Jacques. *Given Time: 1. Counterfeit Money*. Translated by Peggy Kamuf. Chicago: University of Chicago Press, 1992.

Doherty, Thomas. "The Rise and Fall of Catholic Hollywood, or from the Production Code to the *The Da Vinci Code*." In *Moralizing Cinema: Film, Catholicism, and Power*, edited by Daniel Biltereyst and Daniela Trevari Gennari. Abingdon: Routledge, 2018.

Dumit, Joseph. "A Digital Image of the Category of the Person: PET Scanning and Objective Self-Fashioning." In *Cyborgs and Citadels: Anthropological Interventions in Emerging Sciences and Technologies*, edited by Gary Lee Downey and Joseph Dumit. Seattle: University of Washington Press, 1997.

Ebert, Roger. "The Hunted." *Chicago Sun Times*, March 14, 2003.

Ebert, Roger. "*Rampage*." *Chicago Sun-Times*, October 30, 1992.

Ebert, Roger. "Review: *The Night They Raided Minsky's*." *Chicago Sun-Times*, December 23, 1968. Available at: <https://www.rogerebert.com/reviews/the-night-they-raided-minskys-1968>

Ebert, Roger. "Without a Net." *Chicago Sun-Times*, May 24, 2007. Available at: <https://www.rogerebert.com/reviews/bug-2007>

Elsaesser, Thomas. "The Pathos of Failure: American Films in the 1970s." In *The Last Great American Picture Show*, edited by Thomas Elsaesser, Alexander Horwath, and Noel King. Amsterdam: Amsterdam University Press, 2004.

Ercolani, Eugenio, and Marcus Stiglegger. *Cruising*. Liverpool: Liverpool University Press, 2020.

Eszterhas, Joe. *Hollywood Animal: A Memoir*. New York: Alfred A. Knopf, 2004.

Fawaz, Ramzi. "'Beware the Hostile Fag': Acidic Intimacies and Gay Male Consciousness-Raising in *The Boys in the Band*." In *The Boys in the Band: Flashpoints of Cinema, History and Queer Politics*, edited by Matt Bell. Detroit: Wayne State University Press, 2016.

Foucault, Michel. *The Birth of the Clinic: An Archaeology of Medical Perception*. Translated by A. M. Sheridan Smith. New York: Vintage Books, 1994.

Foucault, Michel. *Discipline and Punish: The Birth of the Prison*. Translated by Alan Sheridan. New York: Pantheon, 1988.

Foucault, Michel. *The History of Sexuality, Vol. 1*. Translated by Robert Hurley. New York: Pantheon Books: 1978.

Foucault, Michel. *Madness and Civilization: A History of Insanity in the Age of Reason*. Translated by Richard Howard. New York: Norton, 1988.

Foucault, Michel. "Of Other Spaces." *Diacritics* 16, no. 1 (Spring 1986).

Foucault, Michel. "Preface to Transgression." *Language, Counter-Memory, Practice: Selected Essays and Interviews by Michel Foucault*, edited by Donald F. Bouchard. Ithaca, NY: Cornell University Press, 1977.

Foucault, Michel. *Psychiatric Power: Lectures at the Collège de France*. Translated by Graham Burchell. New York: Palgrave, 2006.

Freud, Sigmund. "Fetishism," In *The Complete Psychological Works of Sigmund Freud, Vol. XXI*. Translated by James Strachey. London: Hogarth and the Institute of Psychoanalysis, 1973.

Friedkin, William. *The Friedkin Connection*. New York: Harper, 2013.

Fry, Carrol L. "'We Are Legion': Primal Dreams and Screams in the Satanic Screen." *Journal of Religion & Film* 19, no. 2 (2015).

Gabbard, Lucina Paquet. *The Dream Structure of Pinter's Plays: A Psychoanalytic Approach*. London: Associated University Presses, 1976.

Galloway, Stephen. *Leading Lady: Sherry Lansing and the Making of a Hollywood Groundbreaker*. New York: Crown Archetype, 2017.

Geary, Robert F. "The Exorcist: Deep Horror?" *Journal of the Fantastic in the Arts* 5, no. 4 (1993).

Gillen, Francis. "Harold Pinter's *The Birthday Party*: Menace Reconsidered." In *Harold Pinter: Critical Approaches*, edited by Steven H. Gale. London: Associated University Presses, 1986.

Greven, David. *Psycho-Sexual: Male Desire in Hitchcock, De Palma, Scorsese, and Friedkin*. Austin: University of Texas Press, 2013.

Gross, Larry. "Whatever Happened to William Friedkin?" *Sight and Sound* 12 (December 1995).

Gunning, Tom. "The Cinema of Attractions: Early Film, Its Spectator and the Avant-Garde." *Wide Angle* 8, no. 3/4 (Fall 1986).
Guthmann, Edward. "'Jaded' Is More Like It / It's got sex, murder and it's all in San Francisco." *SFGate*, October 13, 1995.
Heath, Stephen. "Narrative Space." in *Questions of Cinema*. Bloomington: Indiana University Press, 1981.
Hollis, James R. *Harold Pinter: The Poetics of Silence*. Carbondale: Southern Illinois University Press, 1970.
Humphrey, Daniel. "Gender and Sexuality Haunts the Horror Film." In *A Companion to the Horror Film*, edited by Harry M. Benshoff. Malden, MA: Wiley-Blackwell, 2017.
Jameson, Frederic. "Cognitive Mapping." In *Poetics/Politics: Radical Aesthetics for the Classroom*. London: Palgrave, 1999.
Jameson, Frederic. "Postmodernism, or The Cultural Logic of Late Capitalism." *New Left Review* 146 (July-August 1984).
Kael, Pauline. "The Exorcist." *The New Yorker*, January 7, 1974.
Kael, Pauline. "Urban Gothic." In *Deeper Into Movies*. Boston: Little, Brown, and Company, 1973.
Kelly, Allison M. "A Girl's Best Friend is Her Mother: *The Exorcist* as a Post-Modern Oedipal Tale." *Journal of Evolutionary Psychology* 25, no. 1-2 (2004).
Kermode, Mark. *The Exorcist*. London: BFI, 2010.
Kierkegaard, Søren. *Fear and Trembling* and *Repetition*. Edited and Translated by Howard V. Hong and Edna H. Hong. Princeton: Princeton University Press, 1983.
King, Stephen. "Stephen King's Favorite Films." *BFI*, December 8, 2017. Available at: <https://www2.bfi.org.uk/news-opinion/news-bfi/features/stephen-king-favourite-films>
The Knapp Commission Report on Police Corruption. New York: George Braziller, 1973.
Lacher, Irene. "William Friedkin takes a high-speech chase through his career." *Los Angeles Times*, May 12, 2013.
Lane, Christopher, ed. *William Friedkin: Interviews*. Jackson: University of Mississippi Press, 2020.
LaSalle, Mick. "'Cruising' Back From the '80s." *SFGate*, May 12, 1995. Available at: <https://www.sfgate.com/movies/article/Cruising-Back-From-the-80s-3033280.php>
LaSalle, Mick. "This thriller will have your skin crawling." *SFGate*, May 25, 2007. Available at: <https://www.sfgate.com/movies/article/This-thriller-will-have-your-skin-crawling-2591949.php>
Lastra, James. *Sound Technology and the American Cinema: Perception, Representation, Modernity*. New York: Columbia University Press, 2000.
Leff, Leonard J., and Jerold L. Simmons. *The Dame in the Kimono: Hollywood, Censorship, and the Production Code from the 1920s to the 1960s*. New York: Grove Weidenfeld, 1990.
Lightman, Herb. "Photographing The French Connection." *American Cinematogapher* 53, no. 2 (February 1972).
Lopate, Phillip. *Totally, Tenderly, Tragically: Essays and Criticism from a Lifelong Love Affair with the Movies*. Anchor: New York, 1998.
Ludovici, Chris. "Williams Friedkin's '*Cruising*' Remains a Gloriously Messy BDSM Thriller," *The Spool*, September 25, 2019. Available at: <https://thespool.net/reviews/movies/2019/09/william-friedkins-cruising-blu-ray-review>
Martin, Adrian. "The Sound of Violence." *Undercurrent* 4 (October 2008). Available at: <http://fipresci.hegenauer.co.uk/undercurrent/issue_0407/martin_cruising.htm>
Maslin, Janet. "Review/Film: Random Murder Spree in a Friedkin Thriller." *New York Times*, October 30, 1992.
McDannell, Colleen. "Catholic Horror." In *Catholics in the Movies*, edited by Colleen McDannell. Oxford: Oxford University Press, 2008.

Metz, Christian. *The Imaginary Signifier: Psychoanalysis and the Cinema.* Translated by Ben Brewster. Bloomington: Indiana University Press, 1982.

Miller, D. A. "Cruising." *Film Quarterly* 61, no. 2 (January 2007).

Mitchell, Elvis. "'Rules of Engagement': It's a War Out There, Soldier, and the Uniform is Made of Cynicism and Pain." *The New York Times*, April 7, 2000.

Nelson, Rob. "JitterBug." *The Village Voice*, May 15, 2007. Available at: <https://www.villagevoice.com/2007/05/15/jitterbug>

Newland, Christina Marie. "Archetypes of the Southern Gothic: *The Night of the Hunter* and *Killer Joe*." *Film Matters* 5, no. 1 (Spring 2014).

Ng, Andrew Hock Soon. "Intimate Spaces, Extimate Subjects: The Bedroom in Horror Films." In *Spaces of the Cinematic Home: Behind Screen Doors*, edited by Eleanor Andrews, Stella Hockenhull, and Fran Pheasant-Kelly. London: Routledge, 2015.

Nietzsche, Friedrich. *On the Genealogy of Morality.* Translated by Carol Diethe. Cambridge: Cambridge University Press, 2006.

Parikka, Jussi. *Insect Media: An Archaeology of Animals and Technology.* Minneapolis: University of Minnesota Press, 2010.

Pfefferman, Naomi. "'Killer Joe's' William Friedkin: 'I could have been a very violent person.'" *Jewish Journal*, August 2, 2012.

Pinter, Harold. *Harold Pinter: Plays One.* London: Faber and Faber, 1996.

Prince, Stephen. *A New Pot of Gold: Hollywood under the Electronic Rainbow, 1980–1989.* Berkeley: University of California Press, 2000.

Pristen, Terry. "Friedkin Signing Keeps *Jade* in Lansing Family." *Los Angeles Times*, 18 April 1994.

Quinn, Sally. "Exorcism: Beating the Devil." *Washington Post*, November 6, 1972.

Ramaeker, Paul. "Realism, Revisionism and Visual Style: *The French Connection* and the New Hollywood *policier.*" *New Review of Film and Television Studies* 8, no. 2 (June 2010).

Renner, Karen J. *Evil Children in the Popular Imagination.* New York: Palgrave, 2016.

Ringel, Harry. "The Exorcist." *Cinefantastique* 3, no. 2 (1974).

Rosenblatt, Josh. "Friedkin Continues Career Dive." *The Texas Observer* 104, no. 8 (2012).

Rosenblum, Ralph, and Robert Karen, *When the Shooting Stops . . . the Cutting Begins: A Film Editor's Story.* New York: Viking Press, 1979.

Rotella, Carlo. *Good with Their Hands: Boxers, Bluesmen, and Other Characters from the Rust Belt.* Berkeley: University of California Press, 2002.

Russo, Vito. *The Celluloid Closet: Homosexuality in the Movies.* New York: Harper & Row, 1987.

Rust, Amy. "Plugging In and Bugging Out: The Torturous Logic of Contemporary American Horror." *Quarterly Review of Film and Video* 31, no. 6 (2014).

Sarris, Andrew. "A Devil of a Bad Movie, But Not Diabolical." *The Village Voice*, July 18, 1977.

Schmitt, Carl. *Political Theology: Four Chapters on the Concept of Sovereignty.* Translated by George Schwab. Chicago: University of Chicago Press, 2005.

Schulgasser, Barbara. "This 'Jade' Isn't Even Semiprecious." *San Francisco Examiner*, October 13, 1995.

Sedgwick, Eve Kosofsky. *Epistemology of the Closet.* Berkeley: University of California Press, 2008.

Shapiro, Michael S. "Value Eruptions and Modalities: White Male Rage in the '80s and '90s." *Cultural Values* 1 (1997).

Shapiro, Steven. "Post-Continuity: An Introduction." In *Post-Cinema: Theorizing 21st-Century Film*, edited by Shane Denson and Julia Leyda (Falmer: REFRAME Books, 2016).

Shedlin, Michael. "Police Oscar: 'The French Connection': And an Interview with William Friedkin." *Film Quarterly* 25, no. 4 (Summer 1972).

Snyder, Stephen. "*Cruising*: The Semiotics of S & M." *Canadian Journal of Political and Social Theory/Revue Canadienne de théorie politique et sociale* 13, no. 1-2 (1989).
Travers, Peter. "The Hunted." *Rolling Stone*, March 14, 2003. Available at: <https://www.rollingstone.com/movies/movie-reviews/the-hunted-255683>
Turan, Kenneth. "Movie Review: Friedkin's 'Jade' Mines Familiar Territory." *Los Angeles Times*, October 13, 1995.
Vorkapich, Slavko. "Toward a True Cinema." In *A Montage of Theories*, edited by Richard Dyer MacCann. New York: E. P. Dutton, 1966.
Walker, Gerald. *Cruising*. New York: Stein and Day, 1970.
Williams, Linda. *Playing the Race Card: Melodramas of Black and White from Uncle Tom to O. J. Simpson*. Princeton: Princeton University Press, 2002.
Williams, Linda Ruth. *The Erotic Thriller in Contemporary Cinema*. Bloomington: Indiana University Press, 2005.
Williams, Linda Ruth. "Erotic Thrillers and Rude Women," *Sight & Sound* 3, no. 7 (July 1993), 13.
Williams, Sara. "'The Power of Christ Compels You': Holy Water, Hysteria, and the Oedipal Psychodrama in *The Exorcist*." *Literature Interpretation Theory* 22, no. 3 (2011).
Willis, Sharon. "Disputed Territories: Masculinity and Social Space." In *Male Trouble*, edited by Constance Penley and Sharon Willis. Minneapolis: University of Minnesota Press, 1993.
Wilson, Alexander. "Friedkin's *Cruising*, Ghetto Politics, and Gay Sexuality." *Social Text* 4 (Autumn 1981).
Wood, Robin. *Hollywood from Vietnam to Reagan*. New York: Columbia University Press, 1986.
Young, Damon. *Making Sex Public and Other Cinematic Fantasies*. Durham, NC: Duke University Press, 2018.

Index

Abraham, 80–3, 174
affect, 10, 28, 29, 33, 68, 69, 95, 117, 130, 131
Agamben, Giorgio, 72, 79, 156
Amish, 15, 16, 17, 18
Anglo-American trial, 126–7, 140, 145
authenticity, 1, 2, 8, 15, 19, 20, 26, 45, 65, 75, 177

Balázs, Béla, 92
Bataille, Georges, 116–17
Bateson, Paul, 87–8, 97, 110
Bazin, André, 2, 157
Bell, Arthur, 86, 87, 88, 101
Benjamin, Walter, 158
Bergson, Henri, 131
Berkowitz, David, 98
Bundy, Ted, 138, 139
Buñuel, Luis, 105
Butler, Bill, 125

Chase, Richard, 134, 135, 136
Chion, Michel, 100, 177
claustrophobia, 90, 153, 198
closed film, 30, 36, 43, 50n, 135

Clouzot, Henri-Georges, 4, 5, 6, 186–7, 188, 189, 195
Clover, Carol, 126–7, 144, 147–8, 174
conspiracy, 158–9, 183
contagion, 95, 102, 135, 156, 160, 168, 176, 180
contamination, 95, 109, 160, 194
criminality, 10, 11, 40, 47, 54, 57, 58, 86, 89, 98, 100, 101, 103, 106, 109, 110, 111, 142, 146, 147, 190
Crowley, Mart, 4, 30, 33

D'Antoni, Philip, 45
Derrida, Jacques, 64–5
Diallo, Amadou, 151
documentary, 4, 6, 15, 19, 38, 44, 45, 49, 125, 126, 129, 131, 134, 174, 176, 177
Dylan, Bob, 80–1, 174, 191

Ebert, Roger, 18, 78, 137, 152
Eisenstein, Sergei, 131
erotic thriller, 103, 110
exchange-value, 63, 64, 65, 114, 115
exteriority, 11, 35, 36, 42, 43, 89, 193, 194

fake, 10, 61, 66, 84, 95, 160
fate, 4, 5, 6, 7, 11, 12, 76, 104, 133, 182, 191, 192, 193, 197, 198
fetishism, 106–7, 108, 109
fluidity, 36, 44, 52, 62, 89, 156
Foucault, Michel, 101, 120, 170, 171, 172, 180–1, 190
Freud, Sigmund, 107
Frost, David, 183, 184

Godard, Jean-Luc, 38, 43
Gunning, Tom, 78–9

Hitchcock, Alfred, 30, 45, 90, 100, 119
homophobia, 6, 32, 33–4, 35, 86, 87, 88, 95

improvise, 38, 43, 188
innocence, 19, 20, 24, 29, 81, 89, 101, 111, 113, 115, 119, 120, 127, 153, 158, 160, 178, 180, 189, 192
insanity, 135, 136, 137, 140, 142, 170, 173
interiority, 10, 11, 29, 30, 32, 35, 36, 42, 43, 89, 166, 168, 170, 174, 177, 193, 194

Jameson, Frederic, 61, 64, 158–9
Jesus, 1–3, 132
Jurgensen, Randy, 87, 89, 97, 185

Kael, Pauline, 46, 177, 196
Kierkegaard, Søren, 82–3, 84

Lang, Fritz, 4, 30, 129
Lansing, Sherry, 2, 104, 105
legibility, 27, 58, 89, 97, 100, 178
Letts, Tracy, 4, 11, 112, 152, 156, 157, 158, 159

Lopate, Philip, 54
Lucas, George, 1, 5, 91, 98
Lumet, Sidney, 8, 11, 48, 49, 66, 146, 148, 186, 199
Lynch, David, 164–5, 166, 184

Manichean, 26, 28, 48, 53, 57, 61, 178
McCambridge, Mercedes, 96, 177
mystery of faith, 3, 4, 7, 8, 82, 83, 84, 167, 176, 182, 191, 197
mystery of fate, 7, 76, 191

"Necessary and Possible," 23, 29
New Hollywood, 3, 5, 8, 9, 19, 39, 40, 66, 197
Nietzsche, Friedrich, 114, 116, 120–1, 141
Nixon, Richard, 8–9, 102, 165–6, 178, 182–3, 184, 185
noir, 59, 60, 61, 63, 103

Oedipal, 28, 82, 114, 175
open film, 30, 43

Pazuzu, 96, 167, 168, 169, 174, 176
Petievich, Gerry, 62, 65, 66, 142
Pinter, Harold, 4, 22, 24, 25, 28, 29, 30, 32, 38, 112, 146, 152, 173, 179, 188
Production Code, 8, 10, 19, 21, 32, 37, 39, 41, 175
Proust, Marcel, 125, 181, 198
psychoanalysis, 29, 106, 110

qualified immunity, 47, 49, 79

Reagan, Ronald, 57, 63, 102, 135, 136
reciprocity, 112, 117, 118
Rosenblum, Ralph, 15, 21

Sayoc Kali, 80
Schmitt, Carl, 70–1, 72, 79, 83, 99, 116, 118
scopophilia, 94, 95
Scorsese, Martin, 5, 8, 41, 90, 136, 197, 198
Sedgwick, Eve Kosofsky, 89
Shroud, 1–2, 3, 4, 8, 132
Simpson, O. J., 11, 144, 146–7, 148, 150, 151
sovereignty, 43, 70, 71, 72, 79, 84, 116–17, 118, 133, 158, 159, 160, 183
Stonewall, 35, 87, 91
Stravinsky, Igor, 102

sympathy, 3, 7, 25, 28, 35, 39, 43, 71, 75, 79, 120, 126, 128, 134, 135, 137, 146, 153, 167, 183, 191
synchronization, 100

telephone, 31, 34, 36, 38, 145
Thatcher, Margaret, 102
thin line, 11, 36, 42, 48, 53, 56, 75, 133, 183

vice, 30, 39, 41, 43, 48
Vietnam War, 8, 20, 165, 182
villainy, 60, 127, 180, 196
Vorkapich, Slavko, 130–1, 161n

Watergate, 8, 164, 165, 182, 183
Williams, Linda, 9, 27, 132, 147
Wood, Robin, 88

EU representative:
Easy Access System Europe
Mustamäe tee 50, 10621 Tallinn, Estonia
Gpsr.requests@easproject.com